The Bible and the Believer

The Bible and the Believer

How to Read the Bible Critically and Religiously

———◦———

MARC ZVI BRETTLER

PETER ENNS

DANIEL J. HARRINGTON, S.J.

OXFORD
UNIVERSITY PRESS

OXFORD
UNIVERSITY PRESS

Oxford University Press is a department of the University of Oxford.
It furthers the University's objective of excellence in research,
scholarship, and education by publishing worldwide.

Oxford   New York
Auckland   Cape Town   Dar es Salaam   Hong Kong   Karachi
Kuala Lumpur   Madrid   Melbourne   Mexico City   Nairobi
New Delhi   Shanghai   Taipei   Toronto

With offices in
Argentina   Austria   Brazil   Chile   Czech Republic   France   Greece
Guatemala   Hungary   Italy   Japan   Poland   Portugal   Singapore
South Korea   Switzerland   Thailand   Turkey   Ukraine   Vietnam

Oxford is a registered trade mark of Oxford University Press in the
UK and certain other countries.

Published in the United States of America by Oxford University Press
198 Madison Avenue, New York, NY 10016

Library of Congress Cataloging-in-Publication Data
Brettler, Marc Zvi.
The Bible and the believer : how to read the Bible critically and religiously / Marc
Zvi Brettler, Peter Enns, and Daniel J. Harrington.
p.   cm.
Includes bibliographical references and index.
ISBN 978-0-19-986300-6
1. Bible—Hermeneutics. 2. Bible—Criticism, interpretation, etc. I. Enns, Peter,
1961– II. Harrington, Daniel J. III. Title.
BS476.B597   2012
220.601—dc23   2012003510

1 3 5 7 9 8 6 4 2

Printed in the United States of America
on acid-free paper

Contents

Preface

THIS BOOK ORIGINATED in a symposium sponsored by the Jewish Studies Program at the University of Pennsylvania on October 25, 2010, on "The Challenge of Reading the Bible Today: Can the Bible Be Read Both Critically and Religiously? Jewish, Catholic, and Protestant Perspectives." We would like to thank Professor Jeffrey Tigay, Emeritus A. M. Ellis Professor of Hebrew and Semitic Languages and Literatures, and Professor Beth Wenger, the Chair of the Jewish Studies Program at the University of Pennsylvania, for organizing the symposium and inviting us to speak there. The audience, several hundred students and community members strong, asked probing questions and convinced us that our topic was worthy of publication.

In this book, we are primarily concerned with the Hebrew Bible/Tanakh/Old Testament. (Each writer uses the term that best fits his tradition.) There is no comparable volume about the topic from a Jewish perspective, and in most Christian discussions concerning the Bible and the contemporary believer, the Hebrew Bible is woefully underrepresented, even though the Old Testament constitutes about three-quarters of the Christian Bible. Obviously, the New Testament enters into some of the discussions concerning the Old Testament, in large part because the New Testament authors cite the Old Testament so frequently, thus providing one possible model for Christian appropriation of Israel's story. But our primary focus is on the Hebrew Bible/Tanakh/Old Testament; this will also allow our volume to make a contribution to Christian-Jewish relations as well as to Christian ecumenical dialogue.

The heart of this book is composed of three substantial, self-standing essays in which each author in turn addresses the challenge of reading the Bible both critically and religiously from a Jewish (Brettler), Catholic (Harrington), and Protestant (Enns) perspective. Each writer chose the content and perspective that he felt best addresses the question. There was no formal checklist or template, though we naturally cover many of the same issues. Each of us also made his approach concrete by presenting a sample exposition of a key text or a treatment of a large historical-critical issue or theme. Each essay is accompanied by a short response from the other two authors; we regard these responses as conversations that highlight similarities and differences and reflect on points worthy of further thought and conversation, not as partisan arguments or corrections. A list of suggestions for further reading concludes each chapter.

In these essays, none of us claims to be an authorized or official spokesman for our religious tradition. Rather, we write as practitioners of the historical criticism of the Bible who are also convinced of the ongoing religious relevance of the texts we study. Here we seek to indicate how we try to put together the critical and religious readings of the Bible.

This book is a joint venture. The preface, introduction, postscript, and glossary were written collaboratively. Although each personal essay and response was written by one of us, it was revised in light of the others' comments. It has been a great pleasure for each of us to work with one another.

Brettler's essay benefited greatly from the critical comments of Michael Carasik, Julie Deluty, Yaakov Elman, Tova Hartman, Israel Knohl, Jon Levisohn, Lenin Prado, Ziva Reimer, Peretz Rodman, Baruch Schwartz, Meir Ben-Shahar, Tina Sherman, and Noam Zion, and from many conversations with students and colleagues.

Enns wishes to thank Rob Kashow, Steve Bohannon, and Kenton Sparks for reading earlier versions of this draft and providing many helpful comments. Immanuel Church of the Nazarene; St. Thomas's Episcopal Church in Whitemarsh, Pennsylvania; and St. Matthew's Episcopal Church in Maple Glen, Pennsylvania, provided ecclesiastical contexts that encourage faithful intellectual exploration.

Harrington wishes to thank his students at Weston Jesuit School of Theology in Cambridge, Massachusetts; and now at Boston College School of Theology and Ministry; as well as the communities at St. Peter Parish in Cambridge and St. Agnes in Arlington, Massachusetts, for the opportunity to teach and preach regularly in situations that have challenged him to make explicit how he reads the Bible critically and religiously.

The three of us would like to thank Theo Calderara and Robert Miller, editors at Oxford University Press, for their encouragement and support in the book's early stages. Theo was a wonderful editor, guiding this project to completion. We are also grateful for the outstanding work and support of Sasha Grossman and Leslie Johnson of the editorial and production departments at Oxford University Press. Without their help, this book would not have come together in such a timely and professional manner.

Each of us is cognizant that we have tried to synthesize complex religions into short essays and responses; we do not view this book as the final word on how critical and religious perspectives might be reconciled. In fact, we will judge this volume a success if it spurs further conversation on this topic, both within particular religious traditions and between them.

The Bible and the Believer

Introduction

The Historical-Critical Reading of the Hebrew Bible/Old Testament

THE GOAL OF this book is to show how Jews, Catholics, and Protestants can and do read the Hebrew Bible/Tanakh/Old Testament from a simultaneously critical and religious perspective. This entails explaining the similarities and differences in how biblical texts are read, interpreted, and applied in each tradition. The initial step in achieving this goal is to understand the biblical text's meaning in its original historical setting, using the tools and methods of historical criticism as a necessary preliminary to a sound religious reading.

We use the terms "biblical criticism," "higher criticism," "historical criticism," and the "historical-critical method" more or less interchangeably. In this usage, "criticism" does not have pejorative connotations—our task is not to disparage the Bible or to point out its errors. Rather, we take the term "biblical criticism" broadly to mean the process of establishing the original, contextual meaning of biblical texts and assessing their historical accuracy.[1] This, in turn, might allow those who take the Bible seriously to make informed judgments about its current meaning and significance (or insignificance). Such study is an indispensable step in biblical interpretation.

This approach developed out of "higher criticism," which is an older term used especially to denote the division of the Torah, the first five books of the Bible, or the Hexateuch, its first six books (the Pentateuch + Joshua), into earlier sources. The term "higher criticism" is out of fashion, but the term was used widely in the nineteenth century (and is still heard in some circles) to distinguish it from "lower criticism," which is concerned with establishing the earliest version of the biblical text. For some, higher meant better and more important, as opposed to the menial and supposedly lower mechanical work done by textual critics, who sought to recover the original, or a more original, text. For others, however, it carried the overtones of speculative, biased, untrustworthy, and even irreverent activity, as opposed to the more reverent, solid, and objective work of textual critics. We will thus generally avoid using the terms higher criticism and lower criticism, and we will employ more precise terms such as textual criticism, source criticism, and redaction criticism. "Historical criticism," which means placing a biblical text in its original historical context, is our preferred term. Historical criticism often involves comparing the text with parallel or analogous biblical or extrabiblical texts from the same general geographic area and the same general time period. This helps us better understand what was "in the air" at the time and what may have been the cultural assumptions underlying the biblical text, its authors, and earliest audiences.

Since the middle of the nineteenth century, archaeology has proven to be an indispensable tool for historical criticism. Through excavations and surveys, we now have a better idea of what everyday life was like for the people described in the Bible, the physical conditions under which they lived, and what they believed about themselves and God. We have also discovered and deciphered a large number of texts and artifacts from Israel's neighbors. This growing knowledge of ancient Israel's intellectual and religious context has challenged many conventional, traditional interpretations of the Bible. In recent years, scholars have employed concepts and models from anthropology and the other social sciences to better understand the cultural presuppositions and assumptions of the biblical writers. Thus, one of the main goals of historical criticism is to avoid the types of anachronistic interpretations of the Bible that were, understandably, common in premodern biblical interpretation—although premodern interpretations linger today.

Historical criticism also tries to discern more clearly the nature of events that may have been behind the text. Aware that the Bible contains internal contradictions, and in some cases differs from other ancient, roughly contemporaneous accounts, the method does not assume that the Bible is straightforward history. In this operation, the historians play detective, even if they cannot always arrive at a final answer.

The expression "the historical-critical method" may give the false impression that there is one, unified methodology that is practiced by all critical-biblical scholars. Instead, each scholar employs a variety of methods in combination. In biblical studies, textual criticism means gathering the ancient witnesses in Hebrew, Greek and other ancient languages, comparing them, and then discerning which reading most likely represents what the original author wrote or, at the very least, discerning the earliest form of the text that we can reconstruct. In some cases, all witnesses are problematic because of ancient textual errors; when that happens, scholars offer their best informed guesses (known as conjectural emendations). Philology (the study of biblical languages) seeks to establish the meaning and use of a word, and to determine what it may have meant in the particular context. Form criticism attends to the distinctive literary form and genre of the text, that is, whether it is narrative or discourse, poem or speech, genealogy, prophetic oracle, wisdom instruction, parable, lament psalm, and so forth. It then explores how this understanding of the text's correct genre may be used to guide our interpretation. Source criticism aims to establish if the biblical author may have been using one or more written sources, which he then integrated into his composition. Redaction criticism refers to how and why a biblical editor or redactor arranged his sources and what point he wanted to make by doing so. Rhetorical criticism focuses on how the biblical authors used language and structure to get the readers' attention and/or tried to persuade them to do something. Narrative or literary criticism focuses on the characters and their relationships, the plot, the narrator's point of view, matters of time and space, and so forth.

Many of these methods or operations are not mutually exclusive but represent different ways of approaching a biblical text, and within any one of these critical approaches there can be significant differences of opinion among scholars. Nevertheless, all of the approaches to biblical interpretation have become essential components of the historical-critical method.

The Nature of Historical Criticism

Historical criticism assumes that the biblical text can be read as any ancient text is read, that is, without any special presuppositions concerning what its words mean and how it should be interpreted. It thus uses the tools of language and reason to understand the meaning of a biblical text. Historical criticism tries, first of all, to read the ancient text in its ancient historical context and to discern its original meaning, attending to its language and images, literary form, structure, and message to its original authors, hearers, or readers. Judgments about the ongoing or present-day significance of the text and its religious meaning are then made in dialogue with these historical considerations.

Some distinguished literary critics, philosophers, theologians, and contemporary biblical scholars regard the historical-critical quest as impossible and therefore useless. Sir Edmund Leach, for example, has argued that it is impossible to find earlier sources within a document and that the entire venture is like "unscrambling the omelette."[2] Its undertaking has even been branded as the "intentional fallacy"—the idea that the author's original meaning determines the meaning of the text. That is, some claim that it is a fallacy to imagine that we can determine the intention of an author in the distant past (or in the present) with accuracy. Such critics of biblical criticism argue that once a text leaves the hand of the original author, readers may make of it whatever they find. Moreover, they contend, given the fragmentary state of our knowledge about the ancient world, it is impossible to know enough about the author's intellectual and religious world to ascertain an ancient author's intention or how the text was understood by its earliest readers.

We are sensitive to this charge and do not wish to suggest that biblical criticism claims indubitable knowledge of what mostly anonymous, ancient authors were thinking as they wrote or what ancients understood as they read or listened to the text. Nevertheless, in response to these critiques, historical critics of the Bible argue that we know enough about the world and languages of the Bible (and we hope to know more in the future) that we can offer reasonable and compelling explanations of an author's meaning or a text's function in the original context, and, on that basis, we can certainly disqualify some interpretations of a text as anachronistic, fanciful, and therefore, impossible. We may use corroborating evidence from antiquity to see if certain models that we propose are reasonable.[3] We acknowledge that non-historical-critical insights or applications might be profound, but they do not move us toward understanding the meaning of a biblical text in its original context, which is the aim of historical criticism.

The History of Biblical Interpretation

Biblical interpretation is not a recent phenomenon; it has roots in the Hebrew Bible itself, where later writers adapted, rethought, and, in some cases, wholly reconfigured earlier texts. Jeremiah and the parts of the book of Isaiah known as Second Isaiah (chapters 40–55, mid-sixth century BCE) and Third Isaiah (chapters 56–66, late sixth or early fifth century BCE) take up and adapt words and themes found in First Isaiah (chapters 1–39, mainly eighth century BCE).[4] The books of Chronicles are selective, creative rewriting of material in the earlier books of Samuel and Kings. Psalms often reinterpret earlier biblical passages. The divine attributes in Exodus 34:6–7 are reworked and interpreted in many contexts (see e.g., Jonah 4:2; Psalm 86:15). Indeed, one of the cutting-edge tasks in biblical studies today is called "intertextuality," that is, finding possible links between various biblical texts—an enterprise that characterizes much of classical rabbinic literature of the first millennium.

The discovery of the Dead Sea Scrolls at Qumran in 1947 revealed the existence of a Jewish religious community that not only preserved the oldest extant manuscripts of the Hebrew Bible (by approximately one thousand years) but also cultivated a style of Hebrew language that deliberately imitated the older style of "Biblical Hebrew."[5] Moreover, they have bequeathed to us a particular type of biblical commentary (*Pesharim*) that interprets some prophets and psalms in light of the community's history and life, similar to how many New Testament texts interpret the Hebrew Bible. Other Qumran texts demonstrate various types of interpretation found in later rabbinic texts. For example, the Aramaic *Genesis Apocryphon* fills in details of the biblical text, and the

Temple Scroll attempts to reconcile differing legal traditions found in the Bible. These early interpretations reflect the fact that the Bible, due to its laconic nature and conflicting traditions, demands interpretation.

Meanwhile, other, roughly contemporaneous, Jewish communities were also participating in the process of interpreting and applying what we call the Hebrew Bible. Josephus, in the twenty volumes of his *Jewish Antiquities*, fully recounted the history of the Jewish people from Genesis to his own time (the late first century CE), incorporating biblical and postbiblical sources. In recounting the biblical story, Josephus would, variously, quote his (Greek) Bible verbatim, add interpretative traditions found in other early texts, add his own new material, and reorder the raw material in the text, thus, in essence, rewriting the Bible for a new audience. Philo of Alexandria (early first century CE) tried to show how it was possible to bring together Jewish biblical texts and the key concepts of Platonic philosophy; his interpretations are typically allegorical. In this task, he had a rough contemporary in the author of the Wisdom of Solomon (sometime between mid-first century BCE and first century CE), who also provided a sophisticated interpretation and application of biblical materials associated with the Exodus from Egypt. Other examples of the rewritten Bible from this general time period include *Jubilees*, and Pseudo-Philo's *Biblical Antiquities*. Consciously or not, writers from this period and later periods typically anachronized when they interpreted, making biblical figures and images fit the ideas and ideals of their own period.

The New Testament is heavily influenced by the Jewish Scriptures, especially through their Greek translation known as the Septuagint. The first book in the New Testament, the Gospel according to Matthew, is famous for its "formula quotations" of Scripture ("all this took place in order that the Scriptures might be fulfilled") and its emphasis on Jesus as the authoritative interpreter of Scripture and the Jewish tradition (similar to the role of Righteous Teacher in parts of the Dead Sea Scrolls). The final book, Revelation, is full of allusions to and echoes of the Old Testament. Even though the author John never offers a direct quotation, he delights in using biblical texts and themes and in giving them new twists in light of his faith in Christ. In between those two New Testament writings, the remaining Gospels and Epistles are full of references to the Jewish Scriptures, and, in many cases, they appear to be regarded by both the writers and their readers as authoritative, at least in the sense of providing closure to a theological argument. What unites the many uses of the Jewish Scriptures in the New Testament is the conviction that the key to understanding them is the person of Jesus Christ—a process analogous to what can be found in the Qumran *Pesharim*, where the specific biblical text is interpreted as being fulfilled in the author's time period.

Especially after the destruction of Jerusalem and its Temple in 70 CE, both Jews and Christians turned to the Jewish Scriptures/Old Testament, which were in the process of being canonized, for illumination and support. For the rabbis, the Hebrew Bible, especially its first part, the Torah, provided a firm foundation on which to reconstruct Judaism, and they expended significant creative energy to establish this foundation. Toward that end, they developed sophisticated methods for interpreting biblical texts, following earlier biblical models and ancient Mesopotamian interpretive techniques, and also adopted some of the interpretive methods used in Greco-Roman circles for interpreting classic texts such as the *Iliad* and the *Odyssey*. These rules included arguing from the less significant to the more significant (Hebrew *qal va-ḥomer*, the equivalent of the Latin *a minore ad maius*), finding links between two texts, qualifying the general by the particular and vice versa, arguing from an analogy with another text, and arguing from the context.[6] These rules were helpful in providing a biblical anchor for the rabbis' opinions on matters treated in the Mishnah (ca. 200 CE); the Talmudim of the Land of Israel (completed in approximately the fourth century CE) and of Babylon (completed in approximately the seventh century CE); and various midrashic works that interpret the biblical texts directly.

Jewish biblical interpretation through the Middle Ages was extremely diverse. In legal matters, the Babylonian Talmud was almost always seen as authoritative. On narrative matters, however, there was tremendous creativity. The earliest forms of traditional Jewish commentary, composed in Babylon in the early tenth century, were likely influenced by the Karaite movement, which did not accept that the rabbinic interpretation of the law was authoritative. Unlike Christian medieval biblical interpretation,

rabbinic and classical medieval Jewish interpretation had no single uni-
fying hermeneutical principle.

Jewish interpreters in this era always engaged in close study of the
biblical text in its original languages (Hebrew and Aramaic), and a strong
tradition of philological interpretation developed, influenced by Islamic
study of the Qur'an. But most Jewish interpretation went beyond the literal meaning and often divided into four modes, recalled through the
mnemonic *Pardes* (which means "orchard" in biblical Hebrew and
becomes connected to the Greek word for paradise): *peshat* (contextual
or literal); *remez* (literally "hint"; a type of nonliteral or allegorical interpretation which may include philosophical interpretation); *derash* (midrashic, or homiletical, interpretation); and *sod* (literally "secret," mystical
interpretation). Often the same commentator practiced more than one
of these methods in a single commentary.

Although almost all classical Jewish biblical interpretation was very
traditional, referring back to the methods and interpretations of the Talmudim and Midrashim, there were some outliers. Sa'adya (882–942),
the head (*gaon*) of the Babylonian academy, under the influence of Karaites, wrote a commentary on the Bible, which appeared alongside his
Arabic translation. His commentaries, which included introductions to
the biblical books, were extremely influential in the Arabic-speaking
Jewish world. Especially in Muslim Spain, scholars in the first half of the
second millennium CE engaged in some lower criticism, suggesting that
the Hebrew text, especially outside of the Torah, contained some errors.
These scholars, however, did not advocate changing the text itself to a
more correct or original version. Much biblical exegesis in the Muslim
orbit was influenced by methods and claims of Muslim exegesis of the
Qur'an.

The greatest Jewish medieval commentator was Rashi (Rabbi Samuel
son of Isaac, 1040–1105), who synthesized earlier rabbinic texts into a
very readable commentary. Previous rabbinic commentators were typically atomistic, concentrating on the meaning of the single word. Rashi
helped to develop the method of *peshat* or *peshuto shel miqra'*, literally the
"simple meaning," or what we might call today the "contextual meaning"
of the biblical text. In this method, earlier rabbinic traditions that were

consistent with one another were selected, creating a unified interpretation of an entire unit, rather than focusing on the meaning of each word, which did not add up to a consistent interpretation of the larger unit. His grandson, Rashbam (Rabbi Samuel son of Meir, ca. 1080 to ca. 1160), extended the method and suggested that in some cases the simple biblical reading of the Torah contradicted rabbinic legal tradition. Rabbi Abraham ibn ("son of") Ezra (1089–1164), considered a member of the Spanish school of interpretation (though he wandered widely throughout Europe), suggested in his commentary on Deuteronomy 3:11 that several passages in the Torah could not have been written by Moses. This position would later influence Spinoza. Both Rashbam's idea that the Torah might be interpreted outside of rabbinic norms and ibn Ezra's idea that some of the Torah was post-Mosaic had little traction in the medieval Jewish world.

For the New Testament writers, of course, the Bible that existed was a form of the Jewish Scriptures, which later came to be called the Old Testament. The New Testament authors quote the Old Testament well over three hundred times and allude to it over a thousand times. Indeed, the New Testament can be regarded as an interpretive process of connecting Israel's story with the story of Jesus' life, death, and resurrection. As the Christian movement came to be dominated by Gentiles in the second century CE, the role of the Jewish Scriptures became increasingly problematic and controversial. A small number of Christians, like Marcion (85–160 CE), regarded the God revealed in the Jewish Scriptures to be an inferior deity and thus wanted to jettison the Jewish Scriptures entirely (not to mention portions of the New Testament). He was unsuccessful, however, because that would have meant discarding what had been authoritative Scripture for New Testament Christianity.

Once the Christians decided to keep the Old Testament, they had to determine how to interpret it. The Church Fathers—early Christian writers like Origen (185–254), Ambrose (ca. 340–397), Jerome (347–420), and Augustine (354–430)—followed the lead of the New Testament writers in reading the Old Testament in the light of Christ. In addition, Origen lined up the various Greek versions of the Old Testament and analyzed them (an early example of the first step of textual criticism: collecting the evidence), while Jerome recognized the importance of learning Hebrew in order to translate the texts into Latin. One of their major interpretive methods was allegory, a method practiced in pre-Christian times at Alexandria in interpreting the *Iliad* and the *Odyssey*. But, whereas the Alexandrian pagan interpreters were mainly interested in moral and philosophical applications, the Fathers were primarily concerned with Christology, namely, the person and nature of Christ.

The Fathers approached the Jewish Scriptures, usually in their Greek or Latin versions, as puzzles or mysteries to be resolved under the guiding authority of the "paschal mystery," that is, the saving significance of Jesus' life, death, and resurrection. This master narrative served as the key that would open up the many mysteries of the Old Testament. They regarded the Old Testament as a book of divine promises fulfilled in and through Jesus. Or they viewed it as shadows cleared and illuminated through the incarnation of Jesus, the Word of God. Their approach was neatly summarized by Augustine's dictum that "the New Testament lies hidden in the Old, and the Old is made manifest in the New." The Fathers gave a thoroughgoing Christological interpretation to the Old Testament, and their influence remains strong today, not only in official Catholic and Orthodox Church documents and practices but also in some Protestant circles, for example, within the current movement known as "Theological Exegesis." This contrasts sharply with medieval Jewish biblical interpretation, which saw no single key to understanding the Hebrew Bible and continued to study the text in its original Hebrew and Aramaic.

Another contribution that emerged from the Church Fathers' ("patristic" is the scholarly term) interpretation of Scripture was the idea of the four senses of Scripture, somewhat analogous to the four modes of medieval Jewish interpretation mentioned earlier. According to this approach, an interpreter should look for the literal, allegorical, tropological, and anagogical senses of a biblical text. The literal (historical) sense tells us what happened. The allegorical (theological) sense teaches what is to be believed, primarily about Christ and the church. The tropological (moral) sense involves what is to be done. The anagogical (eschatological) sense concerns where the text can take us: ideally, to heaven. A commonly cited example is "Jerusalem." The word refers literally to the city, allegorically to the church, tropologically to the soul, and anagogically to heaven.[7]

While carrying on the tradition of the four senses of Scripture, Thomas Aquinas (1225–1274), the greatest Christian theologian of the medieval period, emphasized the importance of the literal sense. But unlike modern interpreters, who define the literal sense or plain meaning in relation to the original author and his time, Thomas identified it as what the Holy Spirit—the primary author of Scripture—intended. This identification left the door wide open to spiritual interpretation and to the reading of the Old Testament in terms of promise/fulfillment and shadows/realities. For example, in his famous commentary on the book of Job, Thomas read the text so completely through the spectacles of Christian theology as to suggest that Job's sufferings were really not so serious because he was assured of eternal life with God and the beatific vision—the greatest gift of all.

The Renaissance/Humanist movement associated with Erasmus (1466–1536) and others also laid important groundwork for the histori-cal-critical method. Renaissance humanists encouraged the study of Hebrew and Greek rather than simply relying on the received Latin translation (Jerome's Vulgate). They saw the value of understanding the Bible in (and translating it from) its original languages and encouraged the study of the Greek and Latin classics and the Church Fathers as aids to understanding Scripture. They took a lively interest in the original historical settings of the biblical texts and perceived the differences between that time and their own. They also recognized the value of using Scripture as a means of criticizing the present state of the church, ex-posing its corruption, and bringing about reform. The Christian Hebra-ists, other scholars in this period, interpreted, discussed, and translated nonbiblical Hebrew and Aramaic Jewish texts, especially the Talmud and various Jewish mystical texts.

Although a fierce opponent of Erasmus and a critic of the Renais-sance/Humanist program, Martin Luther (1483–1546), too, sought to use Scripture as a means of bringing about church reform. In place of the traditions and customs that had developed in European churches (especially at Rome and in the papacy), Luther and the other Reformers urged a return to Scripture alone (*sola scriptura*) as a way of recapturing the primitive church's understanding how one is justified before God, at least how Luther understood it. Luther especially prized John's Gospel, Paul's letters to the Galatians and the Romans, and 1 Peter as the New Testament writings that best proclaimed Christ. Luther's problem was not the Old Testament itself, since it was to be reinterpreted in light of Christ. His concern centered on New Testament books that he felt were in conflict with the true Gospel—that is, Pauline theology as he saw it. Thus he regarded the letter of James as "the epistle of straw" because of its apparent contradiction of Pauline theology ("works righteousness" rather than grace, see 2:14–26) and little explicit attention to Christ (see 1:1; 2:1). Luther translated the Bible from the Hebrew and Greek into German, and his translation remains a landmark in the history of the German language. However, he took little or no interest in the ancient historical settings of the biblical books and paid little attention to the gap between the world of the Bible and his sixteenth-century European world, except to criticize both Old Testament Jews and Judaism in his own day as ignorant and superstitious.

By contrast, Luther's contemporary, French theologian and Protestant reformer John Calvin (1509–1564) was trained in humanist studies, which considered the ancient texts' settings. Calvin's commentaries (on most of the books of the Christian Bible, including some Old Testament texts) reflected this training; he was attentive to philological and historical matters and was not bashful about challenging accepted interpretations. For example, a recurrent Hebrew word for God is the grammatically plural *Elohim*. It was common in Calvin's day to see in the plural form an indication of the Trinity. Calvin summarily rejected this reading as being wholly out of step with the historical sense of the word in ancient Israel.

Still, such attention to original context is only superficially related to the rise of biblical criticism in the Christian world, which was marked by a virtual disregard for church tradition and authority. Despite the challenges of the Protestant Reformation to Roman Catholic tradition, there was, nevertheless, a conscious agenda to recover authoritative biblical teaching as reflected in a return to Jesus and Paul. It has not been lost on subsequent observers, however, that Luther's challenge to ecclesiastical authority on the basis of Scripture helped lay the groundwork for the rise of biblical criticism, and it is probably no coincidence that biblical criticism arose several centuries later in Germany, the epicenter of the Protestant Reformation. Careful exposition of the Bible is a consequence of *sola scriptura*, which states that Scripture is the church's final authority, apart from church tradition. Such a posture required the faithful to pay close attention to what Scripture is actually saying. Hence, in retrospect, the Reformation contained within it the germ of critical readings of Scripture. A truly self-conscious critical attitude and methodology, however, would have to wait until the seventeenth century and the rise of biblical criticism proper in the context of developments in European philosophy.

The Emergence of Modern Historical Criticism

As we glimpsed in the preceding survey, modern biblical criticism has deep roots in early Jewish, patristic, medieval, Renaissance, and Reformation biblical interpretation, especially where close attention to the biblical text was prized. However, in some circles of the European Enlightenment a remarkable shift of focus took place. There the Bible ceased to be a way of reforming and purifying the church. Instead, undermining biblical authority became a means of undermining the church's authority and even the authority of the state by which the church, whether Protestant or Catholic, was supported. Among a growing number of liberal Protestant German and British intellectuals, the Bible ceased to be regarded as divine revelation and became a book like any other, to be judged by human reason alone. The locus of biblical interpretation moved from the monastery and the pulpit to the scholar's study and eventually to the German university.[8]

The clearest statement of this new approach to biblical criticism came from the philosopher Baruch (Latinized to Benedict) Spinoza (1632–1677), who was born a Jew.[9] (Although not as thorough and critical as Spinoza, Thomas Hobbes in his *Leviathan* [1651] anticipated some of

Spinoza's points about the Pentateuch.) In the seventh chapter of Spino-za's *Tractatus Theologico-Politicus* ("On the Interpretation of Scripture"), he argued that the Bible should be treated like any other book, that it should be read in the light of philology and history, that readers must attend to the context of a passage within Scripture, and that they must bear in mind the historical circumstances in which the book was written. These con-cerns, of course, have become major principles in modern versions of biblical criticism and no longer provoke much argument.

Spinoza also asserted that the Bible's truth (or untruth) can be recog-nized by the light of natural reason, without the need to appeal to tradi-tion or ecclesiastical authority, and that its miracle stories should be interpreted in terms of what were then regarded as the physical laws of nature. These features of Spinoza's thought can be explained in part by his historical circumstances (he was excommunicated from his local synagogue in the Netherlands) and partly by his philosophy/theology (his pantheistic idea of "nature" as a substitute for God).

The French Catholic priest Richard Simon (1638–1712) is generally regarded as the father of biblical criticism. In his *Critical History of the Old Testament* (1678), he argued, using duplicate accounts of the same incidents and variations in style, that Moses was not the author of the Torah/Pentateuch.[10] Even though he was an opponent of Spinoza and regarded himself as a representative of Christian orthodoxy, he was crit-icized in Catholic circles and expelled from his religious community (the Oratory) in 1678. While Simon found few followers in official Catholic circles, he opened up the possibility that the composition of the Torah was more complicated than had generally been imagined. This paved the way for the works of Jean Astruc (1684–1766) in France and of Johann Semler (1725–1791) in Germany, as well as further developments in Ger-man Protestant circles in the nineteenth century by Johann Vatke (1806–1882) and Julius Wellhausen (1844–1918).

In this setting, in the late 1700s and early 1800s, the quest of the his-torical Jesus was born.[11] In its early stages (Hermann Reimarus, Bruno Bauer, H. E. G. Paulus), the goal was to peel away the ecclesiastical en-crustations in the Gospel tradition and find the "real" Jesus behind the text. The real Jesus turned out to be a disappointed visionary whose plans for revolution against the Romans ended in his execution. His alleged miracles were explained as fantasies or myths based on early Christian imaginative developments from quite ordinary events. For example, his walking on water was supposedly based on his walking by the seashore, and his multiplications of loaves and fishes were allegedly founded on his ability to convince his listeners to share their lunches.

Another important (and problematic) essay on the principles of biblical criticism, "Historical and Dogmatic Method in Theology" (1900), was written by the theologian and philosopher Ernst Troeltsch.[12] He set forth three principles—criticism, analogy, and correlation—that he thought should underlie historical method in theology. Criticism: Religious tradition should be subjected to historical criticism and thus the historian cannot speak of what did or did not happen, only probabilities, that is, what is more or less likely to have happened. Analogy: We must deal with the past according to the same criteria with which we deal with the present (people do not walk on water now, so neither did Jesus). Correlation: All historical phenomena must be interpreted in terms of this-worldly cause and effect (e.g., the Red Sea did not part by a miracle of God but by a strong wind). The application of these criteria to the Bible would seem to rule out direct divine intervention in history and in human affairs—a central theme of the Bible—thus reducing biblical studies to a thoroughgoing exercise in demythologization.

Two major German Protestant biblical scholars of the late nineteenth and early twentieth centuries, Julius Wellhausen and Hermann Gunkel, summarized and extended the previous understanding of the historical-critical agenda and built most of the agenda for the early twentieth century.[13] Wellhausen, a polymath who wrote on the Old and New Testaments and pre-Islamic and early Islamic culture, presented a readable, convincing, and extremely influential summary of source criticism that was eventually translated into English as *Prolegomena to the History of Ancient Israel*. Gunkel (1862–1932) was an early representative of the History of Religions School, which focused on the transmission over time of traditions that lay behind the biblical text, and how the biblical text displays evidence of the stages of transmission. He was instrumental in the development of form criticism (the study of how the formal characteristics of a unit reflect its original social setting or *Sitz im Leben*—German for "setting in life"), which he illustrated especially in commentaries on Genesis and Psalms. It is no accident that both of these scholars were German Protestants.

It is not surprising that, initially, most churches and synagogues reacted negatively to versions of biblical criticism built on the principles of Spinoza and Troeltsch, because, in many respects, they contradicted basic tenets of their traditional faith. However, many of these groups have learned to live with a form of biblical criticism that is shorn of the more radical philosophical and theological propositions offered by Spinoza and Troeltsch. Once among the most adamant opponents of biblical criticism, the Roman Catholic Church, in its recent documentation on the interpretation of the Bible (especially in Vatican II's decree entitled *Dei Verbum*), now regards the historical-critical approach as "indispensable" while insisting also on the need for "spiritual" interpretation. Protestantism and Judaism are diverse movements, with differing points of view regarding historical criticism. But there, too, significant peace has been made, although conservative Protestants and Orthodox Jews are generally less willing to accommodate their traditions to biblical criticism.

Recent years have seen the emergence of a movement that maintains that the moderate form of historical criticism is not sufficiently historical.[14] Some proponents of this approach eagerly point out the errors, contradictions, and moral shortcomings found in the Bible. Others regard the Bible as harmful, or at least irrelevant, today and best ignored. They regard themselves as using historical criticism as a way of rescuing the Bible from overly literal interpreters and misguided persons who claim to be protectors of the Bible.[15]

While we may sympathize at times with some of the critics on either side, we are convinced that it is possible to read the Bible both critically and religiously. Although historically it has been the case that "the scriptural Bible and the academic Bible are fundamentally different creations oriented toward rival interpretive communities,"[16] we do not believe that this should be so. We use the broad understanding of historical criticism, proposed by scholars like John Barton, as outlined earlier: biblical criticism refers to the process of establishing the original contextual meaning of biblical texts with the tools of literary and historical analysis.

Whatever challenges such study raises for religious belief are brought into conversation with religious tradition rather than deemed grounds for dismissing either that tradition or biblical criticism.

This approach underlies our writing in the pages that follow. Now we will move on to showing what reading the Bible—in this case, the Hebrew Bible/Tanakh/Old Testament—both critically and religiously has meant and might mean in the Jewish, Catholic, and Protestant traditions today.

Further Reading

Barton, John, ed. *The Cambridge Companion to Biblical Interpretation*. Cambridge: Cambridge University Press, 1998. Twenty essays by British and American scholars on the methods of biblical interpretation and on biblical books in modern interpretation.

———. *The Nature of Biblical Criticism*. Louisville, KY: Westminster John Knox, 2007. Biblical criticism as establishing the plain meaning of the text with the help of literary and historical analysis.

Brettler, Marc Z. *How to Read the Jewish Bible* (New York: Oxford University Press, 2007). A guide to the Hebrew Bible that shows how historical criticism can make positive contributions to an appreciation of key texts.

Enns, Peter. *Inspiration and Incarnation: Evangelicals and the Problem of the Old Testament*. Grand Rapids, MI: Baker Academic, 2005. Uses the analogy of incarnation to deal with the Old Testament's relationship to ancient Near Eastern literature, theological diversity, and the New Testament.

Frampton, Travis L. *Spinoza and the Rise of Historical Criticism of the Bible*. New York: T&T Clark, 2006. Contends that biblical criticism should be regarded as a product of post-Reformation controversies about the Bible's authority and not simply the invention of Enlightenment rationalism.

HaCohen, Ran. *Reclaiming the Hebrew Bible: German-Jewish Reception of Biblical Criticism*. Studia Judaica 56. New York: de Gruyter, 2010. Describes how various German-Jewish scholars in the nineteenth century responded to biblical criticism, especially to source criticism of the Torah.

Hauser, Alan J., and Duane F. Watson, eds. *A History of Biblical Interpretation*. Vol. 1, *The Ancient Period*; vol. 2, *The Medieval through the Reformation Periods*. Grand Rapids, MI: Eerdmans, 2003, 2009. A survey of the history of biblical interpretation.

Legaspi, Michael. *The Death of Scripture and the Rise of Biblical Studies*. Oxford Studies in Historical Theology. New York: Oxford University Press, 2010. Shows how during and after the European Enlightenment interpreters began to approach the bible critically, thus creating academic biblical studies.

LeMon, Joel M., and Kent Harold Richards, eds. *Method Matters: Essays on the Interpretation of the Hebrew Bible in Honor of David L. Petersen.* SBL Resources for Biblical Study 56. Atlanta: Society of Biblical Literature, 2009. An up-to-date handbook of methods in scholarship on the Hebrew Bible.

McKenzie, Steven L., and Stephen R. Haynes. *To Each Its Own Meanings: An Introduction to Biblical Criticisms and Their Application.* Louisville, KY: Westminster John Knox, 1993, 2nd edition 1990. An introduction, oriented toward students, to the main classical and modern methods used to interpret the Bible.

Perdue, Leo G., ed. *The Blackwell Companion to the Hebrew Bible.* Blackwell Companions to Religion. Oxford: Blackwell, 2001, 2nd ed., 2004. An overview of current Old Testament study based on articles by an international team of scholars.

Reventlow, Henning G. *History of Biblical Interpretation.* Vol. 1, *From the Old Testament to Origen;* vol. 2, *From Late Antiquity to the End of the Middle Ages;* vol. 3, *Renaissance, Reformation, Humanism;* vol. 4, *From the Enlightenment to the Twentieth Century.* SBL Resources for Biblical Study 50, 61–63. Atlanta: Society of Biblical Literature, 2009–2010. A comprehensive survey of the history of biblical criticism.

Rogerson, John. *Old Testament Criticism in the Nineteenth Century: England and Germany.* Philadelphia: Fortress, 1985. The roots of Wellhausen's position.

Sæbø, Magne, ed. *Hebrew Bible Old Testament: The History of Its Interpretation.* Vol. 1, *Antiquity;* vol. 2, *The Middle Ages;* vol. 3, *From the Renaissance to the Enlightenment.* Göttingen: Vandenhoeck & Ruprecht, 1996, 2000, 2008. Detailed essays on various aspects of the history of Old Testament study by an international team of scholars.

Scholder, Kurt. *The Birth of Modern Critical Theology: Origins and Problems of Biblical Criticism in the Seventeenth Century.* Philadelphia: Trinity International, 1990. Argues that the most important positions regarding the understanding and significance of the Bible were staked out circa 1680.

Spinoza, Baruch. *Tractatus Theologico-Politicus* (Gebhardt Edition, 1925). Translated by Samuel Shirley. Leiden: Brill, 1989. Argues that the Bible should be treated like any other book; its truth can be recognized by reason, and miracles are best explained in terms of the laws of nature.

Steck, Odil Hannes. *Old Testament Exegesis: A Guide to the Methodology.* Atlanta: Society of Biblical Literature, 1998. Shows how to approach the historical meaning of Old Testament texts through scientific exegesis.

Tigay, Jeffrey H., ed. *Empirical Models for Biblical Criticism.* Philadelphia: University of Pennsylvania Press, 1985. A collection of essays offering analogies to source criticism, illustrating that it is a reasonable model for how a text was composed.

Troeltsch, Ernst. "The Historical and Dogmatic Method in Theology." In *Religion in History/Ernst Troeltsch,* ed. James Luther Adams and Walter E. Bense, 11–32. Minneapolis, MN: Fortress, 1991. Key essay on the three principles—criticism, analogy, and correlation—underlying the more radical versions of biblical criticism.

My Bible

A JEW'S PERSPECTIVE

Marc Zvi Brettler

Introduction

Judaism is a Bible-centered religion in the sense that the Bible *as interpreted* (rather than the biblical text itself) is primary. Creative Jewish biblical interpretation (*derash*), which often views the Bible as "a fundamentally cryptic document"—a type of puzzle written in special divine speech that must be decoded—was, for centuries, the preferred Jewish method of biblical interpretation. The simple or contextual meaning of the biblical text (*peshat*), which assumes that the Bible is "normal" human speech, was only rarely important.[1]

The Bible-centered nature of Judaism can be seen in a variety of ways. The Torah and selections from the Prophets are read in the synagogue, in Hebrew, on every Shabbat (Saturday) and festival, and many other sections of the Bible, especially Psalms, are integral parts of the liturgy. When the Torah scroll is ceremonially raised in the synagogue, the community stands; if it drops to the floor, the community fasts as a sign of mourning. Yet Judaism is not interested in the Torah, or in the entire Bible, primarily in terms of what the text first meant and how it originated, namely, from a historical-critical perspective. Tikva Frymer Kensky notes that the "centrality of the Torah is more symbolic than real, more celebrated than maintained," and Wilfred Cantwell Smith is correct in his contention in his comparative study of Scripture that "the Bible has not been particularly important in Jewish life."[2] Several critical biblical scholars, including me, are trying to effect a shift, where the Bible itself again becomes central to contemporary Judaism and is studied to the same extent as rabbinic texts and independently of them.

This is a recent development, since only in the last few decades have some Jewish scholars engaged actively in critical biblical study. And many have done so while remaining observant Jews. Yet the different ways that critical study and religious observance can intersect have not been explored extensively, and critical Bible study has often been seen as taboo. For these reasons, the position I present is my own. There is no Jewish pope, acting together with the bishops, to offer official and, in some cases, infallible teachings. Nor is there a universally recognized Jewish Martin Luther. Judaism is best understood as "the evolving religious civilization of the Jewish people,"[3] which takes, and has taken, many different forms.

Because there is no single Jewish position on most issues, even within a single denomination, scholars who discuss issues such as critical Jewish studies—including biblical studies—reconcile critical, academic study and Jewish belief and practice in a variety of ways. Some prefer to compartmentalize scholarly knowledge and religion, simply accepting that the two function on different planes, similar to arguments concerning science and religion. For example, James Kugel claims: "Biblical scholarship and traditional Judaism are and must always remain completely irreconcilable." Others adopt a more postmodern view and insist that all need not be reconciled; it is natural to possess a "messy self." I usually prefer a more synthetic approach, and here I explore the extent to which critical-biblical scholarship and traditional Jewish views and practices may be brought together.[4]

I am writing this essay with some discomfort. As a scholar of religion, I was "trained to keep [my life] out of [my] research" and was taught that a "deep reticence about revealing anything of our own religious stories is very much a part of the discipline and ethos of religious studies."[5] I teach biblical studies from a historical-critical perspective at a secular university founded by a Jewish community, and I believe that the historical-critical method, discussed in the introduction, is sound. I also recognize that my Jewishness infuses my life, including my understanding of the Bible.

My approach to the question of belief and critical study has different answers and emphases than my Christian colleagues. The three of us are not talking about the same Bible. For Jews, the Hebrew Bible is the entire Bible—rabbinic tradition does not have the same status for Jews that the New Testament has for Christians. The Babylonian Talmud, for example, is not printed together with the Hebrew Bible; indeed, rabbinic tradition suggests that it was supposed to remain oral and was not supposed to have the status of a written work. Although rabbinic tradition, in some sense, has the same interpretive role in Judaism that the New Testament has in Christianity, it is much more focused on the biblical texts and not on an individual (e.g., Jesus). These factors make the analogy of Hebrew Bible:rabbinic tradition::Old Testament:New Testament problematic. Additionally, the order of the books of the Hebrew Bible is different from the order of the Old Testament, suggesting different emphases, and the Hebrew Bible canon in the Jewish community is tripartite—Torah, Nevi'im (Prophets, comprised of the Former Prophets, i.e., the books Joshua-Kings and the Latter Prophets) and Ketuvim (Writings)—thus the acronym TNK, or Tanakh. This differs from the four-part Christian canon (Torah, Historical Books, Wisdom and Poetic Books, Prophets), which probably also originated in Judaism. Christian tradition is at best am-bivalent toward "the law" (namely the Torah), while the Prophets, which lead into the depiction of Jesus in the New Testament, are considered the central part of the Old Testament. In Jewish tradition, however, the Torah has been understood as *primus inter pares*, first among equals. In the Catholic canon, some Old Testament books (for example, Esther and Daniel) are longer than those found in the Hebrew Bible, and the Catholic Old Testament contains more books than the Jewish Hebrew Bible, because of the inclusion in the Catholic canon of the Apocrypha (such as the Wisdom of Solomon). These many differences suggest that when Jews and Christians discuss the Hebrew Bible versus the Old Testament, they are not discussing the same book by another name.[6]

As noted earlier, a significant difference between Judaism and Christi-anity, especially Protestantism, concerns the centrality of the Bible. For much of the second millennium, rabbinic texts, especially the Babylonian Talmud, in some ways replaced the Tanakh as the most important writings in Judaism. (The Karaites, a Jewish group that emerged in the second half of the first millennium, rejected the authority of the Talmud and the rabbinite position and offered its own interpretations of the Bible.) The importance of the Talmud for medieval mainstream Judaism is seen in a statement by Jacob son of Meir (also called the Tosafist Rabbeinu Tam), a twelfth-century (ca. 1100–1171) sage who commented on the Babylonian Talmud, especially on the glosses of his grandfather Rashi (1040–1105), whose Talmudic and biblical commentaries have near-canonical status in Judaism. Rabbi Jacob suggested that since the Talmud contains so many biblical verses embedded within it, the *mitzvah* (commandment or obligation) to study the Bible can and should be fulfilled by Talmudic study instead. This ruling was very influential, and, after the first crusade, especially in Franco-Germany, Talmudic study by and large replaced study of the Bible.[7]

This situation did not change until the Jewish Enlightenment, or *Haskalah*, in the eighteenth century. Moses Mendelssohn (1729–1786), who is typically considered the founder of the movement, wrote and edited commentaries on several biblical books. In a highly exaggerated statement, Heinrich Heine said of him: "As Luther had overthrown the papacy, Mendelssohn overthrew the Talmud, and in the same way, for he rejected tradition and proclaimed the Bible to be the fountainhead of religion." However, for a variety of internal and external reasons—especially the fact that it was nearly impossible for Jews to teach the Bible at universities until after World War II—it took a long time for Jews to become part of mainstream biblical studies and thus to engage seriously the issues raised for believers by this type of study. Only with the opening of biblical studies to Jewish scholars in the middle of the twentieth century did a substantial number of Jews enter the guild. Once they entered, they often had to show that they fully fit in, and thus were more critical than Jewish in their approach. Now that Jewish scholars are accepted within the academy they are more comfortable being self-consciously Jewish in their scholarship, developing, for example, a subfield of biblical studies called Jewish biblical theology, parallel in some ways to "regular" Protestant biblical theology.[8]

Much discussion of Jewish critical approaches to the Bible has centered on the thirteen principles of faith of the medieval theologian, physician, and philosopher Moses Maimonides (1135–1204), which are
frequently seen as authoritative within Judaism. In some circles, Maimonides occupies a position analogous to that of Luther or the Magisterium. Abridged forms of his principles are printed at the end of the
morning service of traditional prayer-books (*siddurim*) and are para-
phrased in the *Yigdal* ("May [God] be magnified") prayer. Maimonides'
eighth principle, which concerns the origin of the Torah, reads (in its
most influential, shortened form): "I believe with perfect faith that the
entire Torah we now possess is the one given to Moses our teacher—
may he rest in peace." The ninth principle is: "I believe in perfect faith
that this Torah will never be changed . . ." In the poetic *Yigdal*, most
likely from the fourteenth century CE, they are stated as follows:

> God gave his Torah of truth to His People
> Through his prophet, His faithful prophet.
> God will never exchange or emend
> His law for any other.

Combined, these two principles are typically understood as demanding
belief in the *dogma* that the entire Torah or Pentateuch was revealed
to Moses on Sinai and is perfectly preserved in the current Hebrew
text (usually understood as the Aleppo Codex of the late tenth
century).[9]

Baruch Schwartz, from the Hebrew University in Jerusalem, clearly
contrasts the typical position of the observant Jew with the critical biblical scholar:

> [The Bible scholar] admits the decisive role played by man in the
> creation of the Bible itself, not merely in its interpretation and the
> determination of its normative application, but in the text and its
> transmission . . . The Bible critic knows for a fact about the Torah . . .
> that it is a literarily diverse compilation of separate narrative strands
> and legal compilations, all of which are historically conditioned

human products . . . The Bible is the literary record of earlier, pre-normative stages in Israel's religion.[10]

The Torah, rather than the entire Hebrew Bible, is at the center of his discussion and will be the focus of this chapter. This is because critical methods for the study of the Torah are the most developed and were seen as most threatening to Jewish belief and practice, and because within Judaism, the Torah is the central part of the canon.

The Jewish liturgy speaks of the Torah as *torat ḥayyim*—literally the Torah of life. For me, this is true in several intersecting ways. As an academic biblical scholar, the Bible is my livelihood. In its narratives and laws, especially as interpreted through later tradition, it is my life's guide. I believe that these various senses of *torat ḥayyim* intersect in a constructive fashion, and it is possible to show how certain passages of the Hebrew Bible itself support the historical-critical perspective.

The Meaning of Torah in the Bible, the History of Its Composition, and the Origins of the Idea of a Divine Torah

The short formulation of Maimonides would deny the possibility of both text and source criticism of the Torah. Many Jewish scholars agree with him. These beliefs are based on particular understandings of biblical and rabbinic traditions or, more precisely, biblical traditions as understood by the classical rabbis. For example, Deuteronomy 4:44 states: "This is the *torah* which Moses placed before the Israelites." The meaning of Hebrew *torah* in the Bible, however, is often ambiguous; only in certain late books does it refer to what we call the Pentateuch, the Five Books of Moses, or the Torah. This is likely the case, for example, in Nehemiah 8:2–3:

> On the first day of the seventh month, Ezra the priest brought the *torah* before the congregation, men and women and all who could listen with understanding. He read from it, facing the square before the Water Gate, from the first light until midday, to the

men and the women and those who could understand; the ears of all the people were given to the scroll of the Teaching (*torah*).

The word *torah* means instruction (and not primarily "law") and is often used in the Bible to mean something other than the Pentateuch. Leviticus often uses *torah* in a narrow sense of "ritual law" as in Leviticus 6:2: "Command Aaron and his sons thus: This is the ritual law concerning the burnt offering" (cf. 6:7, 18). Similarly, Exodus 12:49 states: "There shall be one *torah* for the citizen and for the stranger who dwells among you." Given that strangers, that is, resident aliens or travelers, are not obligated to fulfill all of the Torah's laws, *torah* cannot mean (the entire) Torah here. Returning to Deuteronomy 4:44, the decisive question is whether its context suggests a broad ("Torah") or a narrow ("instruction") understanding of *torah*.

The first word of the verse, *wezo't*, "and this," is a deictic or pointing word, and is defined more clearly by the following verses 45–46:

> These are the decrees, laws, and rules that Moses addressed to the people of Israel, after they had left Egypt, beyond the Jordan, in the valley at Beth-peor, in the land of King Sihon of the Amorites, who dwelt in Heshbon, whom Moses and the Israelites defeated after they had left Egypt.

Thus, a reading of Deuteronomy 4:44 in its broader context suggests that "and this" refers to the following legislation in the Book of Deuteronomy only and not to the entire Torah. There is no case in the Torah where the word *torah* unambiguously means Torah. Indeed, critical-biblical scholarship has suggested that in the Torah, *torah* never means the Torah.[11]

Jewish tradition disagrees with critical-biblical scholarship on how to interpret *torah* in Deuteronomy 4 and elsewhere. In fact, in many Jewish communities, after the Torah scroll is read in synagogue, it is raised up and the congregation recites: "And this is the Torah which Moses placed before the Israelites according to God('s instructions), via Moses." This formula is a combination of two unrelated verses: Deuteronomy 4:44, which states: "This is the Torah which Moses placed before the Israel-ites"; and Numbers 9:23, about the Israelites' encampment in the wil-derness, which begins "according to God('s instructions)" and concludes "via Moses." By combining these verses, the new formula insists that the Torah is Mosaic in origin.[12]

It is difficult to date precisely the origin of the idea that the Torah was revealed to Moses by God, an idea known in Jewish texts as *Torah MiSinai* (Sinaitic Torah), *Torah leMoshe MiSinai* (Sinaitic Mosaic Torah), or, more generically, of *Torah min haShamayim* (Heavenly, [or Divine,] Torah); these technical terms do not always have exactly the same mean-ings. It is possible to see some form of this idea concerning divine or Mosaic Torah developing within the Bible itself. Some early biblical books attribute sections of the Torah, but never its entirety, to God. The concept of the divine and/or Mosaic origin of the *entire* Torah appears unambiguously only in the last and latest section of the Hebrew Bible, Ketuvim (Writings), especially Chronicles (dated by most scholars to the fourth century BCE) and Ezra-Nehemiah (fifth century BCE). Both books refer to the Torah (singular) of Moses (e.g., Ezra 3:2; Neh 9:14; 2 Chron 23:18) and to "God's" or "the LORD's Torah" (Ezra 7:10; Neh 8:18; 1 Chron 16:40; 2 Chron 12:1). Nehemiah 8:1 combines these two ideas, referring to "the scroll of the Torah of Moses with which the LORD had charged Israel." Thus, by early in the Second Temple period—the fifth or the fourth centuries BCE, soon after the Torah was canonized and became authoritative—the idea had developed that the Torah was given by God to Moses.[13]

The Bible contains strong internal evidence that the Torah developed over time, and the idea of the Torah as divine and Mosaic developed late in the biblical period. Late biblical texts, from Ezra-Nehemiah and Chronicles, use a technical term, *torah*, or *ha-torah*, "the Torah" in the singular, while earlier texts refer to *torot*, teachings. For example, Leviti-cus 26:46 notes: "These are the laws, rules, and *torot* that the LORD estab-lished, through Moses on Mount Sinai, between Himself and the Israelite people." This change suggests that the idea of a single *torah* replaced the conception of many *torot*. The Hebrew Bible, in some cases, has marginal readings, which provide alternative readings or corrections to the reading found in the main text.[14] In Jeremiah 32:23 and several times in the last section of Ezekiel (43:11; 44:5), the plural *torot*, "instructions," most likely an early reading, has been corrected by a later scribe to *torah*. "Torah" reflecting the scribe's belief that God's word is found in a single document, the Torah. This notion of a single Torah is found several times as the main and only reading of texts that were written later; for example, the poem in Nehemiah 9 refers three times to "your Torah" (singular) (vv. 26, 29, 34). Taken together, these texts suggest a development in the biblical period from *torot*—teachings, to an authoritative, single Torah.

In earlier texts, as noted, *torah* may refer to a specific teaching or even to *part* of what would later become the canonized Torah. For example, 2 Kings 14:6, most likely a sixth-century (Deuteronomic) text, notes of the Judean King Amaziah: "But he did not put to death the children of the assassins, in accordance with what is written in the Book of the Teaching of Moses, where the LORD commanded, 'Parents shall not be put to death for children, nor children be put to death for parents; rather, a person shall be put to death only for his own crime.'" This is a (near) quote of Deuteronomy 24:16. (On this use of *torah*, see also, e.g., Josh 8:31–32; and Deut 27:4–8.[15]) When books such as Joshua and Kings cite what they call *torah*, they are citing D, the main source in the book of Deuteronomy, and never, for example, the Priestly material, which critical scholarship separates from Deuteronomy and which the majority of critical scholars consider to postdate it. This explains why the practice of residing in booths, *sukkot*, in the fall festival of ingathering or Sukkot, legislated in the Torah only in Leviticus 23:42–43, is found only in Nehemiah 8:14–17 and not in earlier books, such as Kings from the First Temple period or soon thereafter.

Chronicles sometimes updates earlier texts from Samuel and Kings, "correcting" them, since, unlike the authors of Samuel and Kings, the Chronicler had (more or less) the complete Torah as we know it.[16] For example, in 1 Kings 8:25, Solomon prays, "And now, O LORD God of Israel, keep the further promise that You made to Your servant, my father David: 'Your line on the throne of Israel shall never end, if only your descendants will look to their way and walk before Me as you have walked before Me.'" Following God here is expressed through the phrase "walk[ing] before me." The fourth-century retelling in 2 Chronicles 6:16 reads: "And now, O Lord God of Israel, keep that promise that You made to Your servant, my father David, 'You shall never lack a descendant in My sight sitting on the throne of Israel if only your children will look to their way and walk in the [path] of My Torah as you have walked before Me.'" The earlier "walk before me" is supplemented by "in the [path] of my Torah" because the Chronicler, but not the earlier author of Kings, possessed an authoritative Torah.

Another case of "correction" by the Chronicler also has a bearing on the development of the concept of a Mosaic Torah. According to 1 Kings 8:65, Solomon dedicated the First Temple on the fall festival of Sukkot, celebrating the festival for "seven days." This week-long celebration fits the legislation of Deuteronomy 16:13: "After the ingathering from your threshing floor and your vat, you shall hold the Feast of Booths for seven days." In the later Priestly tradition, however, a day is added to the festival, as seen in Leviticus 23:36: "seven days you shall bring offerings by fire to the Lord. On the eighth day you shall observe a sacred occasion and bring an offering by fire to the Lord; it is a solemn gathering: you shall not work at your occupations." In reworking the account of the dedication of Solomon's Temple, the Chronicler includes this eighth day as well: "On the eighth day they held a solemn gathering; they observed the dedication of the altar seven days, and the Feast seven days" (2 Chron 7:9). This is clear evidence that the author of Kings did not know the legislation of Leviticus 23, while the Chronicler did, because he possessed the entire Torah.[17]

The development over time of a Torah attributed to Moses is also supported by the words in Malachi 3:22: "Be mindful of the *torah* of My servant Moses, whom I charged at Horeb with laws and rules for all Israel." ("Horeb" is likely another name for Mount Sinai.) Malachi is among the latest prophets, from the postexilic period, and most scholars believe that this verse is secondary and that *torah* there means Pentateuch.[18] Among the classical prophets, only in this Second Temple text does the term "the *torah* of (my servant) Moses" appear—a term which elsewhere is in Chronicles and Ezra-Nehemiah. The absence of this term in earlier prophetic material bolsters the idea that the notion of a Mosaic Torah, identical with the Pentateuch, only developed in the Second Temple period.

Once this idea of a Mosaic Torah arose, it stuck. Thus, over a dozen times the Dead Sea Scrolls (second century BCE–first CE) refer to "the Torah of Moses," alongside less frequent references to "the Torah of God/the LORD." Both Philo (ca. 20 BCE–45 CE) and Josephus (ca. 37–100 CE) understand the Torah to be God's revelation to Moses. Philo typically calls the Torah "the book of Moses," and Josephus in *Antiquities* 4.138 calls the Pentateuchal laws "the most beautiful gift of all the things that He has presented to you" and attributes biblical narratives, such as the creation story, to Moses (1:26). The New Testament, written in the same period, also likely assumes in places that the Torah is Mosaic (see, for example, Matt 19:8; Mark 12:26).[19]

It is thus incorrect to see the idea of the divine, or Sinaitic, origin of the Torah as originating in the rabbinic period. By the early Second Temple Period, the Torah existed as a text (although not all copies were uniform—as discussed later). Following the tradition that Moses tarried on Mount Sinai for forty days and nights (Exod 24:18; 34:28; Deut 9:9, 11; 10:10), clearly he did more than just receive the Decalogue (often misnamed the Ten Commandments), which would take only a few minutes to recite. Thus, picking up on explicit statements that *parts* of the Torah were divine revelation to Moses (see e.g., Exod 20:22; Lev 26:46; 27:34—but never, for example, Genesis!), the idea developed that the entire Torah, viewed as a single document, was divine revelation. As a result, Genesis-Deuteronomy could be called God's Torah, Moses' Torah, or God's Torah via Moses, or simply the Torah. All these terms for this collection of books can be found in the books from the late biblical period but never earlier. The knowledge that the Torah was composite in its origin was likely lost shortly after its redaction or compilation into a single document, and, thereafter, there was no prevarication involved in speaking of the Torah, or God's or Moses' Torah as a unified document. This belief, developed in the Second Temple period, reached the classical rabbis and through them Maimonides and other theologians. Yet I will suggest that it is constructive to return to this "lost" knowledge about the Torah's complex composition.

Dogma and Judaism

A *dogma* is "a principle or set of principles laid down by an authority as incontrovertibly true." Maimonides turned the late Second Temple belief concerning the origin of the entire Torah into a dogma, creating "a whole new way of looking at Judaism." Maimonides' principles qualify as dogmas—he was "an authority," and he notes that "when all these foundations are perfectly understood and believed in by a person he enters the community of Israel." This suggests, quite remarkably, that an individual can be born to Jewish parents but as a result of hetero-dox beliefs not be considered part of the community. In some versions, Maimonides' principles are introduced with the phrase *'ani ma'amin be'emunah shelemah*, "I believe with a full heart," a phrase remarkably similar to the introduction of the Apostles' Creed, which opens "I believe," and the early Church's Nicene Creed, which begins similarly. Thus, according to Maimonides, belief in the divine revelation of the Torah at Sinai is a Jewish dogma, on par with, for example, the belief in the unity of God. This raises both a general and a specific question: What is the status of dogmas in Judaism and of the particular set of principles or dogmas that Maimonides articulated? Given the nature of Judaism, it is not surprising that neither of these questions has a straightforward answer.[20]

Some Christians draw the distinction between Judaism as a religion of law(s) and Christianity as a religion of belief(s), but this is simplistic and unfair to both religions. It is also unclear whether biblical Judaism, as represented in the Hebrew Bible, insists on the importance of belief, as some insist. For example, in later Judaism, Deuteronomy's statement in 6:4, called (after its first word) the "Shema": "Hear [*Shema*], O Israel! The LORD is our God, the LORD alone" is often understood as a dogma or a creed. However, as many scholars have noted, the verse's ending word (*'ehad* "one") is ambiguous and unclear at best, ungrammatical at worst; creeds are typically formulated more carefully. In addition, it is not clear if that verse is self-sufficient or an introduction to what follows, which tells you to love the LORD *through* the fulfillment of certain command-ments rather than commanding love of God as a stand-alone obligation.[21]

It is similarly problematic to see the Decalogue as a collection of dogmas. Although the Bible notes the existence of ten statements (Hebrew *devarim* is best translated as "statements," not "commandments") three times (Exod 34:28; Deut 4:13; 10:4), it is uncertain how the more than ten statements in Exodus 20 and Deuteronomy 5 should be grouped together and reduced to ten. Some traditions see "I the Lord am your God who brought you out of the land of Egypt, the house of bondage" as the first saying and commanding belief; others view it as a broad introduction that does not count among the ten. Still others understand it as an introductory clause which should be read "Because I am . . . you shall . . .," meaning the very beginning of the Decalogue is not a self-standing theological statement, let alone dogma. There is no certain resolution to these ambiguities, and thus the Decalogue may not be used to foster the suggestion that dogmas were central to early Judaism—this despite the importance of the Decalogue in Second Temple Judaism.[22]

Lists of dogmas did not develop until the Middle Ages—there is no precedent to these lists of beliefs in the Bible, in either of the Talmudim or the associated classical rabbinic midrashic literature, or among earlier Jewish philosophers. Maimonides was "the first dogmatist of any lasting influence." It is quite possible that Maimonides' claims should simply be ignored on the grounds that he incorrectly suggested that Judaism has dogmas or key religious principles. In fact, the historian of Jewish thought, Menachem Kellner, has argued convincingly that lists of dogmas were not central to Judaism; they developed in the tenth century under the influence of Islamic and Karaite thinkers and that dogmas continued to develop and become important in the fifteenth century as a result of contact with Christians. Kellner is not alone; the biblical scholar and great Jewish historian Heinrich Graetz (1817–1891), quoting Ernest Renan, viewed Judaism as "a minimum of religion" having "few, or no, articles of faith." Moses Mendelssohn, in his *Jerusalem*, states unambiguously that Judaism does not have dogmas. Other modern scholars, such as Solomon Schechter, disagree strongly, but I find Mendelssohn's view more compelling. At the end of his introduction to *Must a Jew Believe Anything?* Kellner notes:

Must a Jew believe anything? If "belief" is a matter of trust in God expressed in obedience to the Torah, my answer to the question is that a Jew must believe everything. If "belief" is the intellectual acquiescence in carefully defined statements of dogma, the answer is that there is nothing at all a Jew *must* believe.

Elsewhere he notes: "Two individuals can both be good Jews, fastidiously obeying the commandments, while disagreeing over fundamental matters of theology." Kellner is correct, at least with regard to the authority of Maimonides; even in Maimonides' lifetime, many of his books and ideas were controversial, and these controversies continued for a century after his death.[23]

Maimonides' Eighth Principle

The most important part of the eighth principle from Maimonides' commentary on the tenth chapter of Sanhedrin, Tractate Helek, reads as follows:

> The Eighth Fundamental Principle is that the Torah came from God. We are to believe that the whole Torah was given us through Moses our Teacher entirely from God . . . through Moses who acted like a secretary taking dictation . . . All came from God, and all are the Torah of God, perfect, pure, holy and true . . . Anyone who says that Moses wrote some passages on his own is regarded by our sages as an atheist or the worst kind of heretic . . . Every word of the Torah is full of wisdom and wonders for the one who understands it. It is beyond human understanding.

The ninth principle is mainly concerned with the immutability of the Torah; in that context, it notes "that this Torah was precisely transcribed from God." Although some believers understand the Torah to be God's actual speech to Moses, Maimonides states explicitly: "When we call the Torah 'God's Word' we speak metaphorically." This is because as the main Jewish proponent of "apophatic" theology—the idea that God may only be described through negative attributes—Maimonides does not believe that God speaks as humans do.[24]

Even once this typical misreading is corrected, these principles remain highly problematic. As the biblical scholar and theologian Jon Levenson notes: "Like most orthodoxies, Maimonides's eighth principle suffers the embarrassment of contradiction from within the normative sources." These contradictions have been catalogued in detail in Marc Shapiro's *The Limits of Orthodox Theology: Maimonides' Thirteen Principles Reappraised*, where he demonstrates convincingly how scholars before and after Maimonides, from obscure to well-known, disputed his principles concerning an unchanging divine Torah.[25]

Explicit Talmudic evidence contradicts Maimonides: in several places the Babylonian Talmud explicitly states that Joshua wrote Moses' obituary at the conclusion of the Torah along with some other sections of Deuteronomy. The latter opinion that God did not dictate the entire Torah to Moses was extended in some sources, including the Zohar, to suggest that Moses wrote all of Deuteronomy *mippi 'atzmo*, "of his own accord." In b. Gittin 60a, the Babylonian Talmud discusses the opinion that the Torah was given one scroll at a time (*megillah megillah nitnah*) and enumerates seven sections that were only given when the Tabernacle was completed (Exod 40:17), after the revelation at Sinai.[26]

The most famous exposition and extension of these ideas among medieval Jews comes from Abraham ibn Ezra, who suggested that some other verses—including Genesis 12:6, "The Canaanites were then in the land," which assumes that the Canaanites were no longer in the land—must surely be post-Mosaic because during the Mosaic period the Canaanites still occupied Canaan. Several medieval scholars recognized that mistakes must have transpired as the Torah was transmitted. This is explored in detail by B. Barry Levy in *Fixing God's Torah: The Accuracy of the Hebrew Bible Text in Jewish Law*, which cites an important opinion that the *mitzvah* for each Jew to write a Torah scroll is no longer valid since we no longer know the correct text of the Torah![27] The evidence adduced by scholars such as Kellner, Shapiro, and Levy is copious and reliable, indicating that there is no Jewish dogma suggesting either that the entire Torah is Mosaic (and certainly no dogma that it is Sinaitic) or that the standard Hebrew Masoretic Text is error free.[28]

Jewish biblical scholars such as Nahum Sarna and Moshe Greenberg have adduced medieval evidence to support modern Jewish critical-biblical studies. Sarna stated that the development of "Jewish biblical studies reached their apogee in Moslem Spain" where text criticism, a willingness to question divine authorship, and interest in "critical problems of the most sensitive kind" were widespread. For some Jewish biblical scholars, this is very important, because it shows that the modern critical position has precedent in earlier eras.[29]

Some feel comfortable disputing Maimonides on other matters but still see the belief in the divine Torah as central. For some, this is based on the argument that Maimonides was not being innovative but founded his writings on the classical rabbinic text, Mishnah Sanhedrin 10:1. This late second-century text begins, "All Israelites have a share in the world to come" but excludes some Jews, noting: "And these are the ones who have no portion in the world to come: He who says . . . the Torah does not come from heaven." Some see this passage as the *locus classicus* of fundamental beliefs in rabbinic literature. Schechter believed that this passage has "a certain Halachic (obligatory) character." Yet Kellner argues, quite cogently, that the broader passage in Sanhedrin 10:1 reflects various early Jewish debates and polemics and is not intended as a set of dogmatic statements; after all, it mixes dogma and laws, and its supposed central dogmas lack such basics as belief in God. Furthermore, even if it is an obligatory dogmatic belief—a position that I doubt—it says much less than Maimonides' principles. It does not, for example, insist that the entire Torah was revealed on Sinai, and there are many classical rabbinic and later texts that allow for post-Sinai additions. Nor does it insist that the received text has never been open to the natural types of errors and changes that occur when any text is transmitted over time.[30]

In sum, I find myself in agreement with Louis Jacobs, the important twentieth-century British scholar and rabbi:

That MT [Masoretic Text] is always correct and that all ancient variants are due to error is a belief so preposterous that it would hardly have been necessary to refute it were it not for the fact that it is implied in the standard formulation of the eighth article of faith . . . From what has been said up till now it will be obvious that the eighth principle of Maimonides cannot be accepted as it stands by the Jew with even a rudimentary sense of history.

I believe that this view is true and has intellectual integrity. It is supported by key rabbinic texts, and even liturgical texts that have a prominent role in Judaism illustrate how the biblical text has changed over time.[31]

Revelation

To deny that God revealed a complete Torah to Moses on Sinai and that it has been perfectly transmitted ever since does not necessarily deny revelation. Revelation is often understood as the core Jewish experience; in the words of the philosopher Emil Fackenheim (1916–2003): "If revelation must go, with it must go any possible *religious* justification for the existence of the Jewish people." The historian of Jewish philosophy Norbert M. Samuelson has explored extensively the problem of revelation from a historical and philosophical perspective. Largely based on the twentieth-century German Jewish thinker Franz Rosenzweig (1886–1929), he developed a "conception of revelation as a relationship between God and the people Israel out of which arises a form of content information (i.e. communication) called 'Torah.'" Samuelson claims that this idea "reflects far better than its alternatives an authentic understanding of how the term revelation functioned in all of the pre-modern Jewish texts." He is clear that he is outlining a "reasonable belief" that "is more reasonable than any other alternative" and not an absolute position. According to this idea, we now have a Torah that somehow reflects revelation but is not in its entirety the process of that revelation. This would certainly explain why, as critical scholars have pointed out, there are *real* contradictions in both narrative and legal material. This understanding of revelation also permits changes in the Torah text over time and a scholarly search for a more original text, closer to that early revelation. In addition, it allows for more than one revelation. Thus, Samuelson's position may even encourage critical study of the Bible from a Jewish perspective. It would certainly be consistent with the following from Jon Levenson, for whom critical Bible study is essential:

> God's revelation of His Torah does not come in immediate form, but through (and not despite) human language and human culture, specifically the language and culture of biblical Israel and one of its several successors, rabbinic Judaism. The biblical books, for example, are, in part, products of history, and they abundantly display the conventions of composition, attribution, and historiography of the ancient Near Eastern culture in which they emerged. Given the mediate character of revelation, it is impossible to attribute some of the commandments of the Torah to God but others to human culture. All of them deserve to be respected, read liturgically, and studied in detail, for, in theory, they are all owing to divine revelation.[32]

A similar position, insisting on the centrality of revelation, is found in the recently published *Divine Teaching and the Way of the World: A Defense of Revealed Religion* by the Jewish scholar of philosophy Samuel Fleischacker. In defending revelation, he notes:

> There can, accordingly, never be scientific evidence that a revelation has taken place. Scientific evidence establishes empirical facts: facts within nature. Revelation discloses a realm or entity beyond nature . . . Whether an event or text is revelatory or not depends, rather, on how it appears to those inclined to have faith in it. And it is ethical, not empirical evidence that draws the commitment of religious believers.

He also observes: "To make room for revelation we need to make sense of what it might mean for a truth to come from something more radically outside ourselves, more radically different from any aspect of who we are: 'Other' to us, in contemporary jargon."[33] His observations complement those of Samuelson.

These views are consistent with the comments by Benjamin D. Sommer, who observed:

> Revelation was real. The command that Israel perceived at Sinai was real. The rest—whether written by J [the Yahwist source of the Pentateuch] or P [the Priestly source of the Pentateuch], First or Second Isaiah [the author of Isaiah 1–39 and or 40ff.], Akiba or Ishmael [two early rabbinic figures who disagreed on many issues], Rashi [medieval Bible and Talmud commentator] or Ramban [a later Jewish commentator who often disputed Rashi], Moshe Weinfeld [a Hebrew University historical-critical scholar who emphasized the ancient Near Eastern background of the Bible] or Meir Weiss [Weinfeld's contemporary, who emphasized literary study of the Bible]—is commentary. It can add to Torah, but it can't subtract, and so—Go, learn.[34]

An Alternative Position: Sanctity Bestowed by the Community or the Redactor

The position that the sanctity of the text derives from the redactor, or from the community as a whole, which sidesteps revelation by assuming that the Torah is important because the Jewish community made it important, is most closely associated with Zechariah Frankel and Solomon Schechter. For Frankel, considered the founder of historical Judaism—which under Schechter and others developed into Conservative Judaism—*vox populi vox Dei*, "the voice of the people is the voice of God." Solomon Schechter developed this notion into "Catholic Israel," where "catholic" is used in its sense of "universal, general." He claims "that the ultimate source of authority in Judaism is the Jewish people as a whole, in which a consensus emerges as to which aspects of the tradition are permanently binding and which are time conditioned." In Schechter's words:

> Since then the interpretation of Scripture or the Secondary Meaning is mainly a product of changing historical influences, it follows that the centre of authority is actually removed from the

Bible and placed in some *living body*, which, by reason of its being in touch with the ideal aspirations and the religious needs of the age, is best able to determine the nature of the Secondary Meaning. This living body, however, is not represented by any section of the nation, or any corporate priesthood, or Rabbihood, but by the collective conscience of Catholic Israel as embodied in the Universal Synagogue.[35]

Another view holds that the source of the Torah's sanctity is connected to the redactor, the putative editor or compiler of the documents that edited the Torah into a single work. This position is associated with the twentieth-century Jewish thinker Franz Rosenzweig, who, in a famous 1927 letter to the Orthodox Rabbi Jacob Rosenheim, wrote:

We too translate the Torah as a single book, to us too it is the work of one spirit. We do not know who he was; that it was Moses we cannot believe. Among ourselves we identify him by the siglum used by critical scholarship for its assumed final redactor: R. But we fill out this R not as redactor but *rabbenu* [our rabbi, our master]. For, whoever he was and whatever material he had at his disposal, he is our Teacher, his theology, our Teaching.

In this view, rabbinic activity replaces revelation as the act that makes the Torah sacred, and the essence of the "revealed" Torah is to follow the norms generated by the rabbis and connected to the biblical text.[36]

Divine Torah in Contemporary Judaism

Most members of the Reform and Conservative communities do not uphold Maimonides' eighth and ninth principles. In its 1885 Pittsburgh Platform, the American Reform movement adopted a critical stance toward the biblical text, declaring:

We hold that the modern discoveries of scientific researches in the domain of nature and history are not antagonistic to the doctrines of Judaism, the *Bible* reflecting the primitive ideas of its own age, and a time clothing its conception of Divine Providence and Justice dealing with man in miraculous narratives.

This was a complete about-face from its position thirty years earlier: "The *Bible* as delivered to us by our fathers and as now in our possession is of immediate divine origin and the standard of our religion." However, once the 1885 platform was adopted, Hebrew Union College, the Reform seminary, hired critical Bible scholars such as Kaufmann Koehler and Julian Morgenstern, and each became president of the college, giving their critical positions prominence that continues within the American Reform movement.[37]

The Conservative position concerning critical Torah study is more complex. In its earliest years, Conservative Judaism favored only traditional interpretation of the Torah, following the classical rabbinic and medieval sages. This continued with the arrival of Solomon Schechter to head the Jewish Theological Seminary, the emerging Conservative seminary, in 1902. He is well known for his 1903 address "Higher Criticism–Higher Anti-Semitism," where his critique of higher criticism is brutal:

> The genesis of this Higher anti-Semitism is partly, though not entirely . . . contemporaneous with the genesis of the so-called Higher criticism of the Bible. Wellhausen's Prolegomena and History are *teeming with aperçes* full of venom against Judaism, and you cannot wonder that he was rewarded by one of the highest orders which the Prussian Government had to bestow.

Even though a careful reading of this speech, and other works of Schechter, suggests that it is the anti-Semitism and not the theology of source criticism that he found so disturbing, Schechter's position remained dominant within the Conservative movement for over half a century. More recently, the movement and its seminary have begun to embrace biblical criticism of all kinds, and the 1978 book of Robert Gordis, a distinguished Conservative rabbi and biblical scholar, speaks of an "absence of a body of dogmas" in Judaism, though the belief in the oral and written

Torah "as the revelation of God" is crucial, and they are "divinely inspired," though not in the sense of simple dictation. He notes:

> Properly used, both phrases, *Torah min hashamayim* and *Torah missinai*, express a fundamental of Judaism, the belief that Jewish law in its entire history and unfoldment [sic] bears the same relationship to the revelations at Sinai as does a spreading oak tree to its original acorn, in which all its own attributes are contained.[38]

The Orthodox position is by and large closer to that of Maimonides and has been summarized as follows:

> To traditionalists the entire Torah-Book, every word, every letter, was imported by God either directly to the whole people of Israel at Mount Sinai or indirectly through Moses. The fact of revelation is decisive. It is a guarantee of absolute validity, intellectual and moral.

For example, Moshe Bernstein, who teaches at Yeshiva University, wrote in its journal that an "Orthodox Bible scholar" may be an oxymoron and that "we [the Orthodox Jewish community] have axioms more precious to us than those of scholarship." A few years later, in that same publication, however, another Yeshiva University professor defended studying the Bible from a literary perspective. Barry Eichler, currently a dean at Yeshiva, acknowledges that the Bible reacts to ancient Near Eastern laws and notes that this creates "the need to define the uniqueness of the Torah in more subtle yet possibly more profound ways." At the fringes, some practice of textual criticism is allowed, often based on the precedent that rabbinic texts suggest that the Masoretic Text is not perfect. A small number of Orthodox scholars and rabbis have moved away from a literal dictation model. Thus, in a 1966 *Commentary* magazine symposium, Emanuel Rackman, an Orthodox rabbi, later appointed chancellor of Israel's religious Bar-Ilan University, said:

> The most definitive record of God's encounter with man is contained in the Pentateuch. Much of it may have been written by

people in different times, but at one point in history God not only made the people of Israel aware of his immediacy but caused Moses to write the eternal evidence of the covenant between Him and His people. Even the rabbis in the Talmud did not agree on the how.

In a nuanced and thoughtful essay, Barry Levy offers a similar position: "Serious commitment must be given to the notion that God communicated with people in biblical times and the Bible contains the best available record of that communication, the one deemed binding on subsequent generations." These are important, intellectually honest, but minority positions within American modern Orthodoxy; many Orthodox Jews have been influenced by the recent ArtScroll commentaries on the Bible, which deny all elements of critical scholarship and are much more conservative than even many medieval commentators.[39]

Within segments of the Orthodox establishment in Israel there is more openness to critical Bible study. In part, this may be because the community there is so large and powerful, it is not very worried, as is the American Orthodox community, about distinguishing itself from Conservative and Reform positions. In fact, the Bible faculty at the secular Hebrew University in Jerusalem is now almost entirely populated by observant Jews. Also, *living* an observant lifestyle, more than one's beliefs, defines Israeli Orthodox Judaism—and many of these Jews are well educated through the religious school system to understand the diversity of positions concerning issues of dogma in classical Judaism.

In terms of reconciling tradition and criticism, the position advocated first in the 1960s by the late Rabbi Mordechai Breuer has been influential among some traditional Jews in Israel. He fully accepts the idea that the Torah comprises sources but claims that each was divinely revealed to Moses in the Torah. These sources, largely identical to the ones isolated by critical scholars, each have their own perspectives, and only when viewed together do they represent the truth. He asserts, "It is not only the case that the conclusions of critical Bible study do not harm Jewish belief, but they are important and necessary for every student who studies Torah for its own sake," and he understands his method as "sanctification of the secular." For example, he suggests that each of the different narrative strands, such as the two different creation stories in Genesis 1–3, reflect particular aspects of God, and they must be combined to understand God fully. Similarly, different festival laws reflect different important complementary aspects of the festival. His theory has been called the "aspects theory," because different (divine, ancient, properly preserved) sources in the Torah reflect different *aspects* of the divine.[40]

From its very beginning, the theory has been highly controversial. To my mind, its great advantage is that it acknowledges what critical-biblical scholarship has shown—that the Torah has many disparate perspectives that may be seen in more or less continuous written sources that have been redacted together. Yet I do not find this theory intellectually satisfying. Why doesn't the Torah contain a preamble stating that this is why the Bible contains so many voices? In the words of S. Leiman in his critique of Breuer: "One wonders why the Divine Economy could not have come up with a more frugal way of promulgating Torah teaching."[41]

A small number of Orthodox scholars propose instead that revelation should not be confined to Sinai. The feminist Orthodox scholar Tamar Ross, drawing on earlier ideas in Jewish mysticism and in the teachings of Rabbi Kook, suggests "revelation is a cumulative process . . . deviation from the common picture of an absolute and one-time affair at Sinai." This position, which has some precedents in the Jewish world, treats the entire Torah as revelation, though not as Sinaitic revelation, and thus allows the Torah to remain authoritative as divine, though composed of sources revealed over time. The modern biblical scholars Moshe Greenberg and Nahum Sarna have expressed similar views. Greenberg, for example, notes that "the gradual process of God's self-disclosure to man, made evident by modern scholarship, has not diminished the Bible." Sarna, though he ignores hardcore source-criticism in his *Understanding Genesis*, observes: "Surely God can as well unfold His revelation in successive stages as in a single moment of time."[42]

A final position was developed by David Weiss Halivni, who begins with "the premise that the literal surface of the canonical Pentateuch is marred by contradictions, lacunae, and various other maculations whose provenance appears more human than divine." He suggests, based on his understanding of certain rabbinic texts, that the Torah was imperfectly preserved in the First Temple period and the Babylonian exile and that Ezra and his group restored the Torah in the early Second Temple period. This view puts tremendous faith in Ezra—Halivni states: "The religious Jew must trust Ezra in good faith." To me, however, the notion of Ezra as the redactor who restored the Torah is far from proven. The biblical sources we have about Ezra are biased and unreliable, and I cannot muster the faith in Ezra that Halivni requires.[43]

A Different Synthesis: Critical Perspectives, Jewish Observance, and the Written and Oral Law

My position is based on earlier insights; although, until the last few centuries of the critical study of Jewish texts, it would have been considered a heterodox—even heretical—synthesis. The first two points are scholarly beliefs; the final is a personal-religious one:

1. The Torah is a composite text that came into being over time.
2. Even when the Torah came together as a text, once it was compiled or redacted, most likely in the early Second Temple period, its text remained flexible. Only after the destruction of the Second Temple in 70 CE, and perhaps as a reaction to that event, did the Torah text stabilize.[44]
3. I was born Jewish and feel a deep devotion and commitment to Jewish tradition and practice.

The question for me, then, is how my deep commitment to Jewish tradition can fit with my strong scholarly, academic beliefs concerning the origin of the Torah. It is easy to understand the deep religious commitment of the person who believes that the entire written Torah is the record of what was accurately revealed to Moses by God and that the oral law was also revealed then as the authoritative interpretation of the written. Many people with that set of beliefs think that is the *only* situation that justifies *kiyyum mitzvot*—fulfillment of the commandments— but I do not believe that is the case.

As I noted earlier, Judaism is "the evolving religious civilization of the Jewish people." It began in the biblical period and has been changing ever since. As in the evolution of species, at certain points it changed slowly or hardly at all, while at others it transformed markedly. Times of stress and destruction, such as the destruction of the First and Second Temples, tended to cause the greatest changes. Thus, some scholars would say that Judaism began in the Babylonian exile, after the destruction of the First Temple (586 BCE). Although I agree that calamities caused major changes, I do not believe that they are great enough to justify this view—a scholarly convention that cuts Judaism off from its biblical roots. The origins of rabbinic Judaism remain obscure, and some questions have no certain answers, such as the connection of post–Second Temple rabbinic Judaism to the Second Temple Pharisees. Nevertheless, it is clear that the development of rabbinic Judaism, whenever we may date it, reflects a period of great change. In fact, Judaism as it is now practiced is much closer to rabbinic Judaism than to its biblical precursor(s).[45]

Thus, the issue of the authority of rabbinic tradition is really *the* crucial issue for contemporary Jews who are observant. (I am careful not to say "observant with respect to the Law," which often has a negative connotation in Christian views of Judaism. For many Jews, past and present, ritual observance is a source of joy, not a burden.) As a historian of religion, I reject the notion that rabbinic tradition is the only accurate, most ancient interpretation of the ancient Torah texts, and I see other ways of anchoring Jewish practice.

The first is based on the insights mentioned earlier of Frankel and Schechter concerning Catholic Israel—namely, the idea that the people determine the religion. It is not important to me whether particular Jewish practices originated in hoary antiquity and were communicated by God to Moses. These practices were developed within *my* community, by *my* people, and that is sufficient reason for *me* to continue them.

Alternatively, it is possible to believe that the rabbinic tradition, though not Sinaitic, is itself an ancient tradition that is binding. This is surely what Rosenzweig meant when he called the redactor of the Torah *rabeinu*—our rabbi. This view is connected to an important debate in modern Judaism about the origin of rabbinic law, specifically whether it is closely and directly *derived* from the current (and ancient) Torah text, or if it is of independent origin, reflecting ancient custom, and only became *connected to* the biblical text in the rabbinic period. (The fact that the biblical text we now have is not completely accurate presents significant problems for the first view, because the rabbis would be deriving law from an incorrect text.) I believe that the second position has the most merit, and thus by observing these laws, I am associating myself with the ancient Jewish traditions that are typically *presented* as biblical interpretation, taking into consideration their development over time.[46]

The debate over the origin of rabbinic law, and its connection to the biblical text, is summarized well by former Israeli Supreme Court Justice Menachem Elon, who has written the definitive work on Jewish law. He states:

The halakhic authorities and scholars disagreed at various times on this question [of derivation of law from biblical text] of the nature of midrash. Among recent scholars, J. N. Epstein represents the view that midrash merely attributes an existing law to a source in a Biblical verse. "Midrash supports law but does not create law; the law is buttressed by the text but not extracted from the text by means of interpretation." On the other hand, Ḥanokh Albeck asserts that midrash not only supports the existing laws but is also a source for deducing new rules of law from Biblical verses:

In ancient times, when the High court was in existence, whenever a problem came before it for which there was no tradition, they undoubtedly debated and discussed the interpretation of the Torah and on that basis alone they derived their legal conclusion.

Midrashic interpretation, according to Albeck, performed this creative function in all periods.

After noting that there is some truth to both positions, Elon observes:

We cannot determine whether a substantial proportion of laws that were expressed in midrashic form were instances of creative or integrative interpretation; and it is, therefore, impossible to reach any definite conclusion as to how much of the *Halakhah* reflects creative and how much integrative interpretation.

Most contemporary scholars agree with the position that substantial sections of rabbinic literature, though presented as textually derived *from* the Torah, are really prerabbinic traditions that the rabbis wanted to connect *to* the Torah text that they had.[47]

This position has advocates within the Orthodox community as well, including such important figures as Samson Rafael Hirsch (1808–1888), David Zvi Hoffmann (1843–1921), and Isaak Halevy (1847–1914). Hirsch, whose works are full of implicit polemics against critical-biblical scholarship, speaks of the rabbis "produc[ing]" but not "reproduc[ing]" "wisdom" and "truths" from the biblical texts and observes quite explicitly, in his commentary on Exodus 21:2, the beginning of the first biblical law collection:

> This book was to be given into the hands of those who were already well informed in the Law, simply as a means of retaining and of reviving ever afresh this knowledge which has been entrusted to their memories; and also to the teachers of Law as a means of teaching to which the students can go for references for the traditional actual laws, so that the written sentence lying before them would make it easy for them to recall to their minds the knowledge they had only received orally.
>
> The Written Torah is to the Oral Torah in the relation of short notes on a full and extensive lecture on any scientific subject. For the student who has heard the whole lecture, short notes are quite sufficient to bring back afresh . . . the whole . . . For those who had not heard . . . such notes would be completely useless.

Hoffman noted in his otherwise very conservative Leviticus and Deuteronomy commentaries that the purpose of midrash is to reveal how the accepted *halakhah* is hinted at in scripture. Halevy, considered to be one of the founders of the (ultra) Orthodox Agudah movement in Europe, upheld a similar position.[48]

In sum, the idea that rabbinic law is completely and originally embedded in the Torah text that we now have is not the only traditional position, and many traditionalists would feel comfortable with the following summary of the midrashic enterprise by Jay Harris:

> Exegesis of the Torah was the means through which the rabbis established the authority of the extrabiblical laws and practices they inherited; it was the medium they employed to create new laws in their own times; and it was the tool they used to resolve more far-reaching problems, such as contradictions within the Torah, or between the Torah and other biblical books.[49]

This claim that the rabbis often found a justification for their inherited law in the biblical text, rather than their law arising from the biblical text, is also supported by the fact that very often in rabbinic literature the same rabbinic law cites different biblical texts as its source. This is true even when comparing rabbinic laws to sectarian ones, including those known from the Dead Sea Scrolls. For example, various Jewish groups believed in starting the Sabbath before sunset on Friday, a logical idea meant to prevent desecration of the Sabbath; in rabbinic law, this is called *tosefet Shabbat*—adding to the Sabbath. Although different Jewish groups uphold this principle, they "derive" it, or more properly, connect it to different biblical texts, clearly suggesting the law or practice is independent of and precedes its connection to specific Torah verses.[50]

Thus, this evidence makes it clear that the biblical text is not the original source of (all and/or most) rabbinic law. Therefore, the scholarly fact that the Torah text is composite and was preserved improperly, has little, if any, bearing on the authority of rabbinic law. Stated differently, it is quite logical for a Jew to follow rabbinic law as it has developed even if he or she, unlike Hoffman and others, has a fully critical attitude toward the Torah text.

Some medieval Jewish scholars have also decoupled *halakhah* from the written Torah text, though they articulate no rationale for this. This is clearest and most radical in the work of Rashbam, Rabbi Samuel (Shmuel) son of Meir (ca. 1080–1174), the grandson of Rashi. Rashbam sometimes explicated the biblical text against rabbinic interpretation. This is especially salient in his gloss to the law concerning the Hebrew slave in Exodus 21:6, which suggests that a Hebrew slave may work for his master "for ever" (*le'olam*). This contradicts Leviticus 25:40, which says of such slaves: "He shall remain with you as a hired or bound laborer; he shall serve with you only until the jubilee year." Rabbinic interpretation is universal in resolving this contradiction through "creative philology," that is, by assuming that "for ever" (*le'olam*) really means until the jubilee year. Yet, in Rashbam's commentary to Exodus, he glosses *le'olam*: "According to the plain meaning of Scripture, le'olam means all the days of his life." As David Weiss Halivni notes, Rashbam was "textually rigorous in his Torah commentary" but "halakhically sensible and wise in his Talmud commentary." Although Rashbam never clarifies how he justifies these different approaches, he offers an important precedent for studying and explicating biblical texts independently of their rabbinic interpretation.[51]

Even the rabbis sometimes recognize that the oral law, though binding, occasionally differs radically from what the biblical text says, can be late, and does not always reflect the divine will. Gershom Scholem, the late scholar of Jewish thought, especially mysticism, dealt with this in detail in his classic essay "Revelation and Tradition as Religious Categories in Judaism." He based his observations on several stories in rabbinic literature, including a story that Moses sat in the back row of the rabbinic academy of Rabbi Akiva (50–135), who claimed that a certain teaching was "given to Moses on Sinai"—but Moses "did not understand what they were talking about [in the study hall]." A statement in the name of a third-century sage claims, "Torah, Mishnah, Talmud, and Aggadah—indeed even the comments some bright student will one day make to his teacher—were already given to Moses on Mount Sinai." According to Scholem, "Nothing demonstrates th[e] authority . . . of [rabbinic] commentary over author [Moses]" more than the Talmudic story that a sage tried to prove himself correct on a particular legal matter by invoking various divine signs, but the sages did not accept his sign, quoting Deuteronomy 30:12: "It is not in heaven." Remarkably, in the continuation of that story, a sage met Elijah the prophet who noted that

"God smiled [at the divine inability to convince people what was correct from the divine perspective] and said: My children have defeated Me, my children have defeated Me." These rabbinic stories bolster Schechter's idea that the community—in the case of rabbinic literature, the community of rabbis—determines what the Torah really means. They also indicate that following rabbinic interpretations of the Torah (rather than simply following God) was the core of Judaism as it developed. Indeed, one radical midrash quotes God as saying: "Would that they would abandon me but keep my Torah."[52]

I find myself agreeing with Louis Jacobs that an observant lifestyle and belief in the conclusions of critical-biblical studies are commensurate:

> I fail to see why observant Jews cannot take the necessary step of adopting, as many others have done and as I have tried to do in this book, the view that the practical observances of Judaism have as their sanction that this is how the Torah has been developed by human beings in response to the divine will, albeit conveyed through the historical experiences of the Jewish people; that there is a human element in the Torah, which can no longer be seen as an infallible text but still belongs to the way in which God has communicated His will to mankind. If such an approach is not that of Orthodoxy so be it. There is no such doctrine as "Orthodoxy *min hashamayim* [Orthodoxy from heaven, i.e., as a divinely given doctrine]."[53]

Some readers, especially those who are not Jewish, may be perplexed at the amount of space and energy I have just spent on justifying rabbinic law as separate from the Torah text—an issue that my non-Jewish colleagues will not even touch on. I have done so because, for committed Jews who take the Bible seriously, this is *the* issue—in other words, belief in a Mosaic Torah is not important in itself but for undergirding rabbinic norms. I recognize that this is not significant for other religions that take the Hebrew Bible, but not rabbinic law, seriously. It is very important for readers of this volume to recognize that although critical study of the Bible has raised problems, within the Jewish, Catholic, and

Protestant communities, the particular problems it has presented, as well as the solutions offered, have been quite different.

Literalism: The Bible as History and as Science

Jewish tradition is much less concerned with the literal truth and the historical accuracy of the biblical text than is the Protestant tradition. This is true with respect to what would typically be categorized as history and as science.

Historical traditions, namely, narratives that depict a past, were often treated in the biblical period as "clay in the hands of the potter" (Jer 18:4, 6). The book of Chronicles is a creative revision of Genesis-Kings, especially Samuel to Kings, and Deuteronomy often revises narratives found in earlier sources in the Torah. This suggests that the earlier historical sources were seen as flexible rather than absolutely true. Similarly, the fact that non-Torah texts disagree with historical traditions found in the Torah—for example, the many disagreements between the plague narrative in Exodus and in Psalms 78 and 105—implies a malleable view of history.[54]

This is because in ancient Israel, as in other premodern societies, the facts themselves or the historical events were not primary—what could be learned from the stories was primary. This explains, in part, why the classical rabbis were so playful in their engagement with the biblical text, rewriting it so extensively and creatively. Even more drastically, this focus on lessons rather than facts may suggest that Job was a character in a parable (*mashal*) rather than a historical figure—as a narrative of the actual past the text was not paramount. The commentary of Rashi (1040–1105), a type of *Readers Digest* of rabbinical statements, highlights the importance of what the text illustrates rather than what history it reproduces. For example, in the Tower of Babel story, where God "came down to look at" the city and tower under construction, Rashi, citing an earlier midrash, glosses: "He really did not need to do this [because He is omniscient], but Scripture intends to teach the judges that they should not proclaim a defendant guilty before they have seen *the case* and thoroughly understood *the matter in question*." Rashi's glosses here and elsewhere indicate that he read the text as primarily didactic—it uses stories to teach and is not interested in the real past for its own sake. This point is equally obvious from Rashi's initial comments, on Genesis 1:1, where he does not discuss natural science but how the text teaches that the entire world belongs to God, who may apportion it to whomever He pleases, and how the world was created for the sake of Israel or for the sake of the Torah. Although there have been, and continue to be, debates on when the Torah and other parts of the Bible should be read nonliterally, there is a broad consensus within Judaism that the Bible should not always or primarily be read literally.[55]

Thus, most of the scientific theory of evolution has not been problematic for Jewish scholars. In fact, it was embraced by many rabbis soon after it appeared, as fitting with several midrashic and mystical depictions of creation in postbiblical Jewish sources. As Michael Shai Cherry notes in his extensive survey of the matter, "indeed, the vast majority of Jewish theologians adopts the dialogue model and readily admits that the Torah was not meant to be a science textbook." They view it not as "natural history" but as "about morality and our relationship to God." This is because "the Rabbis eschewed a literal reading of the Hebrew Bible, especially concerning the account of creation." Natan Slifkin, an Orthodox Jew, recently wrote:

> It [science] enhances our appreciation of God's handiwork . . . It is a more noble way for God to create and run His world than via supernatural miracles . . . Genesis is best understood not as a scientific account but rather as a theological cosmogony . . . While certain inferences that some people draw from the theory [of evolution] do stand in conflict with religion, the actual theory itself does not.

This contrasts sharply with what Kugel characterizes as the evangelical position: "Scripture speaks directly and literally to us today, without any need for traditional interpretation or ideologically motivated expositors dragging the text hither and yon." There has been some movement, however, in Jewish ultra-Orthodox groups to adopt evangelical positions, perhaps so that Christians will not seem more religious in their outlook than Jews.[56]

The Authorship of Biblical Books

The following passage from the Babylonian Talmud has raised questions for Jews who study the Bible critically:

> Who wrote the Scriptures?—Moses wrote his own book and the portion of Balaam and Job. Joshua wrote the book which bears his name and [the last] eight verses of the Pentateuch. Samuel wrote the book which bears his name and the Book of Judges and Ruth. David wrote the Book of Psalms, including in it the work of the elders, namely, Adam, Melchizedek, Abraham, Moses, Heman, Yeduthun, Asaph, and the three sons of Korah. Jeremiah wrote the book which bears his name, the Book of Kings, and Lamentations. Hezekiah and his colleagues wrote . . . Isaiah, Proverbs, the Song of Songs and Ecclesiastes. The Men of the Great Assembly wrote . . . Ezekiel, the Twelve Minor Prophets, Daniel and the Scroll of Esther. Ezra wrote the book that bears his name and the genealogies of the Book of Chronicles up to his own time.

The passage is difficult to date precisely. For some religious Jews, it has become authoritative. However, others have observed that it is more like an *aggadic* (nonlegal) than like a *halakhic* (legal) passage, and thus it should not be treated as authoritative and binding. This position is bolstered by the fact that significant medieval sages did not treat it as binding. For example, Abraham ibn Ezra used his own insight to propose that Isaiah 40–66 is not by the same author as the previous chapters; he was the first scholar to isolate what later scholars would call Deutero-Isaiah, who did not prophesy like First Isaiah in the eighth and early seventh centuries BCE but in the Babylonian exile (586–538). Despite the widespread belief that David wrote the entire Psalter, or at least the anonymous psalms as well as those attributed to him explicitly, several scholars from the medieval Franco-German school understood Psalm 137 ("By the rivers of Babylon . . .") to be exilic, and explained, based on their context, other psalms as post-Davidic. These scholars correctly perceived the Talmudic statement as a nonbinding opinion rather than a dogma.[57]

As an observant Jew, I recently observed the fast of the ninth of Av, during which the destruction of the First and Second Temples in Jerusalem in 586 BCE and 70 CE is commemorated in a variety of ways, including the liturgical reading of the five-chapter book of Lamentations. The previous passage and other rabbinic writings ascribe the book to Jeremiah, with which it shares some stylistic similarities. Critical scholarship, correctly to my mind, ascribes it to five different anonymous authors. My experience hearing the book was unaffected by my acceptance of the critical opinion. It remains a beautiful, sad, and moving depiction of the tragedy that befell my ancestors. In fact, my critical perspective has enhanced my experience, allowing me to see the different theologies represented in each chapter and their different responses to catastrophe, enriching the book. Authorship of biblical books should not be fetishized, especially on the basis of a single passage in the Talmud.

The passage in the Babylonian Talmud that precedes this one about authorship notes the order of the books in the canon. It says that the order of the major prophets is Jeremiah, Ezekiel, Isaiah, the Twelve, and the order of the Writings is Ruth, Psalms, Job, Proverbs, Ecclesiastes, Song of Songs, Lamentations, Daniel, Esther, Ezra(-Nehemiah), Chronicles. Yet most biblical manuscripts do not follow this order. Tradition has not seen the first part of this Talmudic passage, concerning the order of the biblical books, as definitive, and I believe, that concerning authorship, the second part should not be seen as definitive either. In addition, Jewish tradition is also quite relaxed about whether the prophetic books record exactly what God told the prophet. The predominant idea is "that prophecy is conditioned by the personality and the capacity of the prophet." Indeed, prophets were understood to be free to translate the vision or words they heard, befitting their audience and their individual style.[58]

Inspiration

Given the importance of biblical inspiration within Christianity, some readers may be surprised that I have almost concluded this essay without having discussed divine inspiration. I do not know what it means for a book to be divinely inspired. It is striking that the Talmudic passage from Baba Batra (cited previously) concerning authorship of biblical books says in a quite straightforward way that "Joshua wrote the book which bears his name" and "Ezra wrote the book that bears his name" but nowhere inserts the idea of inspiration, for which a Hebrew phrase exists (*ruach ha-qodesh*, literally "the holy spirit"). Indeed, this term is used in some rabbinic texts concerning biblical books, but not here. As Sid Z. Leiman noted in *The Canonization of Hebrew Scripture*, canonicity involves authority, not inspiration: "a canonical book need not be inspired." Returning to an earlier observation, I treat the Hebrew Bible as the Jewish holy text and appreciate that one of the rabbinic names for it is *kitvei qodesh*, "holy writings," but this holiness for me derives from the community, not from any claim that these books are inspired. I recognize that the idea of the Holy Spirit is very important in early Christianity, appearing over eighty times in the New Testament. It was a much less central idea in rabbinic literature and should not be imported from Christianity into Judaism's understanding of the composition of canonical books.[59]

Conclusions

I find it logical, even compelling, to simultaneously uphold the discoveries of biblical criticism and to live the life of an observant Jew. The Bible itself suggests the validity of biblical criticism, indicating that the Torah came together over time and was only eventually attributed in its entirety to Moses—and thus the Bible, the key Jewish book, supports source criticism. In addition, a careful look at parallel texts in the Bible, such as Samuel-Kings and Chronicles, or Psalms 14 and 53, or 2 Samuel 22 and Psalm 18, illustrates that biblical texts changed over time, and that, inevitably, copying errors crept into the text.[60]

For me, the Bible is a sourcebook that I—within my community—make into a textbook. I do so by selecting, revaluing, and interpreting texts that I call sacred. The Bible is the collection of ancient literature that my community has sanctified. I am selective in using it since I believe that the Bible has come down to us through human hands, and that the revelation which it contains has been, to use the term of David Weiss Halivni, (deeply) "maculated" or tarnished. It is difficult to know how it should be restored, and I respect different Jews and Jewish groups who have attempted to reconstruct it in different ways—just as I hope others will respect my reconstruction, which justifies how I lead my Jewish life, based on how I have made this sourcebook, that all Jews share, into my textbook.[61]

There are no easy principles for converting this broad sourcebook, representing the varied voices within the canon, into an authoritative textbook by which a person chooses to live. Different Jewish groups, living at different times and places, have done this in different ways, and it is important for Jews to respect the various ways that this textbook construction has happened. It is crucial, however, to engage in this reworking so that the ethical problems suggested by a literal reading of certain places of the Bible—xenophobia, misogyny, homophobia—are not transferred into the textbook. There is nothing extraordinary about this move—through its methods of interpretation, rabbinic Judaism has left behind certain biblical texts. For example, the rabbis "abolish" the horrific ḥerem or proscription law of Deuteronomy 7 and 20 by suggesting that we can no longer distinguish Canaanites and their subgroups, who are supposed to be massacred in an act of ethnic cleansing. The rabbis used interpretation to change what they perceived as wrong. The same option is available today. I would also suggest that self-aware Jewish source-critics might say that a particular law is part of only one of many ancient traditions and should be ignored. I am not proposing that we white-out it away, removing it from the Bible (as the deist Thomas Jefferson did in his famous New Testament), but we can imagine that it is printed in tiny font that can hardly be read and followed. It is important to recognize, and to struggle with, the problematic texts contained in the Bible and not to view each as perfect or suitable. After all, even the prophet Ezekiel acknowledged that the Torah contains "no-good laws" (20:25).[62]

Careful readers of this essay will have noted that I avoided using the terms "critical" Bible study or "biblical-criticism" or "the biblical critic" more than necessary, and I would urge others to avoid this term as well. In the introduction, we explained how this term developed and what it means as a technical term.[63] Yet it carries baggage, and most people incorrectly believe that it suggests criticizing the Bible and what it contains. Instead, this essay, like the essays of my colleagues, tries to show how the methods developed within these approaches may fit constructively with people's religious beliefs and may even enhance them.

Criticism in Practice: A Jewish Historical-Critical Interpretation of Psalm 114

The observations that follow reflect how I understand Psalm 114 and thus illustrate how I believe biblical texts should be interpreted critically from a Jewish perspective.[64] The selection of Psalm 114 is intentional: I chose a work from Ketuvim, or Writings, as a counterbalance to the Torah-centric beginning of the essay and as a reminder that even though for Jews the Torah may be *primus inter pares*, Ketuvim is still a fundamental part of the Jewish canon. Psalms is among the most important biblical books for Jews; as in Christian and Dead Sea Scroll literature, Psalms is the most frequently quoted book in rabbinic literature, and many verses and chapters from Psalms are used in prayers. Psalm 114 is part of the liturgical collection called *hallel*, or "praise," comprising Psalms 113–118, which has special importance in Judaism, where it is recited during certain festivals, and this may be the collection mentioned in Matthew 26:30.

As translated in the New Jewish Publication Society (NJPS) edition, the psalm reads:

> 1 When Israel went forth from Egypt,
> the house of Jacob from a people of strange speech,
> 2 Judah became His holy one,
> Israel, His dominion.
> 3 The sea saw them and fled,
> Jordan ran backward,
> 4 mountains skipped like rams,

hills like sheep.
5 What alarmed you, O sea, that you fled,
Jordan, that you ran backward,
6 mountains, that you skipped like rams,
hills, like sheep?
7 Tremble, O earth, at the presence of the LORD,
at the presence of the God of Jacob,
8 who turned the rock into a pool of water,
the flinty rock into a fountain.

Ideally, this rendition should accompany the Hebrew Masoretic Text. Unlike Christian tradition, where various non-Hebraic texts have been seen as authoritative (for example, the Greek Septuagint or the Latin Vulgate), the ancient Hebrew text alone remains authoritative within Judaism and close engagement with the Hebrew text (even if emended) has been a hallmark of Jewish biblical scholarship. Like most psalms, Psalm 114 is not perfectly preserved; I emend the next-to-last word from *lema'yno* to *lema'ynei*. The two Hebrew letters reflecting "o" and "ei" are nearly identical and are often confused, and the Masoretic Hebrew, though not absolutely impossible, is cumbersome. A *Jewish* critical commentary should be based on the MT but not enslaved to it.[65]

This psalm is a self-standing composition. It has four sections of two verses each, yielding a highly symmetrical structure; this symmetry is further heightened by the internal parallelism between vv. 3 and 4, and vv. 5 and 6, and the parallel between 3–4 and 5–6. This core (vv. 3–6) concerning the natural world is surrounded by two verses concerning Israel (1–2) and two concerning God (7–8). Thus this psalm's structure elegantly brings together God, the natural world that He controls, and His people, Israel:

Vv. 1–2: Israel becoming God's dominion at the exodus.
Vv. 3–4: Reactions of sea and hills upon this event.
Vv. 5–6: A question to these geographical entities.
Vv. 7–8: Their answer to this question.

These separate sections, however, are tied together through a variety of means. For example, epithets of Israel are found in vv. 1 (Israel, house of Jacob), 2 (Judah, Israel), and 7 (Jacob). General and specific geographical terms are found in vv. 3 (sea, Jordan), 4 (mountains, hills), 5 (sea, Jordan), 6 (mountains, hills), 7 (earth), and 8 (*tzur* [*NJPS* "rock," but also "mountain"], pool of water, fountain). Water imagery is especially prominent throughout. Unnatural changes also typify this psalm, as noted in the commentary of Kimḥi to v. 8: water-bodies dry up, mountains dance, and flint yields water, suggesting that Israel becoming God's dominion is another unnatural transformation. Finally, the poetic structure seems very simple and monotonous—*every* line is a bicolon where each half is of the same length, and the parallelism throughout is synonymous. There is some variation of word order in some verses (e.g., v. 3), but most verses are structured quite simply, with a verb in the first part that is not repeated in the second (e.g., v. 4, "skipped"), and one word in the first part (e.g., v. 4, *'eilim*, "rams") balanced by a two-word phrase (*benei tzon*, "sheep") to compensate for the missing verb.

The psalm uses relatively simple vocabulary and seems straightforward, yet it contains very striking mythological, or metaphorical, imagery, as well as certain odd grammatical forms in the concluding verses. Stated differently, the psalm is deceptively simple.

Psalm 114 contains insufficient hints about its original setting or *Sitz im Leben*. Given that its central event is the exodus, most modern scholars connect it to some sort of biblical festival commemorating the exodus, though this is not compelling. Its date of composition is debated, but the presence of several likely late biblical Hebrew idioms, and its placement in the last book of the Psalter, suggest that this is likely a postexilic psalm.

Many of these general observations could have or would have been written by non-Jewish critical scholars or by Jewish noncritical scholars. My Jewish perspective is largely one of emphasis—a lot on structure, based on the notion that this informs meaning (not a uniquely Jewish view, though Jewish scholars have shown disproportionate interest in literary issues) and less on hypothetical issues, especially those concerning the psalm's prehistory, such as the original life setting, or *Sitz im*

Leben, of the psalm, which is often emphasized in Christian commentaries. My view on the date of the psalm disagrees with the Talmud and Jewish medieval commentators, but for reasons noted previously, I am completely comfortable with this. I cite the great medieval commentator (Rabbi David) Kimḥi (Radak, 1160–1235) when his interpretations fit the historical-critical method, even though they begin from different premises. In general, I study and cite, if relevant, the main Jewish medieval commentaries whenever I write on biblical texts. (This rarely happens in premodern Christian commentary, which engages less with the simple meaning of the Hebrew text and thus may be less relevant to contemporary Christian critical commentary.) I see myself as partially continuing the work of these medieval commentators, who closely engaged the text for the purpose of elucidating it for the Jewish community. In addition, I would like to set the record straight regarding modern scholars who ignored the medieval scholars and then accidentally rediscovered their insights but did not acknowledge them. Jewish tradition insists: "Whoever cites a tradition in the name of the person who (first) said it brings redemption to the world."[66]

This psalm, by suggesting that Israel became God's people at the exodus, contradicts several Torah traditions that state that this happened either with Abraham or at Sinai. This contradiction highlights my critical perspective, which relishes the multiple views reflected in the Bible. The psalm likely reflects ancient non-Israelite Canaanite traditions concerning the fleeing sea (Hebrew *yam*, a deity in Ugaritic literature). The Bible was very much a part of ancient Near Eastern literature and culture and was influenced by it. The particular constellation of ideas found in the Bible—most found elsewhere and a small number in the Bible—is what makes it unique.

It is essential to consider context when interpreting biblical texts; many interpretations differ one from the other because they interpret the same text within different contexts. A single commentator may offer different explanations of a text within several different contexts and should always make clear what the context is. As a Jewish critical Bible scholar, I offer several contexts. Beginning from the inside, they are of the psalm itself, the psalm as part of the *hallel* collection, the psalm as part of the Psalter, the psalm in the Bible, and the psalm in Judaism; I call these "rings of interpretation." These distinct interpretations highlight how biblical texts' meanings change based on their context, and individual psalms, like most biblical units, may be read, and have been read, in a variety of contexts in both Jewish and scholarly traditions.

The psalm itself is a request for divine help couched in exodus typology; the psalmist is obliquely asking God to reenact the exodus. The Hebrew Bible is often typological, but Jewish scholars have tended not to notice this since they often associate typology with the New Testament. By showing typologies in the Hebrew Bible, I hope I also illustrate how the typologies of the New Testament are a continuation of those found in the Jewish Hebrew Bible. I do not mean to reclaim the New Testament as a Jewish book—though parts of it were certainly written by people who considered themselves Jewish—but to show, for different reasons for Jews and non-Jews, continuities between Judaism and early Christianity. The main image of this psalm, of a powerful God who acted once and can act again, is deeply moving and powerful, and I hope that readers of the psalm along with my interpretation will sense that power. Each ring of interpretation would show how the meaning or main point(s) of the psalm changes, and the outside ring (the psalm in Judaism), citing the *Midrash on Psalms*, would illustrate the audacity of rabbinic interpretation. I hope that these relatively unknown traditions show how the rabbis were not bound by the original meaning of the text, and how successfully they made sure that the text would not remain a dry historical relic but a living text that should inform the religious life of the community.

In some cases, as in Psalm 114, the psalm itself, which highlights God's power and ability to act again, can easily function as a living instructive text—what I would call *"torah."* With other psalms this is more difficult, and the psalm has that function only when recontextualized in one way or another. I include, where relevant, these postbiblical interpretations since Jewish critical interpretation asserts that the text is alive and is not confined to its original meaning and must continue to function as *torah.*[67]

I recite this psalm over twenty times a year on various festivals. I am very aware of its likely original meaning and function, its late non-Davidic origin, and its improperly preserved text. I do not, when reciting it, adopt the position of Franz Rosenzweig concerning reading Numbers 22 liturgically: "All the days of the year Balaam's ass may be a mere fairy tale, but not on the Sabbath wherein this portion is read in the synagogue, when it speaks to me out of the open Torah."[68] It has the same meaning for me in the synagogue and in scholarly circles, but when I discuss it academically, I talk about how the ancient psalmist understood God and Israel; while when I pray it, I recite it to God, and, at good moments, feel how the psalm facilitates the divine presence around me.

Final Thoughts

The historical-critical methods and conclusions are important parts of my study of the Bible as an observant Jew. They represent the main, and often the only, position I use when I teach and when I write academic articles. They help form my identity as a Jewish biblical scholar who wants to understand what the Bible meant in its earliest periods and who tries to integrate those understandings, when possible, into my contemporary life.

As a modern Jew, deeply aware of the history of Judaism and Jewish biblical interpretation, I live under the influence of rabbinic interpretation. The Bible is an ancient text and must be updated—not through emendation or rewriting but through interpretation. In terms of practice, rabbinic law as it has developed, and continues to develop, informs my lifestyle. The rabbinic project, which is interested in making the Bible relevant to later situations, reconciling divergent biblical traditions, and, most significantly, seeing the Bible as a text that must be interpreted in various ways, also determines how I view the Bible: as an omnisignificant text that is not confined to its original meaning. To cite what have, unfortunately, become clichés, there are "seventy faces to the Torah" and biblical interpretation is like what happens when a hammer hits a rock—it shatters into bits (see Jer 23:29), each of which is a legitimate part of the original rock; or, to use another image, from Psalm 62:12 [English v. 11]): "God has spoken one thing, but I have [legitimately] heard two [interpretations]." To my mind, the historical-critical interpretation is one of these seventy faces or two voices. It is the method I enjoy most, that I favor, but it is not, and cannot be, the only method that I, as a Jew, use.[69]

This method makes me more aware of the lasting beauty and truths that are contained within the Hebrew Bible. I thus do not feel hypocritical when in synagogue I receive an *aliyah*; I "ascend" to recite the blessings as the Torah is read liturgically, blessings which include acknowledging having received from God a *torat 'emet*, "a true Torah." For me, this means a Torah that contains profound truths and has, through selection of particular passages at the expense of others and creative Jewish interpretation throughout the ages, been made more true. In the Jewish liturgy, when the Torah is returned to the ark, I recite along with the congregation "Her ways are pleasant ways, and all her paths, peaceful." This is taken from Proverbs 3:17, where it refers to (secular) wisdom (Hebrew *ḥokhmah*), but in rabbinic and liturgical Hebrew, wisdom is understood as the Torah, the ultimate source of wisdom.[70] When I recite the verse in synagogue, the fact that it means something other than its original meaning, which I teach in class when I teach Wisdom Literature, does not bother me at all—biblical interpretations develop over time. Moreover, I truly believe that when properly understood, the historical-critical method supports the notion that Torah can and should lead to pleasantness and peace because by separating the Torah into sources we can highlight particular "peaceful" rather than problematic passages. In the words of the Jewish daily liturgy, I believe *'ashreinu mah . . . yafah yerushateinu*— "how fortunate we are to have such a wonderful inheritance"—namely the Tanakh. And how fortunate I am to live in a generation of Jews who have begun to appreciate the importance of incorporating the understanding of the earliest meanings of the Bible into the rich legacy of the history of biblical interpretation.

In 2003, the Hebrew University Bible scholar Israel Knohl published a book on critical-biblical studies called *The Divine Symphony: The Bible's Many Voices*.[71] To my mind, the metaphor of the book's title captures what I am trying to say. I imagine the biblical text to be like a musical score, combining various instruments, that is, sources. Like many scores, it has been revised over time—sometimes early in its history, sometimes more recently. But a score is useless, at least for me (since I do not read music), without its being actualized. As we know, no two musical performances are identical—just as no two interpretations of the biblical text are identical. Different people, for a variety of reasons, may prefer one performance over another, but there is rarely a universally acknowledged best. In the world of music, it is legitimate to study the strings in the score, or even just the violins—that is similar to source criticism. It is also legitimate to study the score as a whole, and any of its actualizations, reflected in a single performance—this is similar to some redaction criticism or literary readings. What the scholar or listener studies or hears is a matter of preference, though many scholars will insist that studying the history and development of the score, as well as the author's earlier compositions and various recordings of the same piece, adds depth to the meaning of the music. The same is true for biblical scholars, like me, who advocate an appreciation for the historical-critical method—it can deepen the understanding of the text: a text that I love both as a religious text and as the object of scholarly study. In the words of Psalm 119:97: "O how I love Your *torah!* It is my study all day long."

I have unpacked my understanding of the word "symphony" of Knohl's book—but what of "divine"? The Bible contains some of my ancestors' reflections on the divine, and contains, in some form, revelation from the divine, an idea that I accept without fully understanding. Thus, for me, the Bible is a crucial source for understanding Jewish views of God, the Jewish people, the land of Israel, and covenant—that which binds these three entities together—and much more. I believe in a God—and that God is a reflection of both biblical views and their rabbinic interpretation. My personal experience and knowledge of history suggest that God is sometimes, but not always, present; for example, when I pray, I take into account Psalm 69:14 (English 69:13). It reads: "As for me, may my prayer come to You, O Lord, at a favorable moment; O God, in Your abundant faithfulness, answer me with Your sure deliverance." Based on the biblical precedent, I can do no more than hope for me, and for others, such "a favorable moment," when prayers are heard and heeded. The Bible, especially the Torah, is also the work that my community has understood as the source for how God wants me to act. This is true in rabbinic *halakhah*, my community's interpretation of the Bible, and also directly in the divine text, as when the prophet Micah portrays the divine will—what is "good," "what God requires"—as "fostering justice, loving goodness, and walking fully with God" (6:8).

To conclude on a more personal note: Many people believe that the Passover Seder should present me with crises at several levels. As a critical scholar, I do not believe in the veracity of the exodus as described in the Bible, where six hundred thousand males left Egypt (Exod 12:37). I also believe that the so-called ten plagues in Exodus are the result of combining various sources, none of which had all ten. I also know that Psalms 78 and 105 list the number and order of the plagues differently. People then wonder how I, as a mainstream biblical scholar, can sit through the Seder without jumping up constantly and objecting!

For me, the Seder is the later Jewish reconstruction of the biblical story, and such reconstructions are a crucial part of my life, since the historical-critical method is not the only method that I, as a Jew, use when understanding my Bible. Rabbinic tradition is continuing what happens within the Bible itself, where traditions multiply and are interpreted, creating new traditions. The stories that the Haggadah, the text of the Seder, tells are true, but not in a historical sense—they reflect truths about God and about the relation between God and Israel. This claim of lack of literal, historical veracity does not bother me, because I think that Judaism takes its stories, rather than its histories, seriously, and the stories of the Seder help inform my understanding of God. Many of them reflect the beginning of Exodus 10, about knowing God through the divine ability to do wonders—and I see these wonders around me every day. By making me aware of the Bible's richness, the critical method makes me more aware of the complexity and richness of God's world, and it enhances my Judaism.[72]

Response by Daniel J. Harrington, S.J.

In replying to Professor Brettler's essay my aim is not to criticize the Jewish tradition or my colleague's views on it but rather to indicate what is the same and (especially) what is different in the Catholic tradition. I do so in four sections.

Different Bibles

Early in his essay, Brettler notes that the three of us are not talking about the same Bible. The most obvious difference, of course, is that Christian Bibles include the New Testament and Jewish Bibles do not. That makes an enormous and fundamental difference. However, there are other less obvious but very important differences between our Bibles.

In arranging the books of their Bibles, Jews take as their order: Torah, Prophets (Former and Latter), and Writings, forming thus the Hebrew acronym TNK. While Protestant Christian Bibles have the same Old Testament content as Jewish Bibles do, they arrange the books in a different order: Pentateuch/Torah, Historical Books, Wisdom Books, and Prophets. Whatever its historical origin may have been, the Christian order of books suggests a promise and fulfillment theology. That is, whatever has been prophesied or promised in the Old Testament has been (or, is now, or will be) fulfilled in the New Testament.

Catholic (and Orthodox) Bibles follow the same promise and fulfillment order as Protestant Bibles. They do, however, include the so-called Apocryphal or Deuterocanonical books interspersed among the other books: Tobit, Judith, 1 and 2 Maccabees, along with expanded versions of Daniel and Esther, among the Historical Books; Wisdom and Sirach among the Wisdom Books; and Baruch among the Prophets. The inclusion of these books allows a fuller portrait of Israel's history (down to the second century BCE, especially with 1 and 2 Maccabees), an enlarged corpus of wisdom teachings with Sirach, and explicit references to life after death and immortality with the Book of Wisdom, and the entertaining and edifying stories of Tobit and Judith. Their inclusion makes for a bigger (and better, in my view) Bible.

In the Jewish tradition, the five books of the Torah have long had pride of place. And the enormous amounts of time and energy involved in understanding and applying it can be witnessed in the Mishnah and the Talmudim, as well as other Jewish writings throughout the centuries. Among Catholics, however, the favorite parts of our Old Testament include Genesis, the first half of Exodus, the stories about David and Solomon (on their good days), the Psalms, Job, and Isaiah. Most Catholics skip over the parts in the Torah about ritual purity and other legal matters, which have been very important for Jews. Not only do we not read the same Bible, but we also choose to read and emphasize different parts of books that we share. This phenomenon is often called "the canon within the canon." Similar differences occur among Catholic, Orthodox, and Protestant Christians in reading the New Testament.

Different Interpretations

Here I compare Brettler's exposition of Psalm 114 with another by the Catholic scholar Richard J. Clifford.[73] Both commentators are writing for general audiences, though some familiarity with modern biblical studies is assumed.

Much in their expositions is quite similar. That is not surprising, because both are trained in the historical-critical method and have proven to be among the best examples of scholars who can effectively combine the critical and religious approaches to Scripture. In their explications of Psalm 114, they explain the key words and images in the text, analyze in detail the structure of the psalm and how it communicates, note parallels in Canaanite or Ugaritic literature, interpret this text by other biblical texts, highlight the importance of the exodus typology, and suggest ancient Jewish liturgy as the possible origin of the psalm.

They differ in their choice of translations, though both are based on the Hebrew text. This decision, of course, was already made by the sponsorship of the projects in which their commentaries appear: Jewish Publication Society (Brettler), and the New Revised Standard Version (Clifford). Brettler shows respect for precritical Jewish traditional sources in his commentary, while Clifford sprinkles his with references to the Church Fathers. Perhaps the most important difference comes as they approach the theological or religious significance of the psalm today. For Brettler, the central issue in the psalm is to affirm that Israel became God's people at the exodus, rather than with the call of Abraham or with the giving of the covenant to Moses at Sinai. For Clifford also, the exodus typology is key; that is, God's people are freed from slavery in Egypt and led to serve their LORD in Canaan. But for him, this theme and its development in Psalm 114 also have great significance for understanding the Christian celebration of

Easter and baptism. He notes that the waters through which one passes to freedom have traditionally been interpreted as the waters of baptism; that the waters represent chaos and death; and that the resurrection of Jesus (in which one shares in baptism) is a victory over the forces of death.[74]

This comparison shows that the application of the historical-critical method to a biblical text can open up that text to greater understanding and appreciation, can cross denominational religious lines, and can enrich the theologies of the interpreters and the communities in which they stand. That is why recent Catholic documentation on interpreting the Bible has repeatedly insisted that historical criticism is "indispensable," though not completely adequate. Its potential inadequacy comes when one stops with the historical-critical analysis and fails to engage the religious or spiritual dimensions of the biblical text.

Different Concepts of the Bible

Brettler's essay shows very clearly the tensions introduced by the historical-critical method in the Jewish community. Did Moses write the Torah? Are there errors in the Bible? In what sense was the Bible inspired by God? The initial Jewish responses to these questions were generally negative. The negative Jewish responses were matched for the most part by those coming from Catholic officials and theologians. This negativity is patent even in the decrees of the Pontifical Biblical Commission well into the first half of the twentieth century.[75]

In Catholic theology these issues are treated under the terms "inspiration, inerrancy, and revelation"—not major terms in Jewish biblical scholarship. My major source in dealing with them will be Vatican II's *Dei Verbum* and current Catholic theology.[76] Earlier Catholic theology tended to treat inspiration according to the model of "divine dictation." That is, God (or the Holy Spirit) somehow or other made sure that the individual biblical writers wrote directly what God intended. According to this model, the inspiration was mainly communication between God and the writer. However, historical criticism has clearly shown that the composition of the biblical books was much more complicated and communal. For example, the Torah was built up of various written and/or oral sources.

Likewise, the prophetic books are collections of oracles and narratives that had become associated with Isaiah, Jeremiah, or Ezekiel. The book of Proverbs is clearly an anthology of several different collections. As a result of these recognitions, Catholic biblical scholars and theologians now think more in terms of communal inspiration, with reference to those both directly involved in compiling and handing on the traditions and to the communities in which they lived and worked.

Though there are some Catholic defenders of the complete verbal inerrancy of the Bible, in the light of modern critical study of the Bible and modern science, they seem to me to be defending the indefensible.[77] Taking the creation accounts in Genesis 1 and 2 as scientifically inerrant has become impossible for most people today—no matter how beautiful and wise those texts are. Most Catholics today work on the principle of a "limited inerrancy" of the Bible and point to the statement in *Dei Verbum* 11 that the Bible teaches "firmly, faithfully, and without error the truth that God wished to be recorded in the sacred writings *for the sake of our salvation.*" While there is some dispute about whether the council really wished to sanction a doctrine of "limited inerrancy," that is the way most Catholics now interpret it. That is, what is inerrant is what pertains to our salvation, not necessarily the historical or scientific details.

Catholic theology clearly regards the Bible as divine revelation. However, as *Dei Verbum* 2–6 makes clear, what is primary is the revelation of God's person that is gradually unfolded through the Old Testament and reaches its climax in the person of Jesus and the New Testament's witness to him. From this primarily personal revelation of God then flows the "propositions" revealed in the Bible such as the Ten Commandments. In this salvation-historical perspective, *Dei Verbum* describes the books of the Old Testament as divinely inspired and as retaining lasting value, even though "they contain what is only incomplete and provisional" (15).

Different Final Arbiters

Brettler observes that there is no Jewish Magisterium or official teaching position. Early on, his essay brings out the diversity that is present among Jews today and shows itself even in the interpretation of the

Bible. He is, of course, contrasting the situation in Judaism with that in Catholicism where there is a Magisterium; that is, the official teaching office of the Roman Catholic Church consisting of the body of bishops headed by the pope as the bishop of Rome.

According to *Dei Verbum* 10, "the task of authentically interpreting the word of God, whether in its written form or in the form of tradition, has been entrusted to the teaching Office of the Church (*magisterium*), whose authority is exercised in the name of Jesus Christ." The same paragraph, however, also insists that "this teaching office is not above the word of God but serves it by teaching only what has been handed on." In other words, the Magisterium itself must be guided by Scripture and tradition.

With regard to the interpretation of Scripture, the Magisterium might serve as an arbiter or umpire. Its role can be compared to that of the US Supreme Court, whose task is to decide on what is the proper interpretation of the US Constitution in the individual cases that come before it. One of its tasks is to make declarations about the meaning of biblical texts as they impinge on matters of faith and morals. In the very few cases where the Magisterium has exercised its authority on biblical matters, the concern has been not so much with what the biblical texts meant in antiquity (historical criticism) but rather with the implications of those texts for church life in the present and future (its spiritual sense and effective history). For example, in the sixteenth century, the Council of Trent upheld (in the face of opposition from Protestant Reformers) the traditional relationships between various sacraments and certain New Testament texts cited as their biblical foundations: baptism (John 3:5), penance/reconciliation (John 20:23), and anointing of the sick (James 5:14).[78] The issue was not so much the original, historical meaning of these texts, as it was how they were being used in the theological controversies of the sixteenth century.

The goal of the Magisterium's decisions about biblical texts should be to promote the cause of truth, the salvation of souls, and the good of the church. According to *Dei Verbum* 10, Scripture, tradition, and the Magisterium ought to exist in a triangular relationship, since they "are so linked and joined together that one cannot stand without the others, but all together, and each in its own way, under the action of the one Holy

Spirit, contribute effectively to the salvation of souls." Whatever problems it may pose, the living Magisterium can safeguard the integrity of the Bible and direct its use in church life.

Response by Peter Enns

Reading Professor Brettler's essay brought back very fond memories. Most of my doctoral work was done under the guidance of James Kugel and Jon Levenson, two engaging and influential Jewish biblical scholars. As a Gentile—with evangelical roots to boot—studying biblical exegesis and the history of Jewish interpretation with Jewish scholars was a reorienting experience and helped set the course of much of my academic and spiritual thinking about the nature of Scripture.

I quickly learned from Kugel and Levenson how rich, diverse, and creative the history of Jewish biblical interpretation is; a history that begins within the Hebrew Bible itself and continues today (and how well the New Testament fits into those early interpretive trajectories). The common explanation for such a biblically oriented posture is that Judaism is a religion "of the book." Brettler resists such a description, because it does not adequately account for how Scripture has been used in the history of Judaism—often as a point of departure rather than a place to which one must continually return, as it is in the Protestant tradition. What I take away most from Brettler's essay is a penetrating explication of this fascinating dynamic in Judaism between a community oriented toward both its Scripture and the ongoing transformation of that Scripture by means of interpretation.

This attitude toward Scripture surely explains, as Brettler shows, why Judaism is uniquely set up to engage biblical criticism with less cognitive dissonance than either Catholicism or Protestantism. It is certainly true that not all Jews will agree with Brettler's assessment (since Judaism is a diverse faith tradition), but he makes a compelling case, nonetheless. It is also true, as Harrington reminds us, that Catholicism has officially come to terms with biblical criticism, at least in principle, but this has not come without church-wide struggles in addressing the invariable tensions between biblical criticism and biblical authority, which affect both Catholicism and Protestantism. Judaism, however, has built in to its "system" an understanding that "going beyond" Scripture is inevitable, not only because changing intellectual and cultural climates demand it, but also because Scripture was never meant to impede such religious development to begin with. To paraphrase Brettler, authority does not reside in the text but in its interpretation.

As I will suggest in my essay, there is an analogy between how Judaism and the New Testament address the matter of Scripture. For both, Israel's Scripture is of unquestioned importance, but for both the need to transform (recontextualize) that Scripture is patently evident. If the heart of Jewish theology is not really Scripture but Scripture interpreted—which is to say, if authority is not so much located in the words on the pages of the Bible as it is in the interpretation given to those words—one can say something similar about the beginnings of Christianity. To paraphrase Brettler's description of Judaism, Christian faith is not rooted in whether the Pentateuch has a compositional history, it is rooted in Christ. I believe this is true, but here is where things can get a bit tricky for many Protestants. Brettler is correct in laying out the biblical data for a compositional history of the Pentateuch, which serves as an entry point for engaging biblical criticism. (For example, the Pentateuch does not claim to be divinely authored, *torah* never refers to the whole but to smaller portions of legal material such as ritual law or Deuteronomy, and Moses' role is something that does not come into the picture until later books.) Protestants, however, have another biblical datum to consider that muddies the water considerably—Jesus himself seems to have had a view of the "composition" of the Pentateuch that does not allow for much, if any, of a compositional history. For example, in his debates with the Pharisees, Jesus remarks, "Moses wrote about me" (John 5:46).

For some Protestants, statements such as this greatly limit the extent to which source criticism enters into the discussion. Many conservative Protestant Old Testament scholars accept a very limited notion of source criticism. For Protestants to engage in critical scholarship on the compositional history of the Pentateuch, they have the unique burden of framing Jesus' words in such a way as to make that possible while also maintaining theological integrity. For example, one might say that Jesus knew better than to say "Moses wrote" but was accommodating his audience. Or Jesus should not be taken literally here, as if he meant that every word of the Pentateuch was from Moses; perhaps Moses is only responsible for its core. Or "Moses" was simply shorthand for the Pentateuch and should not be understood as a firm comment on authorship. Another option, not typically considered by evangelical Protestants, is that Jesus' view of the Pentateuch was formed by his cultural moment— in other words, Jesus thought Moses wrote the Pentateuch, which is a reflection of Jesus' historical setting and therefore does not determine how the compositional history of the Pentateuch should be understood today. To embrace this last view, Protestants would need to articulate an understanding of the incarnation where there is room to disagree with what Jesus thought of the authorship of the Pentateuch. And this is where it can get tricky.

My point is that Protestants have a view of Scripture and its relationship to biblical criticism that is determined by factors wholly outside the boundaries of Judaism. Having said that, there is a vital lesson to be learned in seeing how Judaism's attitude toward Scripture allows it to address directly the Bible's own properties and therefore, to be deliberate in engaging biblical criticism, more so than is often the case within Protestantism.

In addition to his engaging discussion of Judaism and the composition of the Torah, Brettler discusses several potentially controversial issues to show how Judaism, properly understood, is well situated to absorb the many challenges of biblical criticism and modern thought. For example, Brettler points out the obvious factor that should be seared into the collective consciousness of Protestantism: that the Old Testament reflects on earlier material and changes it for later communities. We see this clearly in how Chronicles addresses both historical and legal traditions. In my opinion, when biblical authors report the same event differently (the New Testament's version of this problem concerns the four Gospels), it has pressing implications for understanding the nature of biblical authority for Protestants that need to be explored more deliberately.

I was struck by Brettler's insistence that Judaism is a nondogmatic faith, in the sense that Judaism does not insist on a set of agreed-upon specific dogmas. Brettler contrasts this to the common evaluation of Judaism as a religion of law (a view that was steadfastly promulgated during the Protestant Reformation and thus contrasted to the Gospel). I recall hearing a similar sentiment expressed a bit more crassly by some of my Jewish classmates at Harvard: "Since I am a Jew, whatever I believe is part of Jewish tradition." I was taken aback that no thought seemed given to a circumscribed tradition that held in check individual preferences. To be honest, I still find it a bit hard to accept Brettler's approving citation of Kellner, "there is nothing at all a Jew *must* believe," because, like all faiths, Judaism has parameters, and I am perfectly happy to call the articulation of any such parameter "dogma." But Brettler's point is well taken, nonetheless: the development of Jewish dogma seems to be more a medieval phenomenon than woven into the biblical fabric from the beginning.

I also appreciate Brettler's struggles with the trajectories set within Judaism by Maimonides' eighth principle (that all of Torah came from God). Protestantism, too, has its traditions, where major voices of the past are seen to invariably determine present conclusions and future directions. The reasoning behind this is self-evident: to deny the past is to deny the tradition, because tradition is the sum total of past events and thinking. Too often, however, adherence to tradition is understood as precluding any sort of progress. Protestants often see this same dynamic at work: fresh ideas are rendered null and void on the sole basis of what past figures said on the subject. I suppose no religious system is immune to this dynamic, but Brettler reminds us of what is true in both Judaism and Christianity: a tradition is *always* in some state of flux. We are always on some trajectory—part of some movement from and transformation of the past. A fully stable tradition is a myth. Indeed, without adaptation, traditions become insulated and eventually die out.

As I see it, the central point of Brettler's essay is the notion that Judaism is "the evolving religious civilization of the Jewish people." Judaism is itself defined by change, development, and adaptation. Evidence of such movement is already seen throughout the Hebrew Bible wherever we observe compositional and/or theological development over time. Brettler asserts that the most significant stage in that movement was not the Babylonian captivity, as is commonly argued, but the transition to rabbinic Judaism, despite the fact that the roots of this transition remain somewhat of a mystery. Rabbinic tradition has shaped contemporary Judaism, meaning that the rabbinic tradition is the dominant, authoritative, and continually developing recontextualization of Israel's faith.

Brettler follows this thought with a most tantalizing—and for any Protestant, familiar—concept. Brettler argues, along with scholars like Jay Harris, that Judaism's rabbinic legal tradition was not anchored in Israel's Scripture. Rather, the rabbis inherited legal traditions and sought to connect those traditions to Scripture. Accepted tradition, in others words, was hooked to Scripture rather than arising from Scripture through exegesis. A common, and ironic, criticism of Protestant groups is that some of its individual practices and theologies are more customs looking for biblical justification than biblically rooted principles. One example is church government. Episcopalians practice a form of apostolic succession of bishops. Congregationalists are governed by the wisdom of the people. In the middle somewhere is Presbyterianism, which is governed by a duly elected body of elders. Each of these forms of government is said to have "clear" biblical support, but surely the matter is more complicated than that. How the various Protestant traditions adopted preferred methods of governance was not determined by simply "doing what the Bible says" but by a variety of cultural and historical factors, with all parties concerned to find some grounding for contemporary practice in the diverse biblical witness.

I was very pleased to see Brettler touch on the issue of literalism and the perennial Protestant stumbling blocks, history and science—and somewhat relieved to see that Protestants are not the only ones who have to deal with literalists rattling their cages. Of course, if one begins, as Brettler does, with the notion that the Bible is flexible in its reporting of history—even being willing to revise history as the Chronicler does— then the science/faith issues that beset Genesis 1–3 become far less pressing, even a bit mundane. Protestants, however, will respond by saying that the Chronicler's revision of Israel's history is nevertheless a telling of an essentially historical story. Genesis is an entirely different matter since scientific and historical studies have led to the conclusion that we are not dealing with historical events.

As I see it, the entire science/faith debate is fueled by disagreements over proper genre identification of the opening chapters of Genesis. The reason why Brettler's Judaism can more easily accept scientific models of origins than some forms of Protestantism can has less to do with the acceptance of historiographical flexibility in the Bible and more to do with a willingness to accept that "history" is not the proper genre label for Genesis. Further, as we have seen before, the Christian canon raises the ante for Christians in a way that it does not for Jews: the apostle Paul, in Romans 5 and 1 Corinthians 15, seems to put a fair amount of theological weight on what Adam as the first human being did (rebellion against God) and consequently what Christ, the second Adam, did to correct the problem (his crucifixion and resurrection).

Let me conclude by engaging Brettler's summarizing statement: "The Bible is a sourcebook that I—within my community—make into a textbook. I do so by selecting, revaluing, and interpreting texts that I call sacred." As I see it, Brettler here articulates a notion that will strike some Protestants as immediately suspect—Brettler and his community seem to stand in judgment over Scripture, declaring what can and cannot, should and should not be transmitted into contemporary religious life. The Bible becomes a religious guide but not without some critical evaluation on the part of the religious community. Brettler would quickly be accused of promoting a view of Scripture that is absent of any notion of biblical authority and any true submission to Scripture as God's word.

There are certainly significant differences between Judaism and Protestantism concerning how biblical authority is articulated, but it might be better to say that for Brettler biblical authority in Judaism is not central (rather than simply absent). But more important, Protestants should not be too quick to play the authority card. The earliest Christian writers— the New Testament authors—each did their own sort of sifting, prioritizing, and reframing of Israel's story. Jesus himself, according to the Gospel traditions, at the very least neutralized, if not abrogated, key Old Testament institutions and practices and was followed in this attitude by

Paul. Cessation of dietary laws, the inclusion of Gentiles without circumcision, decentralizing of Torah, and the end of the entire sacrificial system—these are some examples of views that Jesus and his earliest followers advanced. Fast forward to the Protestant era, and we see selectivity of Scripture as the order of the day. Part of the Protestant dilemma is how to determine how Scripture should be sifted, i.e., where and when Scripture speaks prescriptively or descriptively—the former requires abiding obedience (love your enemies), while the latter reflects ancient culture and either need not or should not be followed today (Abraham passing off Sarah as his sister to save his own neck).

But this distinction is not neat and clean; there is no table of contents to the Bible to tell us what is and what is not to be followed. Making that determination invariably involves a process of sifting, prioritizing, and reframing Scripture for Jews and Protestants alike. The question for Protestants is not whether to turn the source book into a textbook but what that textbook will look like and why.

Further Reading

Bellis, Alice Ogden, and Joel S. Kaminsky, eds. *Jews, Christians, and the Theology of the Hebrew Scriptures*. Atlanta: Society of Biblical Literature, 2000. A wide-ranging collection that highlights differences and commonalities among the different interpretive traditions.

Carmy, Shalom, ed., *Modern Scholarship in the Study of Torah*. Northvale, NJ: Jason Aronson, 1996. A collection of essays, from Orthodox scholars, on the different extents and ways that modern critical-biblical studies and traditional Orthodox positions may be reconciled.

The Condition of Jewish Belief: A Symposium Compiled by the Editors of Commentary Magazine. Northvale, NJ: Jason Aronson, 1989 [1966]. A milestone symposium that surveyed the religious beliefs of key Jewish religious leaders of different denominations. (A more recent survey is "What Do American Jews Believe? A Symposium," *Commentary* 102:2 [August 1996].)

Halivni, David Weiss. *Revelation Restored: Divine Writ and Critical Responses*. Boulder, CO: Westview, 1997. An important argument by a leading scholar of rabbinic texts that the original Torah was "maculated" after it was received and restored by Ezra.

Harris, Jay. *How Do We Know This? Midrash and the Fragmentation of Modern Judaism*. Albany: SUNY Press, 1995. A detailed survey of different methods of traditional, Jewish biblical interpretation.

Heger, Paul. *The Pluralistic Halakhah: Legal Innovation in the Late Second Common-wealth and Rabbinic Periods.* Berlin: de Gruyter, 2003. A historical examination of crucial rabbinic passages that deals with the development of *halakhah*, and thus, the connection between rabbinic law and the biblical text.

Jacobs, Louis. *Principles of the Jewish Faith: An Analytical Study.* New York: Basic Books, 1964. A study of the thirteen principles of Maimonides by the twentieth century's leading British scholar and theologian of Judaism.

Kellner, Menachem. *Dogma in Medieval Jewish Thought: From Maimonides to Abravanel.* Oxford: Oxford University Press, 1986. A survey of the role of dogma and lists of dogmatic principles in medieval Judaism.

Levenson, Jon D. *The Hebrew Bible, the Old Testament, and Historical Criticism: Jews and Christians in Biblical Studies.* Louisville, KY: Westminster/John Knox, 1993. A set of essays from the foremost Jewish scholar of biblical theology that examines what Jewish biblical theology might look like and the fundamental differences between Jewish and Christian biblical scholarship.

Levy, B. Barry. *Fixing God's Torah: The Accuracy of the Hebrew Bible Text in Jewish Law.* New York: Oxford University Press, 2001. A meticulous study, by an Orthodox scholar, of issues surrounding the accuracy of the Torah text.

Schwartz, Baruch J. "Of *Peshat* and *Derash*: Bible Criticism and Theology." *Prooftexts,* 14 (1994): 71–88. An important critique of Halivni's position, containing a passionate argument for the simultaneous acceptance of critical-biblical scholarship and *kiyyum mitzvot* (adherence to the commandments).

Shapiro, Marc B. *The Limits of Orthodox Theology: Maimonides' Thirteen Principles Reappraised.* Oxford: Littman Library of Jewish Civilization, 2004. An examination of the extent to which these principles, which are often perceived as authoritative, were accepted before and after Maimonides.

Shavit, Jaacov, and Mordechai Eran. *The Hebrew Bible Reborn: From Holy Scripture to the Book of Books.* Studia Judaica 38. Trans. Chaya Naor. Berlin: de Gruyter, 2007. The development of the Jewish study of the Bible in the modern period.

Simon, Uriel. "The Religious Significance of *Peshat*." Trans. Edward L. Greenstein. *Tradition* 23:2 (Winter 1988): 41–62. Also at http://www.lookstein.org/articles/simon_peshat.htm. A beautiful argument for the importance of reading biblical texts from both a contextual (*peshat*) and a homiletical (*derash*) perspective.

Sommer, Benjamin D. "Revelation at Sinai in the Hebrew Bible and in Jewish Theology." *Journal of Religion* 79 (1999): 422–451. A very thoughtful exploration of revelation as it appears in the Bible, and its implications for modern Judaism.

2

Reading the Bible Critically and Religiously

CATHOLIC PERSPECTIVES

Daniel J. Harrington, S.J.

IT IS RELATIVELY easy to describe how Catholics are supposed to read the Bible. The major reason is that there is recent, abundant, and intellectually sophisticated, official Catholic teaching on the topic.[1] The Catholic imagination tends toward finding analogies and complementarities wherever possible. The Catholic tradition insists on the integration of faith and reason. Catholics tend toward "both . . . and" thinking. So, on this matter, as on many others, the typical Catholic response is that both critical and religious readings of the Bible are not only possible but also necessary to appreciate fully what Sacred Scripture is.

It has often been said that Catholic social-ethical teaching is one of the world's best-kept secrets. I think that the same can be said of recent Catholic teaching on the Bible and biblical interpretation. Indeed, I suspect that 99.9 percent of Catholics in the world know little or nothing about it. I hope that this essay will remove some of the mystery from it, and put it into dialogue with Jewish and Protestant approaches. While Catholic teaching places its main emphasis on the religious reading of the Bible, it does repeatedly insist that biblical criticism or the historical-critical method (when properly understood) is indispensable in Catholic biblical interpretation.

The Shape of the Catholic Bible

The Catholic Bible is different from the Jewish Bible and the Protestant Bible.[2] All Christian Bibles, of course, include the twenty-seven books of the New Testament: the four Gospels, the Acts of the Apostles, thirteen Pauline letters, Hebrews, seven Catholic or General Epistles, and the book of Revelation (Apocalypse). All the books of the Hebrew Bible appear in the Christian Bible as the Old Testament. However, in Christian Bibles, the Old Testament books appear in a different order from that of the Hebrew Bible. Rather than following the Hebrew order of Torah, Prophets, Writings (with 2 Chronicles 36 as the ending), Christians arrange the books in the order of Pentateuch, Historical Books, Wisdom, Prophets, with the prophecy of Elijah's return "before the great and terrible day of the LORD" in Malachi 4:5–6 [Hebrew 3:23–24] serving as the bridge between the two Testaments. The Catholic (and Orthodox) ordering of the books is basically the same as the Protestant arrangement; both set up a "promise and fulfillment" dynamic between the Testaments. Christians thus regard the Old Testament (especially in its prophecies) as incomplete and as reaching fulfillment in the New Testament.

In content, Protestants follow the Hebrew canon of the Old Testament, while Catholics follow the wider Greek canon of Scripture. Catholic Bibles contain seven Old Testament books over and above those found in Jewish or Protestant Bibles. They are Tobit, Judith, 1 Maccabees, 2 Maccabees, Wisdom, Sirach, and Baruch. In recent years, Protestant publishers have resumed the old practice of including these books (and other books) as a kind of appendix or separate section, under the heading of "Apocrypha" or "Deuterocanonical Books." Orthodox Christian Bibles add a few more books beyond the seven. Moreover, both Catholic and Orthodox Bibles contain fuller editions of Daniel and Esther, following the more expansive Greek textual tradition.

The inclusion of the so-called Apocrypha interspersed among the other undisputed Old Testament books makes the Catholic Bible different from both the Jewish and the Protestant Bibles.[3] The books of Tobit and Judith are now recognized as charming tales (like Esther and Jonah) that provide valuable information about Second Temple Jewish life and piety. The works known as 1 and 2 Maccabees convey important historical and religious data about decisive events in the second century BCE. The book of Wisdom, because of its emphasis on immortality, offers a key element in the development of the biblical hope for eternal life after death. The book of Sirach (also known as Ecclesiasticus) presents the opinions of an early second-century Jewish teacher in Jerusalem about practically everything and bears witness to his efforts at integrating the ancient Near Eastern wisdom tradition and the Jewish biblical tradition. The book of Baruch shows how certain biblical passages—Daniel 9, Job 28, and Isaiah 40–66—were reread and interpreted to shed further light on Israel's experience of exile. The Additions to Esther make that book more explicitly religious, while the Additions to Daniel include the Prayer of Azariah and the Song of the Three Boys, along with the marvelous Greek tales of Susanna and of Bel and Dragon. These additional books make the Catholic Bible a rich resource for the study of Second Temple Judaism. And the inclusion of the Wisdom of Solomon is especially important theologically for its doctrine of immortality, encyclopedic scope of wisdom, attempt to integrate Greek philosophy and the biblical tradition, use of allegory as a method of interpreting earlier biblical texts, and integration of Israel's salvation history into wisdom literature.

Most Catholics continue to use the term "Old Testament" to describe the first part of their Bible. The expression "Old Testament" has New Testament roots (2 Corinthians 3 and Hebrews) and fits with Catholic tradition and theology. In the ancient world (unlike in our twenty-first century), of course, "old" was good. Both Jewish writers, like Josephus and Philo, and early Christian patristic authors made great efforts to prove the antiquity and authority of their religion and their Scriptures. Moreover, each of the modern alternatives carries its own set of problems, at least for Catholics. The Hebrew Bible ignores the Greek texts of the Apocrypha (and the Aramaic portions of Ezra and Daniel), and the fact that in many Christian circles the Old Testament has been the Greek version known as the Septuagint or its daughter versions. Also, the term "Jewish Scriptures" can make these books sound foreign to Catholics, as if they were not part of our Bible alongside the so-called Christian Scriptures (the New Testament). And the First Testament seems only a blander version of Old Testament.

Recent Official Documentation on Biblical Interpretation

The most authoritative modern document on the Catholic reading of the Bible is the "Dogmatic Constitution on Divine Revelation" issued by the Second Vatican Council in 1965. A "dogmatic constitution" is an especially authoritative kind of document because it deals with matters of church doctrine and comes from an ecumenical council involving bishops and theologians from all over the world. The document is customarily referred to by its first two Latin words *Dei Verbum* (Word of God). Its final approval was something of a watershed in the history of the Second Vatican Council. The initial draft (1962) was a very traditional scholastic-theological treatment of the Bible—not at all in dialogue with developments in modern biblical study. When that draft was rejected, the bishops at the council demanded something more in tune with current approaches to the Bible.[4] The six chapters in the version that eventually met their approval deal with revelation, the transmission of divine revelation, the divine inspiration of Scripture and its interpretation, the Old Testament, the New Testament, and Sacred Scripture in the life of the church.

Dei Verbum, of course, did not come out of nowhere. There had been a series of official (and very cautious) letters from popes (encyclicals) on biblical study, beginning with Pope Leo XIII in 1893 (*Providentissimus Deus*). The most important and influential of these letters was *Divino afflante Spiritu*, issued in 1943 by Pope Pius XII. This broke new ground because it recognized the importance of archaeological excavations, ancient philology, textual criticism and translation based on early manuscripts in Hebrew and Greek, aiming to recover the literal (original) sense, attending to the historical circumstances of the biblical writers, studying Scripture in the context of ancient Near Eastern history, and analyzing the different forms or kinds of speech in the Bible. While insisting on the importance of the religious reading of Scripture, this document amounted to the official Catholic acceptance of many of the major concerns of the historical-critical method.

Another significant predecessor to *Dei Verbum* was the 1964 instruction on the "Historical Truth of the Gospels" from the Pontifical Biblical Commission (*Sancta Mater Ecclesia*). Using the principles stated in *Divino afflante Spiritu*, it encouraged the application of biblical criticism to the Gospels while cautioning those who used it not to deny the truth and authority of the Gospels. It also emphasized that the Gospels must be read at three levels: Jesus, the early church, and the Evangelists. While stressing the continuity between the three levels, it also recognized that the Gospel writers and their sources often shaped the traditions about Jesus to deal with problems that had arisen in their own circumstances. These insights, too, were incorporated into *Dei Verbum*.

For our purposes—in keeping with our focus on the critical and religious readings of the Bible—the two most important recent documents come from the Pontifical Biblical Commission. While the commission, composed of biblical scholars, has existed for over a hundred years, it has assumed a variety of forms and purposes. In the early twentieth century, it issued "responses" to questions about the interpretation of biblical texts and topics. Their statements were generally in direct opposition to the positions taken by biblical critics. Today, many of their responses sound retrograde and even embarrassing although they do reflect the mood of fear regarding the "modernist crisis" of the time.

After Vatican II, the Pontifical Biblical Commission was transformed into an advisory committee of prominent Catholic biblical scholars from various parts of the world. It now meets regularly to produce extended essays on topics or themes of special concern to the wider Catholic Church. The two most significant documents related to our theme are "The Interpretation of the Bible in the Church" (1993) and "The Jewish People and Their Scriptures in the Christian Bible" (2002). The former document describes and evaluates the various methods of interpretation, examines hermeneutical questions, notes characteristically Catholic approaches, and considers the place that interpretation of the Bible has in the life of the church. Thus, it deals in some detail with both the critical and religious readings of the Bible. The latter document addresses the place of the Old Testament in the Christian Bible and its interpretation, and also considers how the Jewish people are treated in various parts of the New Testament.

An even more comprehensive presentation of the modern Catholic approach to the Bible and biblical interpretation can be found in Pope Benedict XVI's 2010 apostolic exhortation entitled *Verbum Domini*

(Word of the Lord).[5] This document was prepared on the basis of the October 2008 synod of Catholic bishops devoted to "The Word of God in the Life and Mission of the Church." The synod was intended as an examination of how Vatican II's *Dei Verbum* has affected Catholic church life. Much more than a summary of the synod's proceedings, the pope's exhortation incorporates and synthesizes in a systematic way much of modern Catholic thought on the Bible and its interpretation. *Verbum Domini* is a highly theological document that also places great emphasis on the practical importance of the Bible in church life and in the church's mission. It reaffirms the indispensable character of historical criticism while insisting on the theological or spiritual interpretation of the Bible. In treating the Old Testament, the pope insists on the authority of the Jewish Scriptures for Christians and their status as the word of God. He discusses their relevance for Christians in terms of the continuity between the Testaments, the discontinuity between them, and the themes of the Old Testament's fulfillment and transcendence through Christ.

Clarifying and encouraging Catholic biblical interpretation has been a major concern for Pope Benedict since Vatican II and is an important element in his legacy as both theologian and pope. In practice, Benedict XVI tends toward a spiritual or typological reading of the Old Testament rather than a strictly historical-critical one. Yet he is familiar with the results of historical criticism and uses them often as a starting point. His own approach (and much of recent Catholic teaching) is well summarized by Augustine's famous and oft-quoted dictum, "The New Testament is hidden in the Old, and the Old is made manifest in the New."

How Catholics Regard Their Bible

Catholicism is not a religion of "the book." Islam may well be. And some say that Judaism and Protestantism (with its insistence on *sola scriptura*) are, too. But Catholics view the Bible as primarily a witness to a person, Jesus of Nazareth, the Son of God, and the Word made flesh. Thus, Catholicism is more a religion of a person.

Catholics view the Bible and the church as having existed in a kind of symbiotic relationship from the very beginning. The word *symbiosis* refers to two entities that live together and cooperate in a mutually beneficial relationship. The point can be made by reflecting on the question: Which came first—the Bible or the church? The Bible of the early church, of course, was what we now call the Old Testament. Christians took many theological terms and concepts from it and reshaped them in light of their beliefs about the person of Jesus and his saving significance. The earliest complete documents in the New Testament—Paul's letters— were written in response to problems that had arisen in churches founded by Paul. These letters were in turn preserved in and by various churches, and this process of preservation eventually led to their inclusion in the New Testament. Likewise, the Gospels were developed from oral and written traditions associated with Jesus and handed on in the churches. The Evangelists imposed on these traditions a geographical-theological outline and produced their connected narratives about Jesus. These accounts, alongside the Pauline letters, became the core of the New Testament canon. Catholics regard the Bible as the church's book and the church as guided by the Bible.

The canonical writings that make up the Bible serve as the rule or norm of faith and practice for Catholics but they do not regard the Bible as the only source of divine revelation. According to *Dei Verbum*, "Sacred tradition, Sacred Scripture, and the Teaching Office of the Church are so linked and joined together that one cannot stand without the others, but all together, and each in its own way, under the action of the one Holy Spirit, contribute effectively to the salvation of souls" (10). In this context, "Sacred Tradition" would include not only the teachings of the early Church Fathers and other great theologians throughout the centuries but also the unbroken practice of the church. The "Teaching Office of the Church" (also known as the Magisterium) is composed of the pope and the bishops teaching in concert, as in an ecumenical council. In the case of biblical interpretation, that might mean the Magisterium serving as an arbiter or umpire in disputed interpretations of texts and their pertinence for church doctrine or practice. This power has been used very rarely throughout church history.

Though important elements in Catholic life, tradition and the Magisterium are also bound to Scripture and should not operate apart from it.

Against the background of theological disputes rooted in the Protestant Reformation, Vatican II insisted that Scripture and tradition flow from "the same divine wellspring," and "in a certain way come together into [a] single current and tend toward the same end." Likewise, the Magisterium, or Teaching Office, "is not above the word of God but serves it by teaching only what has been handed on" (*Dei Verbum* 9–10).

Catholics believe the Bible was written by human authors under the guidance of the Holy Spirit. It is the word of God in human language, that is, "the word of God in the words of men." Whereas in the past, some theologians imagined the divine inspiration of Scripture as a kind of divine dictation by the Holy Spirit to an individual writer, recent Catholic theology has (correctly in my view) envisioned the process in more communal terms and refrained from defining the process too precisely. This development reflects the recognition among biblical scholars that most of the Bible is a communal product; the result of scribal circles or schools handing on and reshaping traditional materials until a final editor or redactor put them together in something like their present forms.

Catholics regard the Bible as a trustworthy and inerrant guide on the road to salvation. Again, in the past, some theologians interpreted biblical inerrancy as pertaining to everything, including matters of science or history. Today, most Catholic theologians hold a more restricted view of biblical inerrancy. In this they follow the statement in *Dei Verbum* 11: "we must acknowledge the Books of Scripture as teaching firmly, faithfully, and without error the truth that God wished to be recorded in the sacred writings for the sake of our salvation." While some contest the view that the Vatican Council taught the "limited inerrancy" (only what pertains to salvation is inerrant) of Scripture, it is hard to understand the Bible critically and religiously today without some kind of limited approach. The idea is that the Bible, while inerrant in what pertains to our salvation, is not necessarily inerrant in its worldview or chronology or what we currently regard as the province of the physical sciences. This is surely the view of most Catholics today.[6]

Catholics also regard Scripture as a privileged witness to divine revelation and an occasion for divine revelation. What the Bible reveals first and foremost is the person of God and his will for us. Thus the Bible is not primarily a book of decrees, commandments, or prophecies. Rather, it is a vehicle by which we can come to know the creator of heaven and earth, the one who has entered into covenantal relationship with Israel, and the loving Father revealed by Jesus the Word of God. The Bible, in turn, can serve as a vehicle that can move individuals and communities in certain positive directions.

According to *Dei Verbum* 24, the study of the "sacred page" (another term for the Bible) should be "the soul of Sacred Theology." That same image can also apply to the church's pastoral practice. In other words, the Bible should be at the heart of all Christian life. In response to Vatican II, new and more accurate Catholic translations of the Bible—such as the *New American Bible* and the *Jerusalem Bible* (and their several revisions)— were made widely available. The lectionary of Scripture readings to be used at masses and other liturgical services was thoroughly revised to be much more inclusive of the Old Testament and to provide continuous readings of the Gospels and other New Testament writings. Even the prayers were recast to use a more biblical style and reflect more fully their biblical content. The goal set by Vatican II was that "all the preaching of the Church, as indeed the entire Christian religion, be nourished and ruled by Sacred Scripture" (*Dei Verbum* 21).

Catholics and the Historical-Critical Method

The historical-critical method is a way of investigating biblical texts that attends especially to their original historical settings and what they meant in those contexts. The now official Catholic position is that historical-critical analysis, properly understood, is the indispensable (though not completely sufficient by itself) method for the scientific study of a biblical text. While recent official Catholic documentation shows much more interest in reading the Bible religiously, it seems also to regard historical-critical analysis as the necessary starting point and foundation for the religious reading. Its theological rationale is the incarnation of Jesus the Word of God: "For the words of God, expressed in human language, have become like unto human speech, just as the Word of the eternal Father, when he took on himself the flesh of human weakness, became like unto human beings" (*Dei Verbum* 13).

The way to the acceptance of this approach to Scripture among Catholics was cleared by Pope Pius XII in *Divino afflante Spiritu.* That document proceeded from the recognition that one can use the historical-critical method without affirming the philosophical assumptions of the European Enlightenment thinkers such as Baruch (Benedict) Spinoza, who equated nature with God and denied the possibility of miracles. In affirming historical criticism, the encyclical also affirmed the value of the patristic interpretations of Scripture and the obligation to search for the spiritual or theological meaning of the biblical text.

In that encyclical, Pope Pius XII described the goal of historical-critical biblical interpretation as "to discern and define clearly that sense of the biblical words that is called 'literal'" (15). In this context, "literal" seems to mean what the original author intended. Pius encouraged textual critics' efforts to restore the sacred texts as perfectly as possible, translating from the original languages (Hebrew, Aramaic, Greek) and using the tools of philology and textual criticism to understand better the literal sense of the biblical text. He praised the potential contributions of archaeology toward this goal; and he insisted on trying to determine the peculiar characters and circumstances of the biblical writers, the age or culture in which they lived, the oral or written sources they had at hand, and the literary forms of expression that they used. He was especially eager that biblical interpreters come to know better the mentality of the ancient writers, as well as their manner and art of reasoning, narrating, and writing. To do so, it is necessary to learn and use the languages and cultures of the ancient Near East and the Greco-Roman world.

As noted previously, the theological justification for affirming the historical-critical method in the interpretation of Scripture was the analogy between the Bible and the incarnation of Jesus as the Word of God made flesh (see John 1:14): "For as the substantial Word of God became like to men in all things 'except sin' (Heb 4:15), so the words of God, expressed in human language, are made like to human speech in every respect except error" (20).

In treating the interpretation of Scripture, *Dei Verbum* took over much of what was already said in the papal encyclical *Divino afflante Spiritu*. It, too, insisted on paying attention "to the customary and characteristic modes of perception, speech, and narrative that prevailed at the time of the sacred writer, and to the customs that people of that time generally followed in their dealings with one another" (12).

The 1993 document from the Pontifical Biblical Commission on "The Interpretation of the Bible in the Church" built upon *Divino afflante Spiritu* and *Dei Verbum*. It was mainly concerned with describing in some detail the various literary, historical, and theological methods for interpreting Scripture. In section I.A.2 it points out three fundamental principles of the historical-critical method. It is *historical* because it is applied to ancient biblical texts and concerns the historical processes that gave rise to those texts. It is *critical* because it operates with the help of scientific criteria that seek to be as objective as possible. It is *analytical* because it studies biblical texts as it would study other ancient texts and comments on them as expressions of human discourse. The theological rationale for using the historical-critical method is that this approach will help interpreters to get a better grasp of the content of divine revelation.

Examples of Catholic Approaches to the Old Testament

In my book *Interpreting the Old Testament*, my goal was to explain to a nonspecialist audience how Catholic biblical scholars interpret Old Testament texts critically and religiously.[7] That is, I tried to explain the historical-critical method and to show how it might yield fruit in the lives of those who want to read the Bible both critically and religiously. Thus, I presented chapters on basic literary criticism, historical criticism, archaeology and parallels from antiquity, words and motifs, form criticism, source criticism, redaction criticism, and textual criticism. Also included were chapters on recent English translations, the Old Testament in Christian worship, and the Old Testament in Christian theology. A postscript treated the problems and possibilities involved in canonical criticism and social science criticism.

With each exposition of a method there are examples of texts from the Old Testament that illustrated the method and showed how the texts themselves were greatly illumined by applying the method. Thus, the basic concerns of literary analysis (words and images, characters, structure, literary form, message) served to bring out the artistry involved in the account of Abraham's binding of Isaac in Genesis 22:1–19 and the brilliance of the poem in Isaiah 40:1–11. The section on historical criticism compared the composite narrative in Exodus 14 and the poetic account of Israel's escape from Egypt in Exodus 15, and it discussed what can and cannot be said about the historical events behind those texts. The chapter on archaeology and ancient parallels showed how the Code of Hammurabi illumines certain legal texts in Exodus 21, and how the hymnic/poetic material from Ugarit shows many affinities with the biblical Psalms. The chapter devoted to words and images showed how the biblical vocabulary and the concept of "covenant" reflect various strands present in other ancient Near Eastern cultures. The treatment of form criticism discussed narrative forms such as the "call," as well as legal (commands and cases), poetic (various types of psalms), sapiential (proverbs, instructions, admonitions), and prophetic (threat, reproach, promise) forms of speech. The section on source criticism explained the documentary hypothesis of the Pentateuch, and the section on redaction criticism considered how the author of 1 Chronicles 17 edited the account about Nathan's oracle to David in 2 Samuel 7 for his own theological purposes. And the chapter on textual criticism illustrated, with reference to Deuteronomy 31:1 and 32:43, how the discovery of the Dead Sea Scrolls proved that there was some fluidity in the Hebrew text at the turn of the Common Era. And so on. I chose these and many other examples not only because they represent some of the best fruits of historical-critical study but also because they can and have contributed to the critical and religious reading of the Bible.

The professional biblical journals sponsored by Catholic institutions also demonstrate the predominance of the historical-critical method in recent years. Among the most prominent are *Revue Biblique* (sponsored by the Dominicans' École Biblique de Jérusalem), *Biblica* (sponsored by the Jesuits' Pontifical Biblical Institute in Rome), and *Catholic Biblical*

Quarterly (sponsored by the Catholic Biblical Association of America). All three journals are open to professional biblical scholars regardless of their religious affiliations. As much, if not more, space is given to Old Testament studies as to those that treat the New Testament. Most of the articles and the books reviewed focus on the ancient texts and interpret them according to the textual, literary, and historical operations that constitute biblical criticism today. Both articles and book reviews allow whatever theological messages may be discerned in them to emerge from the texts without forcing Catholic or other theological doctrines upon them. This is not to say that the articles and books have no theological significance. Indeed, they often do. But the goal is to let that significance come from the literary and historical study of the text, not to impose it on them.

These publications illustrate some of the characteristics of Catholic biblical scholarship today. It is international in scope, sees a relationship between scholarship and church life (without needing to make it too explicit), and is committed to Christian ecumenism and to work with Jewish and other scholars. It is all of these things, to a large extent, because biblical scholars have a common methodology—the historical-critical method.

Literary and Historical Problems with the Historical-Critical Method

Whether practiced by Jews, Catholics, or Protestants, there are for religious persons today some serious problems with the historical-critical approach, or at least with some versions. One problem is that according to some literary critics the equation of the literal sense and what the ancient authors intended represents an outmoded (though not necessarily wrong) approach to literature. Recent developments in philosophical hermeneutics and literary theory have cast doubt on the possibility of truly succeeding in the quest for the author's intention. Indeed, the enterprise has won the dubious label of "the intentional fallacy." However, much of today's technical biblical scholarship remains wedded to that quest; its practitioners are well aware of its methodological and philosophical difficulties. They claim in defense (correctly, I think) that through historical-critical study we can at least come close to the author's original meaning, perhaps arrive at an interpretation that takes due account of the ancient context, and (more important) disqualify certain other interpretations as historically impossible.

A second problem concerns finding and using the proper linguistic and cultural background to interpret biblical texts. Two questions immediately arise: which one? and, so what? For the Old Testament, should one privilege Akkadian, northwest Semitic (Ugaritic), Canaanite, Egyptian, or some other language and milieu? For the New Testament should it be the Old Testament, Palestinian Judaism, Hellenistic Judaism, rabbinic Judaism, Greek papyri from Egypt, Greek and Roman classical literature, Greco-Roman philosophy, Gnosticism, or some other milieu? There is something to be said for the value of each and every one of these cultural backgrounds in the task of illuminating the Bible. But which one (or ones) will prove more useful? The ancient Near Eastern and Mediterranean world was very large, and very few scholars can control several other linguistic and historical disciplines besides those needed for biblical studies. The best policy seems to be to do the best one can in whatever area one chooses, respecting what other scholars do in other areas and discerning what approach achieves the best results. The "so what?" question reminds us that in the historical study of biblical texts we are frequently dealing with parallels. And, of course, in geometry, parallel lines never meet. Too often the scholarly appeal to parallel texts fails to establish the real relevance of those texts or artifacts in illuminating biblical texts. Following the lead of Samuel Sandmel, biblical scholars have come to refer to this problem as "parallelomania."

A third (and very important) problem concerns the nature of history as a discipline. Scholars who call themselves historians perform a variety of tasks. One task is editing and publishing ancient texts or artifacts from archaeological excavations. This operation helps us understand better the world of the Bible and its cultural assumptions and limitations. Another task is synthesizing data from the various sources into a coherent narrative. Historians are essentially storytellers, and the great historians throughout the centuries have been effective at both enlightening and entertaining readers. Still, another task for historians is to go behind the texts and artifacts—to play detective and try to discern what "really happened." In these three tasks there is an ever-increasing amount of speculation. Of course, there is nothing wrong with playing detective. But as countless movies and television programs have shown, it often involves following one's intuition and guessing ("hunches"). The problem comes when hypotheses or speculations about the Bible are presented and accepted as established facts on the grounds that "scholars say." Those who practice historical criticism and those who rely on it need to be aware of the limitations of historical detective work and acknowledge them publicly.

Problematic Philosophical and Theological Presuppositions

Perhaps the most significant set of problems for Catholics and other religious persons is connected with the philosophical and theological presuppositions held by some practitioners of the historical-critical method. Their classic statement can be found in the 1900 essay entitled "Historical and Dogmatic Method in Theology" by Ernst Troeltsch (1865–1923).[8] In the essay, Troeltsch articulated what he regarded as the three great principles of historical criticism. This is where the Catholic theological tradition finds its most severe problems with historical criticism.

The first of Troeltsch's principles is criticism itself. That is, history achieves only probability. And so the religious tradition must be subjected to historical criticism. And the historical critic must establish the relationship of the facts in such a way that respects historical contingency. The problem is the implication that historical truth is so contingent that we can never reach the truths of reason (or theology) through historical research. History then becomes just one thing after another. The second principle is analogy. That is, present experiences and occurrences are the criteria of probability in dealing with the past (including the biblical past). The problem is that analogy effectively rules out one-time supernatural events in the Bible such as the exodus, the miracles of Elijah and Elisha, and Jesus' healings and resurrection. For them, another more "rational" and "this worldly" explanation has to be found. The third principle is correlation. That is, all historical phenomena are so interrelated that a change in one phenomenon necessitates a change in the causes leading to it and in the effects it has. The problem here is that this principle rules out appeals to divine action in history, since divine or transcendent causes are not allowed in this kind of historical criticism.

Whatever the merits, Troeltsch's three principles assume a world where the biblical witness is generally discounted on philosophical grounds—a world very different from that assumed in the Bible and in the Jewish and Christian traditions. At least from a Catholic perspective, these principles rest on debatable philosophical presuppositions, and the fact that in some circles they have been elevated to the status of the only criteria for judging what really happened in biblical times is unfortunate and misleading. Their rigid application is incompatible with, and not part of, the positive Catholic understanding of historical criticism as an indispensable tool in biblical interpretation.

When the Catholic documents on the Bible refer to the historical-critical method as indispensable, they mean the approach outlined in *Divino afflante Spiritu* and its subsequent affirmations, which were spelled out in more detail in the 1993 document from the Pontifical Biblical Commission, "The Interpretation of the Bible in the Church." But if the historical-critical method or biblical criticism is taken to mean accepting the philosophical and theological presuppositions of Spinoza or Troeltsch, then the Catholic tradition rejects that version as foreign to and incompatible with the Bible and Christian (and Jewish) theological traditions.

How Catholics Understand the Old Testament

In the Catholic Bible, the books of the Old Testament account for roughly 75 to 80 percent of the total. In New Testament times, the Bible of the early Christians was what we now call the Old Testament, primarily in its Greek version. From the second century onward, the Old Testament has generally been acknowledged as Sacred Scripture by Christians alongside the New Testament. Marcion's attempt to jettison the Old Testament

as a work about an inferior God was firmly rejected by church authorities. However, what to do with the Old Testament has remained a problem (and an opportunity) for Christians ever since.

As Jews, New Testament writers such as Matthew and Paul made
abundant use of Old Testament texts to confirm their statements about
Jesus and about church practice and Christian life. Matthew is famous
for his many "fulfillment quotations." For example, Matthew in 1:22
introduced his quotation of Isaiah 7:14 to "prove" the virginal conception
of Jesus with the formula, "All this took place to fulfill what had been
spoken by the LORD through the prophet." Paul used various biblical
texts (for example, in Galatians 3 and Romans 4 and 9–11) to argue that
the Torah could not do what Christ had done through his death and resurrection in making possible a new and better relationship with God
(justification). In the book of Revelation, John managed to include an
allusion to or an echo of Old Testament texts in almost every verse without ever presenting an exact quotation.

The New Testament writers (and other early Christians) generally
took the paschal mystery (Jesus' life, death, and resurrection, and their
saving effects) as the key to interpreting the Old Testament. In this
respect, they were doing something like what the Jewish group that produced the Dead Sea Scrolls did when they wrote their commentaries
(*Pesharim*) on obscure prophetic texts and psalms in the light of the history and ideology of their own community (probably Essenes). Both
groups regarded the Hebrew Scriptures as authoritative in a general
sense but felt some texts to be obscure and "unfulfilled" in many of their
details. In solving the mysteries (*razim*) of the Bible, they used different
keys: Essene history and life (the Dead Sea community) and Jesus (early
Christians).

The early Christian teachers, known as the Church Fathers (or patristic writers), writing from the second to the seventh or eighth century,
spent enormous amounts of energy studying and interpreting the Old
Testament. They regarded the great figures of the Old Testament as pre-
figuring (as types or shadows) Christ, and they were determined to find
such prefigurations in as many places as possible. They were convinced
that many Old Testament prophecies which seemingly had not been

fulfilled in Israel's history had in fact been fulfilled in and through Jesus. Like Augustine, they were convinced that what lay hidden in the Old Testament had become manifest in the New Testament. In other words, it took the appearance of the person of Jesus to make proper sense of the Old Testament.

Against this background, it is fair to describe the primary Catholic approach to the Old Testament as proceeding "from promise to fulfillment" or "from shadows to reality." The "promise" is to be found in the shadows of the Old Testament, and the "fulfillment" or "reality" in Christ as he is proclaimed in the New Testament. In practical terms, today this approach lies behind much of the selection of Scripture texts in the church's lectionary for Sundays and major feasts. While there are exceptions (especially during Lent), for the most part, it seems that in the lectionary the Old Testament passage has been chosen with an eye toward providing "background" for the Gospel text, and the responsorial psalm serves as a bridge between the Gospel and Old Testament texts.

Various statements in Vatican II's *Dei Verbum* 14–16 illustrate and confirm the primacy of the Catholic promise and fulfillment approach to the Old Testament. While affirming that "these divinely inspired books retain lasting value," it goes on to say that "the economy of the Old Testament was designed above all to prepare for the coming of Christ, the universal redeemer, and of the messianic kingdom." This it did through prophecies and various "types." *Dei Verbum* also claims that in the Old Testament books "the mystery of our salvation is present in a hidden way." However, the document also gives credit to the Old Testament in itself for "its lofty teaching about God and sound wisdom on human life, as well as its wonderful treasury of prayers." It is also said to illustrate God's way of instructing and to convey a vivid sense of God. Nevertheless, these books are judged to "contain what is only incomplete and provisional." What exactly is meant by this statement is not explained. But it appears once more to affirm the traditional promise and fulfillment way of reading the Old Testament.

A more positive, complete, and balanced Catholic approach to the Old Testament can be found in the 2002 document from the Pontifical Biblical Commission on "The Jewish People and Their Sacred Scriptures in the Christian Bible." This document appeared almost forty years after Vatican II and reflects the progress made in Christian-Jewish relations since the council. Moreover, it was prepared by professional Catholic biblical scholars, many of whom had worked seriously on Old Testament texts often in collaboration with Jewish scholars. The Catholic scholars were well suited to appreciate the intrinsic merits and contributions of the Old Testament on its own, without always looking for explicit references to Christ and the New Testament.

That document first affirms that the Sacred Scriptures of the Jewish people are a fundamental part of the Christian Bible. This is clear from the New Testament itself, which would be unintelligible without the Old Testament. The New Testament writers not only appealed to the authority of the Jewish Scriptures and used Jewish exegetical methods in interpreting biblical texts, but they also developed key Old Testament themes such as the revelation of God, the greatness and wretchedness of the human condition, God as liberator and savior, the election of Israel, the covenant, the law, prayer and worship, divine reproaches and condemnations, and the promises (including the kingdom of God and the Messiah).

While noting the prominence of the Christological reading of the Old Testament in the New Testament and in Christian history, the document also observes that the return to the literal sense and the development of the historical-critical method have helped retrieve important insights into biblical texts. It also urges respect for traditional Jewish readings of the Bible and insists that the Old Testament in itself has great value as the word of God. It concludes that there is both continuity and discontinuity between the Testaments, and it shows how none of the great Old Testament themes "escapes the new radiation of the Christological light." Finally, it examines how Jews and Judaism are portrayed in various parts of the New Testament, paying particular attention to their historical situations. While not admitting that the New Testament is anti-Jewish, it does recognize the anti-Jewish potential in some New Testament texts. It concludes that the Jewish Scriptures constitute an essential part of the Christian Bible and warns against taking biblical texts out of context and using them as pretexts for anti-Judaism.

How Catholics Understand the New Testament

While the focus of this volume is the Old Testament, a look at how Catholics understand their Bible as a whole (with the New Testament) may help put their view of the Old Testament in broader relief. In Catholic piety and liturgy, the four Gospels (Matthew, Mark, Luke, and John) are preeminent because they are "the principal witness to the life and teaching of the incarnate Word, our Savior" (*Dei Verbum* 18). Their preeminence proceeds from the assumption that they "faithfully hand on" what Jesus did and taught.

However, *Dei Verbum* and other official Catholic documents insist that the Gospels have to be read and interpreted on three levels: Jesus, the early church, and the Evangelists. This point is made in a long, and somewhat dense, statement in *Dei Verbum* 19: "In composing the four Gospels, the sacred writers selected certain of the many traditions that had been handed on either orally or already in written form; others they summarized or explicated with an eye to the situation of the churches. Moreover, they retained the form and style of proclamation but always in such a fashion that they related to us an honest and true account about Jesus." Reflecting modern study of the Gospels, as well as the symbiotic relationship between the Bible and the church that is typical of Catholicism, this statement leaves room for source criticism, form criticism, and redaction criticism while affirming that there is continuity within the process of tradition about Jesus and that the Gospels tell us the honest truth about Jesus.

The rest of the New Testament consists of the Acts of the Apostles, the thirteen Pauline Epistles, Hebrews, the seven Catholic or General Epistles, and the book of Revelation. In these writings, according to *Dei Verbum* 20, "those matters that concern Christ the LORD are confirmed, his authentic teaching is more fully stated, the saving power of Christ's divine work is proclaimed, the origins and marvelous growth of the Church are recounted, and her glorious consummation is foretold." While prominent in Catholic liturgy today, there is some truth to the observation that Protestants put more emphasis on the Epistles (especially Paul's letters) and Catholics give more attention to the Gospels.

The Spiritual Sense of Scripture

While insisting on the historical-critical method as "indispensable," official Catholic teaching also insists that it is not totally adequate. Besides
establishing the author's intention and the meaning in its original historical context, the interpreter must also consider the spiritual sense of
the text, that is, what the text might mean today for an individual or for
a group. This idea is based on the biblical concept of the word of God as
something living and active, having an effect not only in the past but
also, and especially, in the present and future (see Isa 55:10–11; Heb 4:12).
Ideally, the spiritual sense should flow from the literal sense.

In medieval biblical interpretation, there developed what was called
the "four senses of Scripture"—an approach often used as a tool for
interpreting Old Testament texts. This approach developed at least in
part because of problems created by a literal reading. The four senses are
the literal sense (the basic "facts" of the text); the allegorical sense (what
in the text might pertain to Christ); the moral sense (what might pertain
to right conduct); and the anagogical sense (what pertains to our heavenly hope, or eschatology). This approach was applied eagerly and fruit-
fully up to and through modern times. However, it was open to
arbitrariness and was criticized strongly by the Protestant Reformers
(who, nonetheless, often used it in practice).

The modern understanding of the spiritual interpretation of Scripture has been greatly clarified by the Pontifical Biblical Commission's
1993 document on "The Interpretation of the Bible in the Church." It
insists that the spiritual interpretation of a biblical text must not be alien
to the literal interpretation—that is, to the meaning expressed by the
human author in the written text. Moreover, it defines the spiritual sense
as "the meaning expressed by the biblical texts when read under the
influence of the Holy Spirit, in the context of the paschal mystery of
Christ, and of the new life that flows from it." It also notes, "It is most
often in dealing with the Old Testament that Christian exegesis speaks
of the spiritual sense." To be authentic, a spiritual reading of the biblical
text must keep in mind three things: the literal sense, the paschal mystery, and the present circumstances.

When all is said and done, this approach to the spiritual sense of Scripture is reminiscent of the promise and fulfillment and from shadows to reality ways of interpreting the Old Testament. Although the approach is firmer and more precise about respecting the literal sense, it does come down to assuming Christ as the key to the Scriptures, especially the Old Testament, and privileging the Christological reading of the Old Testament.

Related to the spiritual sense of Scripture is the "fuller sense," or *sensus plenior*. This is the deeper meaning of a text that was intended by God but not consciously or clearly expressed by the biblical author. An example would be the prophecy in Isaiah 7:14 that an *'almah* (in Hebrew a "young woman") would bear a son whose name would be "Emmanuel." Whereas Isaiah and his audience at the royal court in Jerusalem might have assumed that he was talking about a male child (perhaps Hezekiah) to be born from one of King Ahaz's wives, in the fuller sense, the Holy Spirit, speaking through the prophet, was really looking forward centuries later to the virginal conception of Jesus by Mary who was a *parthenos* according to the Greek in Matthew 1:18–25. This sense is obviously a theological accommodation that assumes the Holy Spirit's ultimate authorship of the Scriptures and Christ as the key to all the Scriptures. It serves to explain the inner coherence of the Bible when read from a Christian perspective. It is, again, a form of the promise to fulfillment and shadows-to-realities Catholic approach to the Old Testament.

Inculturation

The word "catholic" means universal, general, pertaining to all. By its very name, Catholicism seeks to touch all the peoples of the world. The issue facing Catholic missionaries is (and always has been) to communicate the message of the Bible as the word of God in such a way as to reach new peoples in their own places and cultural contexts. This is called "inculturation" in theological circles. The starting point of inculturation usually involves translating the Bible into the people's language or teaching a language—English, French, Spanish, etc.—that might be familiar, which also makes it easier to have reliable translations of the Bible on hand. But that is just the beginning.

The more pressing task of inculturation is to learn how to say in the target language what the original biblical language aims to say. This challenge has led to the emergence of "dynamic equivalence" translations of the Bible. Rather than rendering the biblical text in a very literal way ("formal equivalence"), dynamic equivalence translators seek to render the thought content as accurately as possible, without being bound to the Hebrew or Greek syntax and vocabulary. Likewise, teachers of theology must labor to find meaningful equivalents in the target language for those terms and concepts that are essential to their various theological disciplines.

The challenge of the inculturation of the Christian Gospel frequently exacerbates the problem of interpretation. Catholics in India, China, and Africa often find the Old Testament especially "foreign" to their cultures. While they note many similarities between life in ancient Israel and their own experience, they also sometimes protest that the scriptures of Hinduism, Buddhism, and Confucianism, or the experience and rituals of traditional African religions, are their equivalent of the "Old Testament." Consequently, some propose substituting (or adding) those texts or rituals to the assigned Old Testament readings. While Catholic Church authorities have generally resisted such substitutions, one can understand the desire of these new Christians to find and work with a religious past more in accord with their history and experience than the Old Testament.

Actualization: Reading the Bible Religiously

The term "actualization" means to bring the significance of a biblical text into the present. It is here, especially, that we deal with the possibilities and problems involved in reading the Bible religiously. For Catholics, this is an essential component of interpretation and a natural supplement to historical criticism. It can take many forms.

One form is called *lectio divina*, or spiritual reading. Rooted in monasticism, this approach can be used by individuals or in groups. There are four steps. The first step (*lectio*) is to read the text slowly and carefully, asking basic questions about the words and images, the structure, the literary form, the context, and the major theme or themes. The second step (*meditatio*) is to reflect on what this text might be saying to me here and now. The third step (*oratio*) is to say to God in prayer what I might want or need to say here and now on the basis of this biblical text. The fourth step can be either *contemplatio* (enjoying and resting in the spiritual experience) or *actio* (determining what I need to do or change on the basis of my encounter with this text). Again, such reading should take the literal sense as its starting point.

There are several variations on *lectio divina*. One is Ignatian contemplation, named after Ignatius of Loyola, the sixteenth-century founder of the Jesuits and the architect of *The Spiritual Exercises*. Much of the *Spiritual Exercises* consists of contemplations on biblical texts, chiefly from the Gospels. What is distinctive is the emphasis on the religious imagination as a means of entering into the biblical text. In addition to the careful reading of the text, one is expected to apply the five senses to the text where possible. That is, to ask questions such as, what do I see? what do I hear? what do I smell? what do I taste? and what do I touch? The idea is to enter personally and sensually into the biblical scene and become part of it, either as a spectator or as an active participant.

Another variation is the method developed in Latin American Catholic "base communities" in the 1970s. The process begins with an inspection of the current social and political realities, and an assessment of the problems hindering personal and communal flourishing. Next, there is the search for pertinent biblical texts and themes (especially the exodus) that might inspire, encourage, and move the community to positive action. Then there is a return to the people's current situation and an effort to discern in the light of Scripture and prayer what might be the most appropriate response and productive way forward.

The most obvious form of the actualization of Scripture in Catholic circles appears in the Eucharistic liturgy (the Mass). In response to Vatican II, the prayers were rewritten in a more explicitly biblical style. Moreover, the lectionary (the book of Scripture readings) was thoroughly revised to provide a far richer and wider selection of texts. Thus, almost every Sunday, there is a passage from the Old Testament, excerpts from an Old Testament psalm, a passage from one of the New Testament letters, and a reading from one of the Gospels. On weekdays there is a first reading (often from the Old Testament), excerpts from a psalm, and a Gospel passage. The preacher or homilist is expected to take account of the biblical readings and help the congregation see how they might apply the readings to their situation. The hymns sung by the congregation are almost all based on particular biblical texts or themes, many of them explicitly inspired by the biblical psalms. A similar pattern prevails at the liturgies associated with the other sacraments (baptism, confirmation, reconciliation/confession, marriage, ordination, anointing of the sick) and with other church rituals.

Problems with Reading the Bible Religiously

Catholic liturgy and practice make abundant provision for reading the Bible religiously. However, there are some problems. Most Catholics are not very familiar with the biblical texts that are read at liturgies, especially those from the Old Testament. Likewise, many priests and deacons do not feel competent in dealing seriously with Scripture, due in part to deficiencies in their own theological training and continuing education. If we continue to emphasize Scripture in our worship services, we must work at helping our people to become more knowledgeable about and comfortable with the Bible, especially the Old Testament.

Another problem may come from excessive reliance by Catholics on the promise and fulfillment approach to the Old Testament. This can lead to a narrow and false assessment of the Old Testament as merely a book of prophecies about Jesus the Messiah. I once heard a Jewish scholar describe the Christian practice as tearing pages out of his family album. While I would insist that it is my family album, too, I also admit that Catholics' exposure to the Old Testament in their liturgies, while a vast improvement over what it once was, is still woefully insufficient.

During the Sundays in Lent, however, there is something of an exception to the usual promise and fulfillment pattern. In each of the years of the three-year Sunday cycle, there is a sequence of readings that serves to trace the history of God's covenantal relationship with Israel from Abraham (or Adam) to the Babylonian exile of 586. This allows the Old Testament readings to stand on their own and to be taken more seriously for what they say in themselves, rather than merely serve as background or "window dressing" to the Gospel text.

These observations can help us better appreciate the positive value of the historical-critical method even in the religious reading of the Bible. In Catholicism, the two readings are not entirely separate or hostile. As we have seen, this method is primarily understood as an objective way of investigating biblical texts that attends especially to their original historical settings and what they meant in those contexts. However, there is a common humanity between the persons who wrote the ancient texts and us, an existential human connection. Catholics have traditionally referred to this as the natural law (though that term carries too much historical baggage to be helpful today). A better term is our "common humanity" (the *humanum*).

By attending carefully through the historical-critical method to the experiences and insights of the biblical writers and of those persons about whom and for whom they wrote, our own experiences can be greatly enriched, and we may find in the biblical texts material that is genuinely significant for us today. We do this when we read serious ancient (and modern) texts, rather than those in which our concerns are to be entertained or to satisfy personal curiosity. What unites us with the people of the Bible is the common humanity and the religious heritage that we share with those who produced it and those who read it. That allows us not only to understand ancient texts like the Bible but also to identify with and learn from the characters in the Bible. Because, in Catholic theology, the Bible is understood to be the word of God in human language, we have not only the *humanum* (our common humanity) but also the *divinum* (Holy Spirit) to link us to its texts.

Reading a Text Critically and Religiously: The Call of Moses

In Exodus 3, Moses comes to Mount Horeb and discovers a burning bush that is not consumed. A voice from the bush identifies itself as the God of Abraham, Isaac, and Jacob. This God wants to liberate Israel from slavery in Egypt and bring the Hebrews to the promised land of Canaan. He has chosen Moses to be his agent and to lead the people from slavery to freedom. When Moses inquires about God's name, he is told "I AM WHO I AM" (3:14), the God of the patriarchs. Then he instructs Moses to go to the king of Egypt and demand that he let the Hebrews go free.

In Exodus 4, Moses objects, stating he will not be taken seriously by either the Hebrews or Pharaoh. So he is given three signs: his staff turns into a snake and back again; his hand turns leprous and back again; and water from the Nile becomes blood on the ground. The idea is that if God can do these miracles, he can surely get Moses a hearing. Finally, Moses objects because he is "slow of speech and slow of tongue" (4:10). But God reassures him that his brother Aaron can and will speak on his behalf.

In my analysis of Exodus 3–4, I first emphasize that the primary object of Catholic biblical scholarship is to illuminate *the world of the text* as it has come down to us. Next, I suggest that Catholics are willing and eager to read biblical texts in their ancient historical contexts. (But there is a healthy skepticism about the more adventurous hypotheses concerning *the world behind the text*.) Then, I try to show that Exodus 3–4 is an important text in the Catholic Bible. It has been and still is powerful in my own life and so in *the world before the text*.

The World of the Text. Catholics understand the Bible as the word of God in human language; that is, as written by human authors under the inspiration of the Holy Spirit. Approaching a biblical text means analyzing the passage with the tools of philology and literary analysis—two major concerns in Catholic biblical interpretation today. "Philology" concerns the etymology and history of the words and phrases used in the Hebrew, Greek, and Latin texts. "Literary analysis" means respecting the text in its present form as made up of words and images, as having a certain structure, as representing a certain literary form or genre, as situated in a larger literary context, and as communicating a message.

In Catholic and other circles, many heads have been broken and much ink spilled over the divine name YHWH revealed in Exodus 3:14. The philologists want to make something out of its obvious connection to the Hebrew root *hayah* (to be) and to view it as alluding to the role of Israel's God in creation, that is, as "the one who causes to be." The philosophers and theologians for centuries have tried to find in it a reference to God as "pure being" and as an essential concept in Christian metaphysics. Modern exegetes seem to prefer to regard the name as something of an evasion on God's part ("I AM WHO I WILL BE"); and as a challenge to see who this God is from what this God will do in the rest of the book of Exodus, or even in everything that follows in the Torah or in the whole Hebrew Bible.

From a literary-critical perspective, an important concern is the recognition of Exodus 3–4 as a call narrative; a literary form that has parallels in the biblical stories of Gideon, Isaiah, and Jeremiah, along with various New Testament characters such as Mary, Jesus' first disciples, and Paul. Its elements include the sudden appearance of the deity (or an angel), a greeting of sorts, a mission or commission, an initial objection, signs that the commission is authentic and possible with God's help, further objections and signs, and final acceptance. This is the dynamism of biblical religious experience.

The World behind the Text. The term "history" covers a wide range of interests. It can mean finding ancient Near Eastern parallels, determining what sources the biblical authors used and how they used them, or establishing the historical circumstances in which the text was composed. For our purposes, I will limit the discussion to some of the detective work that goes on behind the written text in order to capture the realities to which the text bears witness.

Source criticism is concerned with identifying the written or oral materials behind the text as it has come down to us in the Bible. The so-called documentary hypothesis of the Torah discerns at least four major sources: J (Yahwist), E (Elohist), D (Deuteronomist), and P (Priestly). The classic source-critical analysis of Exodus 3–4 assigns the main narrative in Exodus 3 to E (3:1–6, 9–15, and 21–22) with short passages from J (3:7–8, 16–20), and the main narrative in chapter 4 (through 6:2) to J with short passages from E.[9] There is something to be said for this analysis, but it is by no means entirely persuasive. Catholics are free to take it or leave it. In recent times, some scholars have rejected the whole enterprise in favor of taking the received text alone as the appropriate object of study, while others have worked hard at exploring the even greater complexity that may have been involved in the composition of the Pentateuch.

According to the classic documentary hypothesis, the materials in J and E arose between 1000 and 800 BCE, were joined in the seventh or sixth century, and became part of the Torah during the exile or after the return under the P editor. That still leaves several centuries between Moses and the events narrated in Exodus 3–4. Two obvious questions for the historian: (1) Where did the name YHWH come from? (2) What really happened at Mount Horeb/Sinai to the historical Moses?

In regards to Exodus 3:14 and the name of YHWH, the most important issue for historians is the so-called Kenite hypothesis. The Kenite (or Midianite-Kenite) hypothesis claims that YHWH was originally a Kenite tribal god who became known to Moses through Jethro (his Kenite father-in-law), and through Moses, YHWH was accepted by the Hebrews and became equated with the Israelite "God of the Fathers"— the God of Abraham, Isaac, and Jacob. A distinguished Catholic biblical scholar, Joseph Blenkinsopp, recently provided an elegant defense of this hypothesis.[10] A variation of this hypothesis (which was the centerpiece of a recent PBS production on archaeology and ancient Israel's history) places the Hebrew reception of YHWH as their God at a much later date, which was then read backward to the time of Moses. However interesting either form of this hypothesis may be, it is hardly central to Catholic biblical scholarship and is the kind of hypothesis that evokes Pope Benedict XVI's warnings about the limits of what can really be known from historical criticism.

A more fundamental set of historical questions concerns the relationship between the events described in Exodus 3–4 and the historical Moses. In other words: What really happened, if anything? We know about these events only through the text in our Bibles. If the book of Exodus was put into its present form during the exile or shortly thereafter, then about one thousand years separates the present form of the text from the events it describes. Was the narrative handed on accurately over those thousand years? Or was it created at a much later time? Again, while these are interesting questions, we bump up against the limits of historical study.

The World in Front of the Text. To actualize Scripture means to bring its meaning into the present time and apply it to our lives. That can occur on both the personal and the communal levels. When I was about ten years old, I read in a newspaper that according to the Bible Moses stuttered. I stuttered, too (and still do), and so I was eager to find out if that was true. And so I got a hold of a Bible and found in Exodus 4:10 that Moses resisted God's call for him to lead his people and plead with Pharaoh for their liberation from slavery in Egypt on the grounds that he was "slow of speech and slow of tongue." Many interpreters have understood this to mean some speech impediment on Moses' part.

This verse is part of the narrative in Exodus 3–4 about Moses' experience of God on Mount Horeb and his call to lead God's people. What makes this passage so important is not only its revelation of the divine name YHWH in Exodus 3:14, but also its presentation of the dynamics of religious experience: the numinous burning bush, Moses' curiosity and fear, the concept of holy ground, the call from God, the self-revelation of God, the commission to go to the land promised to Abraham and his descendants, God's promises to be with Moses and to bring about all these things, the displays of miraculous power on Moses' part, his continued resistance to accepting the call, and his final acceptance of it.

Reading Exodus 3–4 as a boy not only gave me personal encouragement but much more significantly opened up to me the whole world of biblical religious experience. It shaped my religious identity. It led me to join the Jesuit order, to study ancient Near Eastern languages and literatures at Harvard University, to be ordained as a Catholic priest, and to teach and preach on Scripture for over forty years. Whenever I get discouraged, I return to Exodus 3–4. Obviously, this text has great personal significance. And a crucial principle in the Catholic tradition of biblical interpretation is that Scripture is to be taken personally and religiously.

Exodus 3–4 contains many rich themes for those in search of a religious reading of the text and points for further personal and communal meditation and prayer. They include fascination with the bush that burned but was not consumed, the idea of holy ground, religious experience as *mysterium tremendum et fascinans* (a mystery that both frightens and fascinates), God's concern with his people's plight and desire to free them from suffering and slavery, the experience of call and commission, concern with the name of God, God's choice of Moses as his unlikely instrument, the despoiling of the Egyptians, the significance of signs from God, and the resolution of Moses' objections.

While trying to communicate my personal religious enthusiasm for Moses and Exodus 3–4, I have also sought to illustrate how a Catholic biblical scholar might approach this text as literature and to raise some questions from a historical perspective. Let me note a challenging observation raised recently by a French Catholic biblical scholar J.-P. Sonnet.[11] The English title of his French article was "Risking One's Life for Beings That Exist on Paper." Sonnet observes that we know Moses, David, Isaiah, Jesus, and Paul mainly as entities on paper, and yet many persons have risked their lives after their example and on their behalf. This phenomenon, I think, raises the study of Scripture from the academic playground to the existential and theological level—where, I think, it belongs.

Patristic Interpretation

In all the recent Catholic documents on the interpretation of Scripture that endorse the historical-critical approach, there is also high praise for the Church Fathers as interpreters of Scripture. In many periods of church history, they have functioned as the equivalents of the Jewish rabbis. The title "Church Father" is generally bestowed on early Christian theologians from the second to the seventh or eighth centuries CE who wrote in Greek, Latin, or Syriac, and whose works are regarded as generally orthodox (as opposed to heretical or gnostic). The most prominent figures include Origen, Clement of Alexandria, John Chrysostom, Basil, Gregory Nazianzus, Ambrose, Augustine, Jerome, Ephrem, and Aphrahat.

Their interpretations of Exodus 3:1–4:17 provide a sample of their interests and offer something of a contrast to the historical-critical approach.[12] The Church Fathers were careful and critical readers of Scripture, insofar as they were particularly concerned with understanding and explaining certain peculiar features in the biblical texts: Who was the angel of the LORD? What was the significance of the bush? Why was Moses commanded to take off his shoes? And so on. They were not, however, historical critics in the sense of how that term is used in this book. Their focus was primarily the world of the biblical text. They took the text as a given, worked from it, and were mainly interested in edifying their readers and confirming them in their Christian faith.

For the Fathers, the world behind the text was not the literature and culture of the ancient world, as it is for historical critics today. Rather, their concern was the Christian narrative, which they regarded as standing behind the text not only of the New Testament but also of the Old Testament. They found the Christian story almost everywhere. They did so not only by what they considered literal readings but also (and especially) by interpreting one biblical text by another and by allegory. Thus, they were far more interested in the religious or spiritual reading of the Bible than in what we today consider the historical-critical reading of it. They were fascinated by Christian theological matters: the various names for God, the meaning of YHWH/ "I AM WHO I AM," the workings of the Trinity, the morality of despoiling the Egyptians, and the meaning of Moses' miracles.

As for Moses' speech impediment in Exodus 4:10, Augustine notes that Moses could and did become eloquent suddenly, "when the LORD began to speak to him." Origen takes it as symbolic of the Jews' inability to give reasonable explanations of the precepts of their Law and of the predictions of their prophets. In another place, Origen associates Moses' condition with his not having yet been circumcised in the lips, and sees in it the need for Jews to apply allegory to their practice of circumcision of the foreskin. This small sample illustrates the Church Fathers' great interest in and curiosity about the text of the Old Testament, as well as their theological passion to interpret it in terms of Christian theology. It also illustrates their unfortunate tendencies to theological supersessionism and anti-Judaism, that is, to assume that Christians have replaced Jews as the people of God, and that the Old Testament Scriptures are meaningful only in terms of the Christ-event.

Conclusion

For those seeking to read the Bible both critically and religiously, recent Roman Catholic teaching on biblical interpretation can provide a good framework. By accepting many key elements of the historical-critical method, it encourages us to place the biblical texts in their original historical contexts and to grasp as best we can what the biblical writers were trying to say to their original audiences. By also insisting that the task of biblical interpretation does not end with determining the text's meaning in the past, it challenges us to consider its significance for today and invites us to engage in a religious or spiritual reading of it.

In interacting with the Old Testament, however, perhaps Catholics in the future might be more open to using the historical-critical method, as they come to understand it and to delve more deeply into the existential or transcendent human values in the texts. There are many untapped riches in these texts, and the historical-critical method can help Catholics to recover them. The Christological reading of the Old Testament is as old as Christianity itself, and it will not (and cannot) disappear. However, our appreciation for Old Testament texts may be greatly enriched by taking them more seriously on their own merits rather than always forcing them into a promise and fulfillment theological schema. It is also necessary (and in keeping with Vatican II's *Nostra aetate* 4) to discourage the theological supersessionism and anti-Judaism that have too often accompanied it. Then perhaps we will see more clearly both the human and the divine significance of those texts for us, too.

Allow me to end with a personal testimony. Most of my adult life has been taken up with both the critical and the religious readings of the Bible. I entered the Society of Jesus (Jesuits) at age eighteen (1958) and showed an ability for languages and literary studies. The first experience of reading John's Gospel in the original Greek was a thrill I will never forget. I became seriously interested in biblical studies around the age of twenty-one (1961), when a wise Jesuit dean suggested that biblical studies was "the coming field" in Catholic circles and that I should think of pursuing it. That was the best advice anyone ever gave me. An even greater thrill was reading the whole Old Testament in Hebrew. In the Jesuit academic course and in my doctoral studies at Harvard University in 1965–1969 (with course work at the Hebrew University in Jerusalem and at the Dominican École Biblique de Jérusalem), I had the privilege of working with some of the greatest scholars of their generation (Catholic, Protestant, and Jewish), professors who approached the Bible with both critical consciousness and religious respect.

For over forty years, I have taught courses in biblical languages, late Old Testament and early Jewish writings, all parts of the New Testament, and topics in biblical theology. Throughout this time, I have edited *New Testament Abstracts*, which provides access to all the major biblical periodicals and the most recent books in the field. I have written over fifty books, many articles, and book reviews. I have edited an eighteen-volume series of technical commentaries on the New Testament by Catholic scholars (Sacra Pagina). All the while, I have been active as a Catholic priest, preaching on biblical texts every Sunday at two different churches in the Boston area and on weekdays within my local Jesuit community. On any given day, I find myself going back and forth between the critical and the religious readings of the Bible. I do not find them contradictory, and I am convinced that each approach can and does enrich the other in many ways.

Response by Peter Enns

The Roman Catholic tradition has an ancient and robust history of biblical interpretation, and Professor Harrington's excellent essay gives us a succinct and studious introduction to it. Particularly with respect to the theme of this book, Roman Catholic biblical interpretation has been an invaluable guide, because both spiritual and critical readings of Scripture are prominently featured in its history. There is simply no area of biblical studies where Catholic scholarship has not made some major and lasting contribution; a point that has not been lost on this Protestant throughout my own academic career. As Harrington outlined, historical criticism has an official, recognized, and respected place in Catholic tradition. Not only does this promote an attitude of openness toward scholarly advances in our understanding of Scripture but also lends considerable credence to criticisms of modern scholarship when offered (which Harrington does at various points by alerting readers to potentially unhelpful philosophical precommitments in some versions of historical criticism).

As for religious readings of Scripture in the Catholic tradition, Harrington rightly mentions two central examples. First and foremost is the ultimate Christ-centeredness of Scripture, a point demonstrated in the

New Testament, the earliest recorded witness to Christ. This ultimate focus does not deflect from the need to address the always-present critical readings of Scripture, and bringing the two into conversation is part of the Catholic (and Christian) hermeneutical and theological journey—always underway, never arriving. Second is the ancient contemplative practice of *lectio divina*, where Scripture is the font of deep spiritual contemplation, an exercise of the heart rather than simply the head. Contemplative readings never had strong support in Protestantism, owing to the Reformation's emphasis on Scripture as a source of propositional theological knowledge (a by-product of *sola scriptura*). Enlightenment philosophical influences also had a major role in marginalizing contemplative practices, not only in Protestantism but also in Roman Catholicism. It is only in recent decades that contemplative practices are making a popular comeback, thanks in large part to the influence of Thomas Merton and more recently, among others, Cardinal Carlo Maria Martini, Thomas Keating, Richard Rohr, and the Protestant Richard Foster.

Harrington is right to remind us of this tradition, and Protestants would do well to listen, because one of the greatest stumbling blocks in the Protestant tradition is its focus on right thinking to the exclusion of much else. Of course, no one should want to marginalize right thinking, but there is much more to communion with God than having well-articulated theological arguments. In other words, God does not simply "enter through the head" and then work his way to the other human faculties. It may be that God addresses his creatures in various ways, and that at times the head must play catch-up—be a student of the heart, so to speak, not its master. The Protestant tendency has given pride of place to a precise intellectual articulation of the faith—glimpsed in the history of Protestantism, where doctrinal articulations are the basis of divisions. I do not mean to minimize the intellectual exercise of Christianity, but, as I discuss later, when intellectual heels are dug into the soil, the kind of intellectual flexibility that serious interaction with biblical criticism requires is less likely to happen.

At any rate, one hoped-for result of Harrington's essay would be to nudge Protestants, who need such nudging, to come to terms with the tremendous theological, critical, and Christological sensitivity built into

Roman Catholic biblical interpretation, and so to be open to fresh ways of thinking.

With these sentiments as background, there are three general points where I would like to extend Harrington's discussion somewhat.

Promise/fulfillment pattern. This pattern is a common way of describing the relationship between the Testaments in the Christian Bible (whether Protestant or Catholic). Indeed, the New Testament writers go to great length to present the Good News in terms of God's long-standing purposes extending back to the very beginnings of Israel's history. Jesus is the promised messiah who fulfills God's redemptive mission. With this, however, we stumble upon an irony. The promise/fulfillment pattern is (obviously) distinctly Christian; yet, as we have seen in Introduction, the manner in which Jesus is said to fulfill the Old Testament very often evinces a creative handling of the Old Testament.

A word commonly used to describe this creative use of Scripture is "midrash" (Hebrew, investigation or study). Midrash is typically restricted to particularly Jewish ways of handling Scripture that attempt to fuse past and present, and by employing a variety of techniques to do so.[13] Therefore, promise/fulfillment, as presented by the New Testament authors in their engagement of the Old Testament, rests firmly in Jewish ways of reading. Of course, this is hardly a surprise since the earliest New Testament authors had certainly not made a sharp division with Judaism and, in fact, saw themselves as simply continuing Israel's story. And, as we will see in my essay, early Judaism was beset by its own set of problems of appealing to ancient Scripture to address entirely new circumstances.

To say all this is not to suggest that the promise/fulfillment pattern is devalued. It is, however, a step toward acknowledging what, hermeneutically speaking, lies behind this pattern. Such a recognition may—and I say *may*—provide some ground for Jewish–Christian dialogue, or, at least, mutual respect and admiration, because both traditions employ similar techniques to make their theological points and are rooted in the same story. I do not, however, want to say that a recognition of shared interpretive approaches is a sufficient ground for full-scale ecumenical dialogue, because, at the end of the day, Judaism and Christianity are

two distinct religions with legitimate and obvious differences, most nota-
bly, their opinion on Jesus of Nazareth. Nothing is gained by ignoring
that fact, nor lost by stating it.

Spiritual sense of Scripture. Reading Scripture, not as a source of
theological or historical information but as a means of communion
with God, is a long-standing tradition in the Christian church, going
back at least to the early Desert Fathers and Mothers—and some would
argue modeled by Jesus himself in his periods of seclusion. The central
question, however, is how spiritual and critical readings are related—or
if they are at all. On one level, one can say that there is no strain between
them, or at least there need be no strain, but I am not sure critical readings let us off the hook that quickly. One can conclude that these two
approaches are after different things and designed for different reasons. However, a critical reading casts doubt on the integrity of readings that are not rooted in historical contexts. And, here, I am not
thinking of how specifically historical-critical issues affect interpretation (e.g., three-part authorship of Isaiah, the documentary hypothesis).
Spiritual readings of Scripture are not beholden to basic contextual
issues. Instead, verses, clauses, or individual words are used as fertile
soil for spiritual contemplation.

I hope it is clear that I consider spiritual readings of Scripture to be a
core Christian path to spiritual growth. But biblical criticism has introduced a compelling approach to reading Scripture that by definition pre-
cludes readings that do not pay attention to literary or historical contexts.
The point of biblical criticism is to say, "No, you can't just read this psalm
or this verse in Genesis in any way that strikes you as spiritually significant." As far as I am concerned, biblical criticism is in no position to
make such a sweeping determination, but if your focus is on how religious and critical readings can co-exist, the relationship between the two
will have to be articulated in a compelling way. To put it differently, one
would need to lay out how spiritually sensitive and critically informed
readers could flip the switch inside of them, to move from one type of
reading to another. How does one justify one reading over the other at
any given time? On one level, it may be enough to say, "A spiritual reading
is going to happen now, because I am in church, or alone in my living

room." But this, too, brings the problem to the fore: critical scholarship questions (directly or indirectly) the legitimacy of spiritual readings.

Here is the central issue, as I see it. Continuing to practice spiritual readings without somehow integrating biblical criticism unwittingly supports the bifurcation of the two that we see in critical circles. Saying "spiritual reading is something you have to get over" and "spiritual and critical readings are both legitimate but must be kept separate" operate from the same assumption: the two readings are at odds. As far as I see it, the question then becomes whether there can be some mutual influence between the two—a proposal that is anathema to either.

Distinguishing between the world of, behind, and in front of the text. A final point of Harrington's essay that I want to touch on is the relationship between these three "worlds" involved in reading. Harrington understands the world of the text to pertain to philological and literary issues, i.e., focusing on meaning of texts in their linguistic and literary contexts. So, read the Hebrew text and pay attention to what is happening in the context. That context can include not just the surrounding verses but, at least in principle, whole books and even interaction between various books of Scripture. The world of the text, in other words, includes the text of Scripture as a whole.

This is distinguished from the world behind the text, which is the purview of historical criticism. Unlike the world of the text, Harrington cautions that one must be careful not to allow spiritually disruptive assumptions to determine interpretive conclusions (e.g., miracles don't happen, people don't rise from the dead). Archaeological studies have greatly and permanently affected how modern readers interpret Scripture, but the data also have to be interpreted, and this is where what one brings to the text must be made plain. For example, it is one thing to conclude, correctly, that ancient Mesopotamian creation myths and Genesis 1–3 share similar ideologies that (along with other reasons) indicate that the latter are not to be read as historical. It is quite another matter, however, to say that acknowledging the mythic nature of the story means that it has no abiding theological value. To speak this way reveals a philosophical precommitment, that historical accounts are of more religious value than nonhistorical, or that any God worth his salt would never stoop so low as to express deep truth in mythic ways. Oddly, this precommitment is shared by both fundamentalists and liberals, which is a lesson to all of us that bad philosophy can be found at either end of the ideological spectrum.

The world in front of the text is what many refer to as "application" or "actualization," which is related to the spiritual sense mentioned earlier. Included is a grounding in the history of interpretation, where Christians today can benefit from the insights of earlier, less cluttered times. Central here, too, is the focus on the paschal mystery as the key to true Christian spiritual insight to Scripture. As we saw, one can ask how specifically this last interpretive world is related to the previous two—whether there is some point where all three draw off of each others' energy, so to speak— but that will not be resolved here. Perhaps, at the end of the day, there is more mystery in all of this than can be captured in books and essays.

My points can be summed us thus: Where the dialogue needs to continue is precisely in those areas of strength in Roman Catholic approaches to Scripture—Christ-centered and spiritual readings—and where those readings and biblical criticism can, and must, be in conversation for mutual benefit.

Response by Marc Zvi Brettler

I read Father Harrington's essay with a sense of jealousy—if only theological matters were so centralized in Judaism! I had to spend most of my essay sorting and sifting and synthesizing three thousand years of texts and beliefs—from the earliest texts in the Bible to what some Jewish thinker said yesterday. Harrington's essay reflects the authoritative teachings of the Catholic tradition—those which preceded and made way for the revolutionary teachings of the Second Vatican Council, the teachings that emerged from that council, and those that followed, especially from "The Jewish People and Their Scriptures in the Christian Bible," and through Pope Benedict XVI's *Verbum Domini*. His essay thus had the luxury of focusing on the content of clear Roman Catholic Church teachings, how they developed, how they relate to various types of criticism, and how these teachings may affect the religious life of the individual Catholic.

The three contributors to this volume understand that part of our project is to open an ecumenical dialogue on the issue of critical-biblical interpretation and faith. I am a relative newcomer to this venture and believe that it can only take place when each person represents his or her tradition unapologetically from within. I find it greatly disturbing when the world's religions, or monotheistic religions, or even "just" Judaism and Christianity are presented as minor variants of each other.[14] This is patently false. In that context, although I do not use the term "Old Testament," I applaud Harrington's use of the term and his justification of it—that it has "New Testament roots" and "fits Catholic tradition and theology." It is not only that we use different methods from our traditions to evaluate critical-biblical studies, but we also study different Bibles. The use of the term Old Testament properly highlights this. And, although it has become fashionable to employ more neutral terms such as Jewish Scriptures, Harrington correctly points out some of the problems with these terms; and, in any case, when writing from a Catholic confessional perspective, the use of the term Old Testament is not only justifiable but also essential. This is especially true in an essay that most laudably notes earlier Catholic interpreters' "unfortunate tendencies to theological supersessionism and anti-Judaism."

The self-conscious use of the term Old Testament helps to bring out the major difference between my perspective and Harrington's and, indeed, between the Jewish and Catholic (and perhaps even the broader Christian) perspective on this issue. Harrington notes this difference by citing what he calls "Augustine's famous and oft-quoted dictum": "The New Testament is hidden in the Old, and the Old is made manifest in the New." This is especially important now, given that, as Harrington states, it reflects the approach of the current pope. Thus, from a Catholic perspective, the New Testament offers a lens through which the Old Testament can or should be read. For some Jews, the rabbinic tradition is similar (as I explain in detail in response to Enns's essay), but for most Jews, this is not the case. In addition, even to the extent that Jews may read the Hebrew Bible in relation to rabbinic tradition and might believe (to paraphrase Augustine), "The Oral Law [rabbinic tradition] is hidden in the Written Law [the Torah], and the Written Law is made manifest in the Oral Law," as Harrington's further observations make clear, the New Testament is not really similar to rabbinic tradition. He notes: "Catholics view the Bible as primarily a witness to a person, Jesus of Nazareth, the Son of God, and the Word made flesh. Thus, Catholicism is more a religion of a person." This means that the main distinction between Catholicism's and Judaism's view of the Old Testament/Hebrew Bible is not only whether the book finds some sort of fulfillment in Jesus, but also whether the book is important as a book (Judaism), albeit an interpreted book, or as a witness to an individual.

Although Moses plays a significant part in the Torah, and elsewhere in the Hebrew Bible, he is important for the roles he plays, especially (but not only) as a lawgiver, not as an individual. It is noteworthy that Malachi 3:22 (English 4:4) does not emphasize the importance of Moses as a person but as the giver of the Torah: "Be mindful of the *torah* of My servant Moses, whom I charged at Horeb with laws and rules for all Israel." Stated differently, even though the Qur'an calls both Jews and Christians (at that point, Catholics) "People of the Book," they are people of the book in very different ways. Jews venerate the book's teachings; Catholics venerate Jesus, the main character.

This point is further clarified and emphasized in Harrington's discussion of J.-P. Sonnet's article, "Risking One's Life for Beings That Exist on Paper"—a wonderful article with a wonderful title. Here, too, what seems like a commonality is ultimately significantly different. Jews are enjoined in certain situations to risk their lives *'al kiddush ha-shem,* "for the sanctification of the [= God's] name." This is most typically understood to mean that when faced with a situation where a Jew is asked to commit idolatry, murder, or incest (and adultery), he or she should die rather than commit that infraction. *Kiddush ha-shem* was also frequently invoked by Jews who preferred to be killed rather than to convert during the Crusades, and modern Jewish liturgy refers to those who died in the Holocaust—for being Jewish—as having died *'al kiddush ha-shem.* I know of no case of a Jew risking his or her life over the historicity of David or Isaiah; these particular figures are mentioned by Sonnet because they prefigure and prophesy about Jesus, and their historicity has an impact on the truth of Jesus' witness for the Christian community. Thus, the title and content of Sonnet's article also highlight one of the most important differences between Jews and Catholics, which Harrington clarified for me: Catholics (and Protestants, too) are a people who maintain the importance of certain people mentioned in the Bible; Jews highlight instead the teachings of the Bible. A comparable Jewish article might be titled: "Risking One's Life for Select Ideas Written on Parchment (as Interpreted by the Rabbis)."

Harrington notes that "the primary Catholic approach to the Old Testament" is to see it "as proceeding 'from promise to fulfillment' or 'from shadows to reality.'" Fulfillments are more important than promises, and realities are more important than shadows. Thus, this statement suggests that within the Catholic tradition, the New Testament is more important than the Old. Jews, especially in the late nineteenth and early twentieth centuries, suggested that this explained why Christians were so excited about using critical methods to essentially disembowel the Jewish Bible, and some Jews continue to uphold this position. From my knowledge of New Testament scholarship, this is not a fair claim—most Christians, including Catholics, are equally critical toward all parts of the Bible; although, as Harrington observes, the New Testament (studied critically) may be more important than the Old Testament (studied critically) to Catholics, and this, indeed, is reflected in the liturgy and the lectionary.

Given that the Bible *interpreted* is crucial within Jewish tradition and rabbinic tradition is more important than the Bible itself, Harrington's observation that "the Bible should be at the heart of all of Christian life" cannot be easily appropriated by Jews. In fact, his summary of the "now official Catholic position" that the historical-critical method "is the indispensable (though not completely sufficient by itself) method for the scientific study of a biblical text" also does not translate easily into Judaism, which might say instead that the historical-critical method is an acceptable method, within reason, but never supersedes the centuries-long Jewish interpretation of the text.

Harrington discusses authentic spiritual readings of the biblical text; this is a Jewish goal as well, found in rabbinic literature, most medieval commentary, and in most synagogue sermons, and would seem to be a Jewish-Catholic commonality. Yet here, too, there is a significant difference. He notes that such Catholic readings "must keep in mind three things: the literal sense, the paschal mystery, and the present circumstances." Jewish spiritual readings, up to now, very often only kept in mind the text and the present circumstances, and ignored the literal sense; however, I advocate that new Jewish spiritual readings can and should be based on the literal sense. More generally, Jewish spiritual readings are more diffuse than Catholic ones. They (obviously) do not focus on the paschal mystery, and there is no single item that replaces the paschal mystery as a point of focus.

It is not the case, however, that Catholicism and Judaism differ sharply in all of the matters we are examining. Much of what Harrington says about Catholicism resonated deeply with me, and, in several cases, the word "Jew" or "Jewish" could replace his "Catholic." This is the case, for example, when he writes that "Catholic social-ethical teaching is one of the world's best-kept secrets"—the same is true of Jewish rabbinic teachings.

Another unexpected similarity between the Catholic and Jewish traditions concerns the role of later tradition in interpreting the Bible in an authoritative manner. I cite various traditions about the authority of the classical rabbis. As Harrington notes, Vatican II's *Dei Verbum* says that "Sacred tradition, Sacred Scripture, and the Teaching Office of the Church are so linked and joined together that one cannot stand without the others." This, too, is similar to the rabbinic understanding of the connection between the Oral Law and Written Law. If this part of *Dei Verbum* began "Sacred Scripture and Sacred tradition as reflected in the classical rabbis," it could be a Jewish document. Indeed, some Jewish traditions see rabbinic tradition as the continuation of prophetic tradition; for example, *Seder 'Olam Rabbah*, a rabbinic work of historiography, notes that prior to Alexander the Great "prophets prophesied with the Holy Spirit; hereafter, incline your ears and obey the sages' words."[15] Here, too, the Catholic and Jewish traditions stand closely aligned, in contrast to the Protestant *sola scriptura* tradition. Yet, there are important differences within the similarities—as *Dei Verbum* states, these traditions are "linked and joined together" to "contribute effectively to the salvation of souls." Although "salvation," understood, at least, as enjoying a beneficent afterworld, is a theme in rabbinic Judaism, it does not have the prominence that it has in Catholicism, and it is not salvation through an individual. Stated differently, the linking together of biblical and postbiblical traditions and teachings has fundamentally different purposes in Judaism and Catholicism.

I see significant parallels between Harrington's treatment of the call of Moses and my treatment of Psalm 114. I spoke of various circles or rings of interpretation: the psalm itself, the psalm as part of the *hallel* collection, the psalm as part of the Psalter, the psalm in the Bible, and the psalm in Judaism. This is similar, though not identical, to his "the world of the text," "the world behind the text," and "the world before the text." Specifically, his insistence on including "patristic interpretation" is similar to my inclusion of "the psalm in the Judaism." I sense several differences of balance. Harrington includes as a separate section "the world behind the text"; I do not. Material that stands behind my text is included in the "psalm itself," but only to the extent that I believe it is relevant for the interpretation of the text. In general, I believe that Jewish scholars are generally more interested in the text and its posthistory rather than the text and its prehistory. In explaining his inclusion of a Christological reading, he asserts, "The Christological reading of the Old Testament is as old as Christianity itself, and it will not (and cannot) disappear." There is, again, no single item in the history of interpretation that I as a Jew must include, and from my perspective as a Jew, cannot disappear.

In his Further Readings, Harrington includes the recent book of the Australian Jesuit scholar Antony Campbell, which shows how critical study of the Old Testament can assist readers today in understanding what may appear to be difficult and problematic scriptural texts in ways that are beneficial to modern faith and do not endanger it. I believe that this expresses my personal feelings and experience as a Jewish critical Bible scholar as well. For a Jewish audience, I would offer an additional observation concerning the importance of the historical-critical method: it allows me to understand rabbinic texts better. These texts often respond to contradictions in biblical texts, gaps in texts, and disparate traditions found in the Bible. Rabbinic tradition treats as *apparent* contradictions what modern critical scholars see as contradictions deriving from different people and different traditions. I would therefore extend Campbell and suggest that critical study of the Hebrew Bible is enormously helpful to understand what problems the classical rabbis and the medieval Jewish interpreters were responding to, and thus may be even more important to Judaism than to Catholicism.

Harrington's clear essay helped me clarify my positions and outline significant similarities and differences between typical Jewish and Catholic positions; we can better understand what we share and how we fundamentally differ when discussing the Old Testament and the Hebrew Bible. I hope that other Jewish scholars will follow Harrington's essay and especially his bibliography, including his own works, and will produce comparable books within Judaism. I noted in my essay the reasons why this field is so underdeveloped in Judaism, and we are much in need of books with titles like *The Scriptural Documents: An Anthology of Jewish Teachings; The Jewish Discussion of Biblical Hermeneutic; How Do Jews Read the Bible?; Biblical Interpretation in Crisis; The Historical Critical Method in Jewish Exegesis;* and *Jewish Principles for Interpreting the Scripture.* I hope that the present volume will spur such publications, illustrating still further Harrington's claim, which I believe true for Judaism as well, that "each approach can and does enrich the other in many ways"; as I tried to show here, the manner of this enrichment in Judaism is different from Catholicism.

Further Reading

Béchard, Dean P., ed. *The Scripture Documents: An Anthology of Official Catholic Teachings.* Collegeville, MN: Liturgical Press, 2002. An excellent collection of translations of official Catholic documents that record the Church's recent efforts at promoting and guiding study of the Bible.

Benedict XVI, Pope. *Verbum Domini. The Word of God in the Life and Mission of the Church.* Ijamsville, MD: Word Among Us Press, 2010. The pope's apostolic exhortation in response to the 2008 synod of Catholic bishops on the word of God in the life and mission of the church.

Boadt, Lawrence. *Reading the Old Testament: An Introduction.* New York: Paulist Press, 1984. Treats the original contexts, ancient Near Eastern parallels, literary features, and religious and theological features of the individual books.

Campbell, Antony F. *Making Sense of the Bible: Difficult Texts and Modern Faith.* New York: Paulist Press, 2010. Explores what happens when familiar interpretations of biblical texts clash with history, archaeology, science, scholarship, and good sense.

Curtin, Terence R. *Historical Criticism and the Theological Interpretation of Scripture: The Catholic Discussion of a Biblical Hermeneutic: 1958–1983*. Rome: Gregorian University Press, 1987. Describes Catholic debates in the late 1970s and early 1980s about the use of historical-critical methods in interpreting the Bible.

Duggan, Michael W. *The Consuming Fire: A Christian Guide to the Old Testament*. Huntington, IN: Our Sunday Visitor, 2010. A representative Catholic treatment of the Old Testament books, with links to the New Testament and invitations to meditation and prayer.

Fitzmyer, Joseph A. *The Interpretation of Scripture: In Defense of the Historical-Critical Method*. New York: Paulist Press, 2008. Seven essays by a distinguished Catholic biblical scholar on the positive aspects of the historical-critical method.

Hahn, Scott W. *Covenant and Communion: The Biblical Theology of Pope Benedict XVI*. Grand Rapids, MI: Brazos, 2009. Drawing heavily on the pope's many writings on biblical interpretation, the book argues that Benedict XVI, Joseph Ratzinger, has successfully synthesized modern scientific methods and spiritual exegesis.

Harrington, Daniel J. "Biblical Criticism." *Oxford Bibliographies Online*. New York: Oxford University Press, 2011. An annotated bibliography treating the nature, history, practice, and problems of biblical criticism.

―――. *How Do Catholics Read the Bible?* Lanham, MD: Rowman & Littlefield, 2005. Places biblical criticism in the context of modern Catholic approaches to the Bible, especially as articulated in Vatican II's "Dogmatic Constitution on Divine Revelation" (*Dei Verbum*).

―――. *Interpreting the Old Testament: A Practical Guide*. Wilmington, DE: Michael Glazier, 1981. Explains and illustrates the various methods of biblical criticism, with reference to the Old Testament.

Prior, J. G. *The Historical Critical Method in Catholic Exegesis*. Rome: Gregorian University Press, 1999. Maintains that the historical-critical method has been and will be an essential and indispensable (though limited) part of Catholic biblical exegesis.

Williamson, Peter S. *Catholic Principles for Interpreting Scripture: A Study of the Pontifical Biblical Commission's*. The Interpretation of the Bible in the Church. Rome: Biblical Institute Press, 2001. Detailed analysis of the Pontifical Biblical Commission's 1993 document leads to twenty basic principles for the Catholic interpretation of Scripture.

Protestantism and Biblical Criticism

ONE PERSPECTIVE ON A DIFFICULT DIALOGUE

Peter Enns

THIS CHAPTER EXPLORES Protestant religious faith and its dialogue with a critical reading of Scripture. After defining what I mean by "Protestant," I will focus on some obstacles to that dialogue and then look at two broad examples where critical and Protestant readings of Scripture are particularly difficult to bring together but where the dialogue must continue. Along the way and at the end of this essay, I will offer some thoughts on the path I have taken to bring critical and religious readings of Scripture into dialogue.

Getting Our Bearings

What Is a Protestant, Anyway?

The first challenge is to define Protestantism and its view of the Bible, and that lands us right away in a bit of a mess. Protestantism means different things to different people because it refers to diverse movements and traditions stemming from the Protestant Reformation. Today, Protestantism includes American young earth creationists, liberal German Lutherans, mainline Methodists, Chinese Pentecostals, Korean hyper-Calvinists, Moral Majority Baptists, emergent church hipsters, and many others.

There is certainly no single Protestant perspective on how to read the Bible. In fact, the history of Protestantism is marked by conflict over what it means to read the Bible "correctly," and the plethora of theological traditions and denominations are a testimony to that conflict.[1] This stands to reason because Protestantism was conceived out of conflict, getting its start when Martin Luther famously challenged what he saw as Roman Catholic failure to submit to Scripture. This same spirit of protest continues among various iterations of Protestantism, all claiming to be (more) faithful to Scripture (than others). Unlike in Roman Catholicism, there is by definition no official Magisterium to settle theological disagreements. Protestants choose instead a direct appeal to the clear word of God. And, unlike Judaism, Protestantism has no Talmudic or midrashic tradition (as wide ranging as they are) around which discussions of biblical interpretation can take place. Rather, Protestantism's various movements stem from influential founders (like Martin Luther and John Calvin) who attracted a following within their particular social, political, geographical, and religious moments—each movement looking to recover Scripture as the supreme authority of their faith. With such beginnings, theological diversity can hardly come as a surprise.

Just as Protestantism has no one view of how the Bible should be understood, there certainly is no one view of how present Protestant faith should be in dialogue with the many pressing challenges of biblical criticism. At one end of the Protestant spectrum is fundamentalism. This movement arose in the late nineteenth and early twentieth centuries to stress the "fundamentals" of the Christian faith (mainly dealing with the authority of the Bible and the deity of Christ) that were thought to be in jeopardy in the face of biblical criticism. Fundamentalism was born as an opposition movement, and thus has a long history of spirited, nonnegotiable opposition to biblical criticism as an enemy of the Christian faith. At the other end of the spectrum are those Protestants for whom this entire discussion is passé and tedious. How faith and biblical criticism can be in constructive dialogue is a question met with a look of quaint curiosity, a relic of an earlier generation that has not yet gotten over it. This group, conventionally referred to as "liberal," tends to be found among mainline denominations.

Given such a range of views, we need to limit our definition of Protestantism by focusing on Protestants who are most likely to have an interest in how faith and biblical criticism can be in dialogue. That definition moves us along because it eliminates the two extremes mentioned. Included in this narrower definition are many in mainline churches and many who would identify themselves as evangelical—a term more difficult to define each passing day, as that movement experiences its own identity crisis.[2] With respect to the Bible, evangelicals hold a variety of opinions, from a literalist, inerrantist view (barely distinguishable from fundamentalism), to more progressive views, some of which have significant overlap with liberal views. What unites evangelicals, however, is a commitment to a high view of Scripture, meaning that the Bible bears the stamp of divine authority and therefore must be heeded.

Even when limiting Protestantism to this multidenominational middle group, we are still left with a spectrum of attitudes about what it means to read the Bible faithfully vis-à-vis biblical criticism. Some appreciate the need for the conversation but may also tend toward a default position of suspicion regarding critical readings of the Bible, and thus their appropriation of critical scholarship may be more piecemeal—addressing the issue only when forced to do so. Others are more deliberate in synthesizing faith and critical scholarship but with various degrees of dis-ease. For example, some may experience discomfort over specific issues (Did the exodus happen? Is Adam a myth?). Still others may experience a general cognitive dissonance—a constant background noise or discomfort that may eventually come to the foreground.

I aim in this chapter to keep this broad middle group in mind as much as possible; however, there is a slight focus on the conservative end of the spectrum, because those Protestants exhibit more cognitive dissonance than others and are, perhaps, in greater need of the type of conversation this book intends to promote. By attending to a more conservative population, I also hope that issues will be addressed that others on the spectrum will identify with as well. To round out our definition, the Protestants I have in mind are a middle group that feels on some level the tension between reading the Bible with the eyes of faith and of biblical criticism. These Protestants are committed to taking the Bible seriously, but they also sense—maybe reluctantly—that the modern study of the Bible is a challenge that cannot be ignored.

Some in this middle group address these tensions on a sophisticated level—those who have seminary or advanced degrees in Bible study or theology, and for whom, perhaps, older, conservative responses to biblical criticism ceased to have explanatory power. But such tensions are not limited to those with formal education in these areas. Anyone who has taken an Introduction to the Bible course at the college level, or has watched the History Channel or PBS, or read *Time* or *Newsweek* around Christmas or Easter, will have been exposed to some broad themes of biblical criticism that challenge conventional Protestant positions. Few with an interest in the Bible, can avoid the historical problems— brought to light through scientific and archaeological progress in the eighteenth and nineteenth centuries—with the creation and flood stories in Genesis. (The mythological Babylonian flood stories are typically presented in college introductory courses as Exhibit A for reading the biblical flood story as myth.) The problem of the historical Jesus is not simply an academic topic, but, thanks to Dan Brown's *The Da Vinci Code* and New Testament scholar Bart Ehrman's appearances on *The Colbert Report* and *The Daily Show*, it is very much a part of public consciousness. It is hard to avoid critical views that are both persuasive and threatening to the Protestant audience I have in mind. Exposure to biblical criticism can begin for them a long and unsettling spiritual journey.

A Paradox

So, can these Protestants read the Bible religiously and critically? They can—and, indeed, I would argue that they must—but they will need to make their way through a paradox. They must embrace the Protestant spirit of challenging the status quo while also taking a hard look at the status quo in Protestantism (at least their own version of it). In other words, they must be willing to turn the Protestant spirit inward to discern what sorts of adjustments might need to be made to their familiar ways of thinking.

Making such adjustments is very difficult, if the last hundred or so years of conflict are any indication. After all, if one's faith is rooted fundamentally in a sacred book where God speaks to you, which is a core Protestant conviction, then biblical criticism is bound to create some trouble, particularly when the basic historical reliability of the Bible is called into question. The problems are familiar: the creation and flood stories are not history but myth; Abraham is not a historical figure but a legend; Moses, if he existed, did not lead slaves out of Egypt nor did he write the Pentateuch; the exodus and conquest narratives are at best distorted histories, if not outright fabrications. Similar problems exist in the New Testament, such as whether the Gospels or the book of Acts are accurate historical accounts or biased theological impressions by later Christian communities. I am not prejudging the answers to these questions, and biblical criticism is hardly unified in its answers. Biblical criticism is not above reproach nor is it the guardian of the final word. Nevertheless, these and other questions are entirely valid—indeed, the very stuff of Scripture's modern study—and with good reason, even if they are hardly friendly to traditional Protestant positions.

The cause of at least some Protestant tensions, however, may not be the arrival of biblical criticism onto the pleasant shores of Protestantism. The cause of discomfort may rest with Protestantism itself, because in Protestantism the Bible is pressed into the role of supreme religious authority in a way that Scripture may have trouble supporting. Judaism, Roman Catholicism, and Protestantism all have long histories of deep respect and reverence for Scripture, but Protestantism, especially as it developed in the nineteenth century, required something more of the Bible than Roman Catholicism or Judaism did, and much more than biblical criticism allowed.

What follows in the next section is further prodding into why Protestants have the particular problems they do with biblical criticism. Knowing the obstacles is necessary for processing how Protestant faith and a critical reading of Scripture can be in dialogue. I isolate three factors that I feel are important to this discussion, although there are certainly others: (1) The Reformation rallying cry of *sola scriptura*; (2) the nature of the Christian Bible; and (3) Protestant identity coming out of nineteenth-century "battles for the Bible."[3]

The Bible and Biblical Criticism: Three Obstacles for Protestantism

Sola Scriptura

One factor that contributes to the tensions between Protestant faith and biblical criticism seems inevitable given Protestantism's beginnings. A clarion call of the Reformers was *"sola scriptura,"* Latin for "Scripture alone," meaning that, since Scripture and Scripture alone is God's word, it is therefore the church's final authority on all matters pertaining to faith. This slogan is sometimes misunderstood, particularly among fundamentalists, as a rejection of all church tradition in favor of the Bible. Rather, it refers to Scripture's role as the final arbitrator concerning what traditions are faithful to the biblical witness. This does not imply, however, that Scripture's meaning is plain and simple, provided we just get out of the way and let the Bible speak. The best of the Protestant tradition has always understood *sola scriptura* as a statement of Scripture's *primary* (not "sole") role in guiding the church theologically. For example, the Wesleyan tradition speaks of Scripture as one quadrant among four, the other three being tradition, reason, and experience. Likewise, the Episcopal tradition speaks of a three-legged stool of Scripture, reason, and tradition. So, theology is more than simply turning to see what the "Bible says." What the Bible says is accessed by individuals in light of their experience of God, their ability to reason, and their tradition (which includes, in the broadest sense, the Christian tradition as a whole).

Despite this generous understanding of *sola scriptura*, few were ready for the upheaval introduced by biblical criticism in the nineteenth century (more on that later). For Scripture to function authoritatively as Protestants required, it had to be seen as revelation from God to humanity and therefore qualitatively different from any other sort of communication. Biblical criticism, however, pointed out that Scripture was not unique among other religious texts and ideas of the ancient world. Protestants expected this God-given Bible to be generally clear and consistent in order to guide the church, but biblical criticism introduced ambiguity and diversity to biblical interpretation. Protestants assumed that Scripture must be truthful and trustworthy, because it is God's voice speaking, but biblical criticism pointed out errors and contradictions. For Protestants, some conformity in interpretation with the grand tradition of the church was vital, but biblical criticism privileged no ecclesiastical tradition and instead critiqued tradition in light of intellectual and scientific discoveries. Protestants valued the role of reason, though chastened by Scripture and the guidance of God's spirit, but biblical criticism valued human reason unaided by supernatural or ecclesiastical interference. The Bible could not function as the church's final authority, as Protestantism required, if biblical criticism was correct.

The Protestant problem is exacerbated by another factor. One of the great ironies of *sola scriptura* is that it eventually led to a bewildering disunity among Protestants rather than the unity of all gathered around the unambiguous, authoritative word of God. This seems unavoidable in hindsight. Once one says, "We will *only* listen to what *God* says in the *Bible*," one is bound to pay close attention to the Bible. And as any decently trained seminarian has observed, if one reads the Bible, one discovers that the Bible is not as clear as advertised. It is not that easy to understand what the Bible is authoritatively saying, because it is open to legitimately diverse interpretations. That is why there are various and sundry Protestant subgroups clinging to "biblical authority," while arriving at polar opposite conclusions about what the authoritative Bible says. Such divisions are part of the Protestant experience and can become heated, which is why Protestants form new churches and denominations, establish insulated Bible colleges, create vigilant seminaries, and—more than once in history—kill or mistreat those with whom they disagree. After all, this is God's book, God's means of communicating to the church. A lot—indeed, everything—is at stake in how one handles this authoritative text.

Perhaps the most arresting irony is that the Protestant spirit and its insistence on *sola scriptura* are linked to the rise of biblical criticism. Surely it is no accident that the same soil from which the Reformation sprung, Germany, is also where biblical criticism was nurtured and fed one hundred years or so later. The same iconoclastic spirit that drove Martin Luther and others to reject Catholic authority was applied in later European scholarship (under the influence of Enlightenment philosophy) to all ecclesiastical authorities. And Luther's translation of the Bible into German, thus putting the Bible directly into the people's hands, was surely a two-edged sword. Once everyone has access to Scripture, its interpretation becomes a matter of personal inquiry, not monitored by the church, and interpretive chaos ensues. Hence, the Protestant Reformation had a hand in opening the door to the secularization of biblical studies.[4]

Sola scriptura has been hard to live by, as the history of Protestantism has shown, and biblical criticism raised the ante considerably. Among the Protestants I focus on in this chapter, the Bible's status as the final religious authority continues to be a deep impulse. Biblical criticism, which introduces novel readings and extrabiblical evidence to inform interpretation, is often seen as undermining that authority. Thus, biblical criticism remains a common foe or at least a distant and awkward conversation partner.

The Nature of the Christian Bible

A second factor that has introduced tensions between Protestantism and biblical criticism is the nature of the Christian Bible itself.[5] Throughout history, Christians have read the Bible as an unfolding and unified story of salvation, culminating in the birth, life, death, and resurrection of Jesus of Nazareth—in other words, Scripture is read as a coherent whole. Traditionally, Judaism has not shared this same conviction, as noted Jewish biblical scholar Jon Levenson reminds us: "Whereas in the church the sacred text tends to be seen as a word (the singular is telling) demanding majestically to be proclaimed, in Judaism it tends to be seen as a problem with many facets, each of which deserves attention."[6]

Levenson's comment points to an important and telling difference between how Jews and Christians view the Bible, and this observation goes a long way to explaining why Protestants have an uneasy relationship with biblical criticism. Throughout its history, Jewish biblical interpretation has been well aware of the tensions and contradictions in the Bible, and although they expended much energy in addressing them, those efforts were free of the dogmatic angst that preoccupies Protestantism. The

Jewish Bible is complex, and its many peaks and valleys, gaps and gashes are invitations to engage the text and so to connect with God through conversation, argument, and struggle. Hence, biblical criticism—although historically still challenging for various strands of Judaism—is less of a problem, at least insofar as Judaism, too, points out the peaks and valleys, gaps and gashes of the Bible.

For Protestants—and indeed the Christian tradition as a whole—the Bible is not there to set the church on an exegetical adventure during which one discovers God through interpretive struggle. The problems of Scripture are minimized, because the Bible is ultimately a coherent grand narrative that tells one and only one story with a climax: the crucified and risen Son of God brings Israel's story to completion. The New Testament authors go to great lengths to explain how Jesus of Nazareth completes Israel's story and gives it coherence. Taken as a whole, the Christian Bible has a singular message.

If the Bible, ultimately, has a singular message, one can see why biblical criticism would cause problems. Biblical criticism does not unify the Bible but breaks it down into its various and conflicting messages by focusing on the particular historical settings in which the texts were first written or uttered. For example, the two creation stories of Genesis 1 and 2 have different theologies because they were written at different times for different reasons, and to understand them well means respecting their disunity. Chronicles is an alternate account of Israel's history that differs prominently from its predecessor, the Deuteronomistic history (especially 1 and 2 Sam and 1 and 2 Kings). Chronicles was written no earlier than the late fifth century BCE, that is, well after the Israelites returned to the land from captivity in Babylon, to address pressing concerns of the early Second Temple period; namely, how the present community saw itself vis-à-vis Israel's glorious past. The Gospels give us conflicting versions of Jesus' life and teachings, at least in part because they were written in different communities and addressed different concerns. The critical impulse to deconstruct the Bible's unity by focusing on the points of origin of its various writings, rather than on the finished product we have before us, impedes the Christian proclamation of a unified message, and thus partly accounts for resistance to biblical criticism on the part of Protestants.

Ironically, one particularly pressing issue that challenges the Protestant notion of the unity of Scripture comes from an unexpected source: the way the New Testament authors themselves use the Old Testament in establishing the connection between the Gospel and Israel's story. Simply put, the theological unity of the Christian Bible is not self-evident but owes something to the creative thinking of the New Testament writers. Critical scholarship, especially since the discovery of the Dead Sea Scrolls in 1947, has given some clarity to this phenomenon by pointing to similar creative techniques and tendencies in the Jewish literature produced during or near the New Testament period.[7] How the New Testament authors use their own Scripture poses challenges to the Protestant view of Scripture as a unified whole. We will look at this issue more closely later.

Protestant Identity in the Nineteenth Century

The third obstacle to Protestantism's constructive engagement with biblical criticism is the contentious legacy of the nineteenth century, when the "battle for the Bible" began. In the span of about twenty years, three independent, technical, and powerful forces converged to challenge the historical reliability of one book of the Bible, Genesis: First, there was the emergence of the theory of evolution, made famous by Darwin's publication of *Origin of Species* in 1859. Second, there was the publication in 1878 of Julius Wellhausen's documentary hypothesis, which argued that the Pentateuch was written one thousand years after Moses. Third, in 1876, there was the decipherment of Babylonian myths about creation and a flood that uncomfortably resembled Genesis.

Each of these forces was a handful by itself, but together they had a powerful impact on Protestant identity by challenging the basic historical reliability of Genesis in particular, and by extension the Bible as whole. In fact, there is no greater challenge to Protestant views of the Bible than this challenge to historical reliability. Conservative Protestants invested a lot of energy in battling these three attacks on the Bible, and the memories of those battles are etched in the minds of many Protestants till today. To read the Bible critically—which means *engaging* these three factors rather than *fighting* them—is too hard a pill to swallow for many Protestants. Maintaining pure boundaries against these forces was and is often a primary concern.

To understand the animosities that created these boundaries, we must first be clear on the nature of the threat these three issues posed to the Protestant consciousness at the time. First, Darwin's theory that apes and humans share common ancestry was profoundly unsettling to many, let alone *sola scriptura* Protestants, who looked to Genesis to settle the question of human origins. By the eighteenth century, the fossil record had shown that the earth was millions upon millions of years old—far older than most people had believed and far older than a literal interpretation of the Bible allows. But Darwin's work raised the conversation to an entirely new level. To say the least, evolution cast into serious doubt the historical credibility of the creation narratives in Genesis 1–3, especially the story of Adam and Eve. At stake was not simply the historical reliability of Genesis in general but whether Adam was the actual cause of the fall of humanity that Jesus died on the cross to undo, as Paul famously argues in Romans 5:12–21. In other words, evolution was seen to undermine not just Scripture but also Christianity. It is not hard to understand how unsettling this was.

The second factor was the maturation of European biblical criticism and its influence on biblical scholarship in the United States. The most pressing issue was the argument that the books of the Bible were written much later than traditionally thought. Further, some individual books showed clear evidence of having more than one author, with long histories of oral and written tradition, before reaching their final form. The most famous examples were Isaiah, Daniel, and, most important, the Pentateuch.

The traditional view of the authorship of the Pentateuch was that one man, Moses, living in the middle of the second millennium BCE, was solely (more or less) responsible for writing the first five books of the Bible. After a century or so of serious academic discussion, the issue came to a boiling point in the work of the German Old Testament scholar Julius Wellhausen (1844–1918).[8] Wellhausen stood on the shoulders of many biblical scholars before him, offering a compelling synthesis and extension of the insights of others. Wellhausen argued that the Pentateuch was not one document but originally four, written over several hundred years beginning in the tenth century BCE. These documents were spliced (or redacted) together, somewhat carelessly, about one thousand years after Moses lived. Perhaps most controversial was Wellhausen's theory that the Law of Moses was written in the postexilic period by a group of priests, zealously determined to put Israel's religion under the thumb of their own political authority. The Law of Moses, in other words, was propaganda. The specifics of Wellhausen's work no longer dominate the academic landscape, but at the time his theory caught on, and the conservative backlash was considerable. This was understandable, since Wellhausen stripped the Pentateuch of any significant historical meaning. Even today, for some, to cede any ground to Wellhausen is a sure sign of apostasy.

The third factor was the growing field of archaeology in ancient Israel and the surrounding area, that is, biblical archaeology. Archaeology introduced external data—texts and artifacts from the ancient Near Eastern world, Israel's neighbors and predecessors—to biblical study. These findings have helped us more fully understand the intellectual and cultural climate in which the Bible was written. They have also challenged core Protestant beliefs about the Bible.

The first and most famous of these findings is the Babylonian text known as *Enuma Elish*, which means "When on high," the first words of this ancient story, written in Akkadian, a distant and far older cousin of biblical Hebrew. This story has elements that are clearly similar to the story of creation in Genesis 1 (for example, darkness precedes creation, light exists before the heavenly bodies are formed, and a solid structure overhead keeps the heavenly waters at bay). Also groundbreaking was the discovery of two other Babylonian texts, the epics of *Atrahasis* and *Gilgamesh*. These texts contain flood stories that are so similar to the biblical story in Genesis 6–9 that scholars routinely consider the biblical story to be dependent on them.

One can scarcely overstate the impact that these discoveries had on Protestant assumptions about the authority of the Bible. That the rather bizarre, Babylonian creation and flood myths were so disturbingly similar to Genesis raised the obvious question of the historical value of Genesis 1–11 as a whole. If the Bible can look so much like these pagan myths, how can they still be God's holy, revealed—and therefore unique—word? The stories of the early chapters of Genesis may have seemed fanciful to modern readers beforehand—with a talking serpent and trees with magical fruit. But now there was external, corroborating evidence that Genesis and pagan mythologies were connected, at least indirectly.

These three factors—Darwin, Wellhausen, and Babylonian myth—had a profound impact on Protestants and reactions were swift and unyielding. Questioning the fundamental historical value of any part of the Bible was by extension an attack on the God who wrote it. Many saw the church on a slippery slope to unbelief: doubting Genesis was only a few steps removed from casting doubt on most anything the Bible says, including Jesus and the resurrection. After all, if God is the author of all of Scripture, undermining one part undermines the whole. Protestants sensed that the trapdoor to the slippery slide to unbelief was cracking open and it needed to be slammed shut. Clear battle lines were drawn and conflict ensued. Generations of traditionally minded biblical scholars dedicated their entire careers to defending the Bible from these threats, and separatist Bible colleges and seminaries began dotting the landscape with greater density. The nineteenth-century challenges were met with resistance, not engagement, and with lasting results.

Initial resistance to these challenges led to the establishment of sociological boundary markers that persist until today.[9] Many Protestants have been carefully schooled in these earlier conflicts and see themselves as part of a tribe that continues to distinguish itself from those who caved in to these insidious influences. For this reason, any suggestion that the Bible be read religiously *and critically* may from the outset be deemed an attack. Engaging critical scholarship would require a redrawing of those sociological boundaries, a rewriting of ecclesiastical narratives. That process is usually threatening to a personal or group narrative, but all the more so if those narratives include very clear ideas about ultimate significance, the nature of the universe and one's place in it, God, and eternal life. Conflict will continue until engagement of critical thinking becomes part of the narrative rather than deemed as a threat to the tribe's existence.

In my estimation, such change is already underway, which also explains why there is some soul-searching, even volatility, in some Protestant (specifically evangelical) circles. The way forward, I feel, is for these Protestants—whose identities were shaped by the factors discussed earlier—to decide to create a culture where critical *self*-reflection is valued rather than seen as a threat. There are biblical critical insights that are widely accepted, virtually unanimously, but may also disturb familiar Protestant theological categories. Revisiting those categories would promote constructive conversations in denominations, colleges, and seminaries, rather than defensiveness. Protecting boundaries—although always tempting—is not the best way to preserve faith.

Self-examination may require looking outside the main themes of the Protestant story to see what wisdom can be gained from examining how other faiths handle biblical criticism. For example, Protestants could learn from a Jewish dialogical approach to engaging the Bible rather than focus on "getting it right"—where God is encountered in the conversation of reading rather than treating the Bible as a sourcebook of infallible historical information. I think, too, that there is much Protestants can learn from the contemplative (*lectio divina*) part of the Roman Catholic tradition. Needing to get the Bible right, fretting over whether one is getting it right, and what God thinks of us should we get it wrong stem from spiritual and emotional dysfunction, not health—from a false and wounded self, not mature piety. Spiritual masters, not only of Christianity but also of other faiths, are quick to remind us that living in your head and attempting to control others and God, even through Scripture, hinders communion with God and spiritual growth. It is a great Protestant irony that one's devotion to Scripture can wind up being a spiritual barrier.

The way forward, in other words, will have to include willingness on the part of Protestants to evaluate how well things are working and to make changes where necessary. Some might say that such a program would compromise the very Protestant spirit. I disagree. I think it calls upon the true spirit of the Reformation but turned inward, not on the enemy lurking outside the walls. Searching self-evaluation is the first step toward a true synthesis between Protestant religious readings of

Scripture and critical readings. The Protestant predicament, however, is that looking inward may also be the hardest step to take.

Biblical Criticism and Protestant Faith in Conversation
Moving Forward

We move now to two broad areas that have proved perennially difficult for Protestants and where a synthetic approach to reading Scripture is sorely needed: (1) The creative way that the New Testament writers interpret the Old Testament; and (2) the difficult historical problems that beset the Old Testament. Both of these issues are in tension with Protestant notions of Scripture (as I defined Protestantism at the outset) in the following ways: they allow extrabiblical evidence (not *sola scriptura*) to frame issues of biblical interpretation and they undermine Scripture's unity. By engaging synthetically critical scholarship, the defensive legacy of Protestantism over the last one hundred and fifty years is called into question.

These two issues bring to the table the same challenge for Protestants: How can a book that is believed to be God's word appear to behave in ways that don't sit comfortably with that belief? How can a book that is inspired by God bear such striking similarities to questionable ancient customs and beliefs? How can one read with religious respect a book that suffers from so many challenges and problems? In other words, why does the Bible so fail to align itself with Protestant expectations that regular Protestant defenses of Scripture are necessary?

Bridging the gap between critical readings of Scripture and religious readings will require reorienting readers' expectations of how they feel God's word should behave. Protestants generally recognize, on some level, that Scripture is a product of the times in which it was written and/ or the events took place. This seems straightforward enough, but it is precisely here where problems can arise for Protestants. We have learned much about the Bible's historical setting over the last several generations. With that knowledge the Bible has taken on more of an unavoidable and uncomfortable "down-to-earth" rather than "divine" feel: the Bible can at times look disturbingly similar to the literature and religious ideas that we find in other ancient cultures, as we glimpsed with the Babylonian myths.

One way to get more comfortable with this down-to-earth feel of the Bible is to be reminded of the central mystery of the Christian faith: the incarnation of Christ.[10] A basic Christian (not just Protestant) belief is that Jesus of Nazareth was God in human form, both fully and truly human and fully and truly divine—however mysterious and ultimately inexplicable that confession of faith may be. In the history of Christianity, theologians have suggested that the Bible can be spoken of in a similar way: the Bible was written in particular times and places and reflects those settings, but it is also a "divine" book, meaning the writers were inspired by God and so the Bible carries with it divine authority. Scripture is a thoroughly human *and* divine product.

Comparing Jesus with the Bible tends to start more debates than it ends, and it certainly does not settle how the Bible should be interpreted in its particulars. Rather, the comparison provides a general frame of reference for how Protestants today can approach the Bible as a religious text that also embraces *as God's word* the limits, quirks, and other oddities that are part and parcel of its historical settings. In fact, one should gladly accept that the Bible will bear the marks of its ancient historical settings—after all, Jesus himself was thoroughly human and so looked, talked, acted, and thought like a first-century Palestinian Jew. Thinking this way can help Protestants come to expect of Scripture the same sort of embrace of the human that, according to orthodox Christian teaching, Jesus himself willingly took on—even to the point of emptying himself of his divine prerogative and becoming a servant, as the Apostle Paul puts it in one of his letters (Phil 2:6–8).

Of course, speaking of Jesus and the Bible in this way is metaphorical. Jesus was a man, and orthodox Christianity speaks of him as having divine and human natures. The Bible is a collection of writings, and so it does not have natures but is the product of divine and human speech. Simply stated, Christianity affirms that Jesus is God incarnate whereas the Bible is not. Still, this "incarnational analogy" between Jesus and the Bible is a deep, Christian instinct found as early as the Church Fathers.[11] For modern readers, the analogy can help ease the cognitive dissonance of those who have a high regard for Scripture *and* see the need to engage the humanity of Scripture that biblical criticism so relentlessly points out.

How the New Testament Authors Handled the Old Testament

One of the three obstacles preventing Protestants from accepting biblical criticism, mentioned earlier, is the overall character of the Christian Bible. The New Testament writers saw Jesus of Nazareth as Israel's Messiah, the chosen one of God—indeed, God's own Son—and therefore the concluding figure of Israel's story. The Christian Bible, in other words, is a unified, coherent two-part story beginning with Israel and ending with Jesus.

The New Testament authors were quite relentless in demonstrating unity between the Old Testament and the Gospel. According to one count, there are about 365 direct citations of the Old Testament in the new and about one thousand allusions.[12] In fact, there is hardly a significant section, theme, or character from the Old Testament that, in one form or another, is not presented by the New Testament authors as fulfilled or exemplified in Christ. At various points in the New Testament, Jesus is described as the new and improved Moses leading his people to a new country; the final king of David's line; the ultimate object of Abraham's faith; the new Adam; the ultimate prophet, priest, and sage; the sacrificial lamb, even the temple itself; God's companion at creation in whom all things are created anew; the end of the law; Israel's shepherd; and the suffering servant of Isaiah. The list goes on, and each of these themes could be expanded in a variety of directions.

All of this is fine as far as it goes, but as students of the New Testament are well aware, the New Testament writers took some clear liberties in bringing Israel's story and the Gospel into such thorough alignment. Even casual readers of the New Testament will notice the problem by comparing how a New Testament author uses an Old Testament passage with what the Old Testament author is saying in his context ("How did Paul get *that* out of Isaiah?!"). Not to put too fine a point on it, but for modern readers the unity of the Christian Bible is more an imposition rather than a self-evident fact. For many Protestants, watching how their own Bible behaves can be very challenging. If the Bible is truly the church's authoritative guide, why do the New Testament writers take such liberties with it? Why do the New Testament writers not share Protestant convictions of what Scripture should be? To illustrate this Protestant dilemma, consider the following brief examples.

Matthew 2:15 and Hosea 11:1. Of the four Gospel writers, the author of Matthew is particularly concerned to show how Jesus' life and teachings fulfill the Old Testament in many specific and, for us, unexpected ways. A clear example is Matthew 2:15, where Matthew speaks of Jesus' trek to and from Egypt as a boy to escape Herod's edict to kill male children. Matthew claims that Jesus' return from Egypt after Herod's death fulfills the words of the prophet Hosea where God says, "Out of Egypt I called my son" (Hosea 11:1, quoted in Matt 2:15). One need only turn back to the book of Hosea to see that the prophet was not talking about the boy Jesus or anyone else in the future. He was simply alluding to the past event of Israel's exodus from Egypt. Hosea refers to Israel as "God's son" (see also Exod 4:22), whom God delivered from Egypt by his love.

What drives Matthew to read Hosea's words as referring to the boy Jesus—when they clearly refer to Israel—is his prior conviction that Jesus is the Son of God, raised from the dead, and therefore the proper focus of all of Scripture. In fact, this conviction captures the central focus of how the New Testament writers read the Old Testament. Whatever modern readers might think about the New Testament claims concerning Jesus is beside the point; for the New Testament writers, Jesus' crucifixion and resurrection was the point of departure for reading the Old Testament. Believing that Israel's story finds its fulfillment in Jesus, the New Testament writers went back to their Scripture and reinterpreted it in light of that conviction.

Furthermore, Jewish approaches to interpreting Scripture at that time were marked by considerable creativity and had been for centuries. Scripture was seen as a source of divine guidance with hidden mysteries that required subtle, inventive means to uncover. Various Jewish groups (one famous example being the Dead Sea Scroll community) looked to Scripture to help them make sense of their present circumstances by appealing to the past, to the story of bygone days. The need to bridge past and present encouraged a flexible attitude toward interpreting Scripture, since Scripture was being called upon to address circumstances for which, from a historical-critical perspective, it was not written.[13]

We will come back to that last point a bit later. I only wish to say here that Matthew's handling of Hosea did not come out of thin air but demonstrates well both his Christian convictions about Jesus and his approaches to biblical interpretation that he shared with his Jewish contemporaries. One of those approaches is a "hook word," or a technique for demonstrating the interconnectedness of Scripture (and the interpreter's skill in pointing them out). Matthew hooks his conviction that Jesus is the "Son of God" to a "son of God" passage in the Old Testament. The fact that Hosea 11:1 also refers to an escape from Egypt further alerted Matthew that some sort of connection with Jesus was there to be made. Matthew's use of Hosea, however, is less likely due to the presence of a hook word in a random passage but more likely arises from an internal logic that may not be immediately apparent to us. Since "son" in Hosea refers to Israel, Matthew may be expressing his conviction that Jesus' life was a reenactment of Israel's story. It seems that for Matthew, Jesus is the exemplary Israelite, the one truly worthy to be called "Son of God" and therefore worthy of Matthew's readers' full assent.

Such speculation, however, may be left aside. What is clear is that Matthew appropriates Hosea's words in a way that Hosea certainly would not have recognized. The unity between the Gospel and Hosea is forged by Matthew on the basis of his conviction that Scripture's true subject matter is Christ—regardless of whether the Old Testament author understood that. The unity between Israel's story and Christ is anchored not in what Hosea says but in how Matthew reads Hosea.

Galatians 3:11 and Habakkuk 2:4. In Galatians, Paul argues that Christians are justified before God by faith and not through human effort in keeping the law. For Paul, this includes the circumcision of males—a rite of initiation into the Israelite community commanded by God (see Gen 17:11–14; Exod 12:48). There were Jewish Christians in Galatia, however, who insisted that faith is all well and good, provided Gentiles follow God's law in the Old Testament and become Jews first by getting circumcised.

Paul would not budge. Anyone who says that circumcision is a require-
ment for being right with God is preaching a false gospel and is therefore
worthy of condemnation (1:8). Circumcision is not a sign of obedience to
God but a "yoke of slavery" (5:1), a desertion from true faith in God (1:6),
and an undoing of the benefits of Christ's death and resurrection (5:2).

Paul's view certainly seems irreconcilable to the Old Testament,
where not only was circumcision commanded but the law as a whole
was a cause of celebration: a "lamp to light one's path," as we read in
Psalms 18:28 [Hebrew v. 29] and 119:105. Paul's conviction was that the
law had its place but was no longer binding now that Jesus had arrived.
Alone this is enough of a problem, but Paul makes a grander claim: the
marginalization of the law is already embedded in the Old Testament.
Israel's story, despite appearances to the contrary, points beyond the law
to Jesus. Therefore, Israel's story and the Gospel are ultimately one story.
Paul argues for this unity through a creative handling of his Scripture,
and his use of Habakkuk 2:4 is one celebrated example.

In Galatians 3:11, Paul cites Habakkuk 2:4: "The (one who is) righteous will live by faith." Paul uses this verse to support his case that one's
right standing before God is a matter of faith and not the individual's
effort in keeping the law. At first glance, Paul seems to have a point,
since Habakkuk speaks of living by faith. A look at the context of Habakkuk, however, will help us to appreciate the problem. The prophet
Habakkuk complains to God about the injustice perpetrated by Israel's
leaders (1:1–4). God promises to address the situation by sending the
hated Babylonians to teach Israel a lesson (1:5–6). This is not the solution Habakkuk had in mind, so he asks God to reconsider (1:12–2:1). Beginning in 2:2, God responds by telling Habakkuk, in essence, "Don't
worry. I know all about the Babylonians, and they will get what they
deserve, too."

Paul cites only the last part of 2:4, but the beginning of the verse
refers to the Babylonians as "proud" and not having a "right spirit" in
them. Verse 5 continues by saying that their wealth is treacherous and
they are as arrogant and greedy as death itself. Tucked in the middle of
this condemnation of Babylonian wickedness is that portion of verse 4
Paul cites. In context, the righteous who live by faith that Habakkuk likely

refers to are *Israelites who are faithful to God's law in contrast to the Babylonians.* "Faith" in 2:4 does not mean "believing" in God, as Christians might be prone to think, but means steadfast *faithfulness* demonstrated by one's actions. In other words, Habakkuk is saying that those who are righteous are those who live *faithfully* according to God's law—not like Israel's leaders who pervert the law through violence and injustice (1:2–4) nor like the arrogant and proud Babylonians. To be righteous is now, as it always has been, a matter of "faithfulness" to God's standard of justice, or to his law.

How then can Paul call upon Habakkuk 2:4, which commends as righteous those who keep the law, to support his argument that law keeping is now contrary to God's will? For the same reason we saw in Matthew 2:15: the prior conviction that Jesus is the risen Son of God now sets the standard for how Scripture is to be read. To modern tastes, Paul seems to be misusing Habakkuk's words. From Paul's point of view, however, Habakkuk's words must be reframed in light of the Gospel. Further, as we saw with Matthew, Paul's creative engagement of Israel's ancient text was hardly remarkable at the time. Paul's Jewish opponents certainly had no place for a Christ-centered reading of Habakkuk, but they would not have objected to Paul for failing to follow "proper rules of interpretation."

Romans 4 and Genesis 15:6. Our third example is from another of Paul's letters. In chapter 4 of Romans, Paul argues that Abraham was not so much the father of law-keeping Israel but of all those who have faith. After all, Paul argues, Abraham himself was not a law-keeper since he lived centuries before the law was given. Instead, Abraham must have lived by faith. Since Abraham was a man of faith, not law, Paul argues that the Gospel was embedded in the Old Testament all along. In making his case, Paul returns three times to Genesis 15:6, which he presents as an anchor for his understanding of Abraham: "And he [Abraham] believed the LORD, and he [the LORD] reckoned it to him [Abraham] as righteousness."

As with the previous example, Paul seems to have a good point: is not Abraham declared righteous by God for believing? On closer examination, however, Genesis 15:6 is not about believing in God as a matter of the emotions or the will, as Christians might mean when they talk about believing in God for salvation. Rather, Genesis speaks of Abraham *trusting* God (a better translation of the Hebrew) to do something specific, namely, give him offspring in his old age. For Paul to extrapolate from Genesis 15:6 a general principle that faith rather than law justifies one before God takes more from this verse than it is prepared to offer. Furthermore, "righteousness" in the Old Testament is not someone's inner status before God, as Paul seems to say in Galatians. Instead, it refers to actions that are "in the right." This can mean adherence to the law or, as we see in Genesis 15, an act of trusting God. In fact, God himself is referred to as "righteous" when he acts faithfully toward his people (for example, Ps 4:1).

God promises to give Abraham offspring and Abraham responds, "I trust you to do that." God says, "In this act of trust, you have done well [you are righteous]." The heart of the exchange is this: Abraham trusts God to deliver on his promise and God commends him for it. If it were not for Paul, readers would pass this verse with hardly a pause.

Paul is no fool. He certainly understands the contours and details of Abraham's story, as any other trained Jew would have. Yet, true to his conviction that Israel's story must now be rethought in view of the death and resurrection of Christ, Paul reads Genesis with fresh eyes. One might object that such a forced reading would work against Paul, for who would be convinced by such shoddy use of Scripture? But that is a modern way of thinking. Again, such creative handling of biblical texts was not simply Paul's invention but part of Jewish tradition regarding how Scripture was to be treated.

This last point is worth stressing. Jews and Christians have read the Hebrew Bible differently, and understandably so, since they have very different religious convictions. What they shared, however, was the same general viewpoint that Scripture was to be read with a fresh set of eyes to account for present circumstances. Put differently, in their formative periods, Jews and Christians both exhibited a similar type of creative energy in showing how their respective stories were the true continuation of ancient Israel's story. Both struggled to embrace a text that, simply put, was not really written for them. After all, the Hebrew Bible assumes that securing the land and keeping it was of prime importance. All of the good things that were to happen to Israel, then and in the future, assumed their place in the land with king and cult firmly established.

Neither Judaism nor Christianity fit that description. The Israelites returned to a land occupied and governed by Gentiles and would live under those circumstances for centuries. Then, after the destruction of the Temple by the Romans in 70 CE, they began to disperse. The struggle to be "people of the book" under circumstances the book never envisioned prompted Jews to engage its tradition in creative ways to maintain their identity as the people of God. The great literary achievement of this process is the Babylonian Talmud. Judaism, in other words, is the response of a people to their Scripture in light of changing circumstances.

The New Testament is something like a Christian Talmud. I am not suggesting, of course, that the Talmud and New Testament are interchangeable, and we can all walk hand in hand into an ecumenical sunset. I am suggesting that both the Talmud and the New Testament share a similar posture toward Scripture: it is to be read in light of sudden and unplanned-for paradigm-shifting events. For Judaism, the promise of continued presence and divine blessing in the land was lost during the exile and subsequent return to foreign occupation. Many early followers of Jesus, judging by the Gospel stories, were expecting Jesus to be a conventional messiah—a military figure poised to lead his people to religious and political independence. They were certainly not expecting Jesus to die a criminal's death, let alone rise from the dead. Christ's death and resurrection were game-changing developments that prompted the early Christians to reflect afresh on the significance of Israel's story for them. The precipitating events were different for Jews and Christians, but the general question those events prompted was similar: in view of changing circumstances, how do we continue to be a part of Israel's story? The New Testament bears persistent witness to how those followers of Christ answered that question.

How the New Testament authors used the Old and why they said what they said is an enormous subject. I raised it here because, in my estimation, it is one of the more difficult topics for Protestants to wrap their minds around while maintaining their convictions about the Bible, namely, its authority. On the one hand, the New Testament authors display an attitude of clear respect toward their Scripture; on the other, they handle it in ways that would seem, to Protestant ways of thinking, to betray that respect. The way forward is not to minimize the creative handling of the Old Testament by the New Testament authors in order to subsume Scripture under Protestant dogma. Rather, the handling of Scripture by New Testament authors must be explained in terms of the ancient setting in which they lived and wrote. In that setting, what the New Testament authors did makes sense. The challenge, therefore, is for Protestants to realign their convictions to reflect how their Bible actually behaves and not how they feel it should behave.

The Old Testament and the Problem of History

Biblical criticism has had a profound impact on our understanding of the historical nature of the Old Testament. As we saw earlier, the convergence of three factors in the nineteenth century (evolution, biblical criticism, and biblical archaeology) generated deep concern for many about the historical reliability of the Old Testament in general and Genesis in particular. Was the cosmos created in six days (Gen 1)? Were Adam and Eve real people (Gen 2–3)? Did early humans really live hundreds of years (Gen 5)? Was there a flood that covered the entire earth (Gen 6–9)? Did the languages of the world result from a failed tower-building project (Gen 11)? As students of the Old Testament know only too well, hardly a corner of the Old Testament has been unaffected in some way by modern historical investigations. Although few scholars dismiss outright any authentic historical underpinning of the Old Testament as a whole, most accept that the Old Testament authors do not recount events as modern historians do but as storytellers, and so the historical accuracy of the Old Testament should not be taken at face value. Rather, intersection between the biblical text and historical events must be discerned on a case-by-case basis.

The problem of the Old Testament and history has been the greatest challenge of modern biblical criticism to traditional Protestant notions about the Bible and largely accounts for why there has been such a tense relationship between biblical criticism and Protestantism. After all, if the Bible is God's word, at the very least, one should expect it to be accurate in its reporting of history, or, as some insist, absolutely free from the slightest historical error. What is left unstated is that equating God's word and historical accuracy is an assumption about how the Bible ought to be and not an assessment of what the Bible is. Further, just what constitutes historical accuracy is rarely made explicit. Presumably, what is operating under the surface is an assumption that good history writing (the kind God would certainly engage in) would be up to snuff with modern expectations of accuracy. But, as we saw in the matter of the New Testament's use of the Old, imposing modern assumptions onto ancient texts creates more problems than it solves. Protestants must be willing to learn to be comfortable with how the Bible actually behaves rather than presuming how it should behave and then massaging the data to align with that theory.

Such a mind-set is necessary, because the historical problems with the Old Testament are pervasive and beyond reasonable doubt. In fact, even a survey of the issues would be far too much ground to cover in this chapter. Instead, I would like to focus briefly on one difficult historical issue that illustrates the problem: the exodus from Egypt. The exodus is presented in the Old Testament as a historical event of miraculous proportions that led to the founding of Israel as a nation. Through a series of plagues and the splitting of the Red Sea, Yahweh delivered a band of slaves to Mt. Sinai, where he gave them the law and tabernacle—standards of morality and worship to distinguish the Israelites from all other nations. Then, after forty years in the wilderness, the Israelites entered Canaan, conquering one city after another in relatively short order until the land was in their possession.

Biblical scholars are in general agreement that the story of the exodus and conquest is an embellishment of a distant historical event that bears modest similarity to the biblical account—or, perhaps, is simply a fabrication. Archaeologically, there is no positive, direct evidence for Israelite presence in Egypt or a massive departure of about six hundred thousand men (see Exod 12:37–38 and Num 1:46). If one adds to that number women and children, plus others (see Exod 12:38), the count could exceed two million. It is typically considered unlikely that a group that large, which then spent forty years wandering around the wilderness, would leave Egypt (population around three million) without a trace in either Egyptian literature (or that of other nations) or the archaeological record.

On the other hand, there are indirect suggestions that some type of authentic historical memory lies behind the story. The Joseph story represents well some aspects of Egyptian life. There was a clear Semitic (not identifiable as Israelite) presence in Egypt at a time roughly corresponding to the Joseph story, and Semitic slaves were used to labor on building projects in the Nile Delta (where the Israelites were enslaved according to Exodus). The names Moses, Aaron, Phinehas, and others are of Egyptian origin. The storehouses Pithom and Rameses (Exod 1:11) are clearly historical and their locations have likely been identified in the Nile Delta. There seems to be some sort of "memory" of Egypt in the biblical story, although, as scholars remind us, this falls short of proof that the exodus happened as the Bible describes it.

The archaeological evidence for the conquest of Canaan is also problematic. The archaeological record presents a far more complex picture than we find in the book of Joshua. The best-known problem is Jericho, which was destroyed by Joshua according to Joshua 6, but according to the archaeological record was neither occupied nor destroyed anywhere near the time depicted in the book (thirteenth century BCE). The same holds for Ai and Jerusalem. Two other cities, Hazor and Lachish, were destroyed according to the archaeological record but about one hundred years apart, not soon after each other as we read in Joshua 10:31–32 and 11:13. For these and other reasons, biblical archaeologists commonly conclude that "Israel" was not a discreet, massive, outside population that imposed itself upon the Canaanite population, but rather largely Canaanite in origin, perhaps influenced by a small group of outsiders (who may have come out of Egypt). The fact that Israelites shared with Canaanites things such as pottery style, alphabet, and a name for God (the Canaanite high god was called El, which is also used of Israel's God over two hundred times in the Old Testament—over three hundred times if we include the references to Bethel "house of El") lends further credence to the notion that Israel grew out of Canaanite culture.

The biblical story taken literally does not sit well with these kinds of archaeological data. We also have literary evidence that raises similar problems. The way Moses is portrayed in Exodus bears clear similarities to two well-known stories from the ancient Mesopotamian world. The Egyptian tale of Sinuhe (who may have been a historical figure) comes from Egypt's Twelfth Dynasty (about 1800 BCE), about three to five hundred years before anyone would date the life of Moses. The broad story-line of Sinuhe is familiar to anyone acquainted with the story of Moses.[14] Both Moses and Sinuhe flee Pharaoh's wrath over a murder; they both wind up in tent-dwelling communities and marry a chief's oldest daughter, and both return to stand before Pharaoh. Of course, these similarities are not so striking to make us think that the biblical author copied from Sinuhe. There may be some direct connection between them, but no one knows for sure. What is unlikely, though, is that Moses' life coincidentally followed a similar pattern. It is more likely that the Moses story is patterned after themes seen in the older tale of Sinuhe.

The legend of Sargon (ancient king of Akkad, 2300 BCE) is quite similar to Moses' birth story in Exodus 2:1–10. Of humble birth, Sargon was placed by his mother in a reed basket lined with pitch, set afloat on a river, was found by the king's water drawer who raised him as his son, and eventually became king. These similarities are striking and suggest that something other than the reporting of history is going on in Exodus. Neither of these examples is evidence that Moses is a purely literary figure, but they do suggest that the Moses of Exodus is known to us today through the lens of a literary convention of the time.

My purpose here is not to defend or detract from a historical basis for the exodus or the man Moses. Rather, I demonstrate that the pressure is on Protestants to find a way to talk about the historical character of the exodus in view of the archaeological and literary evidence that, at the very least, gives it more the feel of a story than of a historical report. Faced with these challenges, some evangelical Protestant scholars content themselves with making the case for the historical plausibility of an Israelite presence in Egypt and eventual presence in Canaan, and therefore the "basic historical reliability" of the biblical story.[15] Such arguments have value, to be sure, but it must be admitted that speaking of the exodus story as historically plausible guts it of any sort of authority over historical matters, as Protestantism has traditionally understood it. Instead, this approach admits that the historical evidence is of such a nature that one can aim no higher than "plausibility" for the biblical story.

"Plausibility" also leaves unanswered how much of the exodus story reflects a historical core. Is it a minimal hint of history? For example, a few dozen Semitic slaves leave Egypt and spin a tale over the years that grows into a miraculous deliverance story? That is a plausible thesis, as are others. The echoes of Egypt mentioned earlier really do not tell us one way or another whether the biblical exodus account is historically plausible. It may be an essential fabrication given an Egyptian flavor. We do not know. At any rate, defending the plausibility of the exodus is a concession to these pressing historical problems. The present state of the evidence is so compelling that plausibility seems to be a necessary interpretive strategy.

Further, the historical issues surrounding Exodus run deeper than archaeological artifacts or literary parallels to Moses. The exodus story echoes the so-called cosmic battle myth known from other, older, texts of the ancient world. Those texts speak of a primordial battle between the gods, where one god emerges as victor and therefore high god of the pantheon and ruler of the cosmos. The Israelites portrayed the deliverance from Egypt as another "cosmic battle."

One can begin to see this by stepping outside the exodus story for a moment. For example, Psalm 77:16 [Heb v. 17] describes the Red Sea as "writhing" and "convulsing" at the "sight" of God. This is more than a vivid use of poetic language. In other ancient stories, the sea is a symbol of chaos and is personified as a divine figure vanquished by the warrior high god. In *Enuma Elish*, mentioned previously, the chaos figure is called Tiamat.[16] The high god Marduk cut her in half and with one-half formed the sky and with the other half the earth. In Canaanite religion, the chaotic sea is called Yam, and he is defeated by the high god Baal. The Red Sea in Psalm 77 is not convulsing because of a bad storm but having a panic attack at the sight of the warrior Yahweh who has come to defeat it. By depicting the parting of the Red Sea this way, the writer conjures up images of this well-known ancient image of a primordial divine battle—which is to say, the warrior-god who defeated the sea is now fighting for Israel by defeating the sea once again.

The imagery of Psalm 77 becomes a bit clearer when we turn to Psalm 136:13. We read there that Yahweh "cut the Red Sea to pieces," which echoes more clearly Tiamat's fate at the hands of Marduk. Dividing the sea asunder echoes in Israel's creation story. In Genesis 1:6–10, God divides the waters of chaos (called "the deep") into two separate bodies of water: waters above the firmament and waters below (verses 6–8). Unlike *Enuma Elish*, the sea in Genesis is not a divine being but an impersonalized chaotic force that Yahweh splits in two. In Genesis 1:9–10, we see a second splitting of the sea. This time the waters below are parted to reveal the dry land beneath. The Red Sea incident, likewise, is a parting of waters to reveal dry land beneath (compare the wording of Gen 1:9 with Exod 14:21).

Tying the Red Sea to the ancient cosmic battle is a theme seen elsewhere in the Old Testament (for example, Job 9:8, 26:7–13, 38:1–11; Ps 93:3–4; Isa 27:1, 59:9–11), which indicates that this theme was a key way in which the Israelites thought about the exodus. Of course, we need to be perfectly clear that this in and of itself does not prove that there was no departure from Egypt and crossing of the Red Sea. The presence of a plausible historical core would have to be determined by considering other factors. The bottom line, however, is that the exodus story in the Bible clearly has literary, theological, and mythic qualities. Any grappling with the historical value of the exodus story needs to account for these factors. Whatever else we can say, the exodus story is doing something other than reporting history. This is the inevitable conclusion to which biblical criticism leads and to which Protestantism must adjust.

Cosmic battle overtones can also be seen elsewhere in Exodus. Pharaoh was considered a divine figure, the earthly manifestation of the high god of the pantheon. Much of Exodus is actually a battle between Yahweh and Pharaoh about which of these "gods" will call Israel his own. Pharaoh wants Israel to stay and "serve" him as slaves. Yahweh wants the Israelites released so that they can "serve" him on Mt. Sinai (see especially Exod 7:16). "Serve" is a pun on the Hebrew word 'avad, which can mean to serve as slaves or to serve in the sense of worship.

Exodus, in other words, is an account of the battle between the true God Yahweh and the false god Pharaoh over whom Israel will serve: Pharaoh as slaves or Yahweh on Mt. Sinai as worshippers.

The story of the plagues (Exod 7–12) continues this divine battle theme. The plagues are not random displays of power but a series of pointed attacks meant to undermine Egypt's socio-religious structure. This battle is an utter mismatch from the beginning, but Yahweh prolongs the battle so his power might be on full display (see especially Exod 9:15–16). In the very first plague, the Nile is turned to blood. The Nile was Egypt's source of survival, and this act wreaked economic havoc. The Nile was also personified and worshipped as a god. By turning the Nile to blood, Yahweh was showing mastery over the god responsible for Egypt's very existence. The goddess of childbirth, Heqet, was depicted with the head of a frog, and so the plague of frogs (second plague) foreshadows the death of the Egyptian firstborn in the tenth plague. The mother and sky goddess, Hathor, was depicted as a cow (fifth plague on livestock). The hailstorm (seventh plague) shows Yahweh's supremacy over the Egyptian gods associated with storms (e.g., Seth). Pharaoh was considered to be the earthly representative of the sun god Re (or Ra), and in the ninth plague Yahweh blots out the sun. Osiris is the Egyptian god of the dead, yet Yahweh will lay claim on the firstborn of Egypt by putting them to death (tenth plague).

The "battle of the gods" theme is amply summarized in Exodus 12:12: "For I will pass through the land of Egypt that night, and I will strike down every firstborn in the land of Egypt, both human beings and animals; *on all the gods of Egypt I will execute judgments.* I am the LORD." This is not rhetoric. Exodus is a battle scene between Israel's God and the gods of Egypt. Israel's God—the God of a first homeless and then enslaved people—marches into the territory of the superpower of the day, toys with its king and gods, and then delivers a crippling strike in the tenth plague. The final blow, as we saw, occurs at the Red Sea. Yahweh splits the Red Sea, as he had split the sea/chaos in primordial times, thus defeating Egypt's entire army and bringing freedom to Israel (Exod 14:15–18).

Again, whatever historical core there may be to the exodus story, the story itself is clearly addressed in literary conventions of the time, which includes nods to stories from other ancient cultures. It is a noble enterprise, which I genuinely support, to continue to explore the basic historical reliability and plausibility of the book of Exodus. But, at the end of the day, we are left with a story that does something other than simply report events. Exodus is a theological statement that uses idioms of the day to paint a portrait of Israel's glorious beginnings and of the God they serve. The question that gets to the heart of the matter for Protestants is not "Did *something* happen?" but "What is the historical character of God's word? What do we have the right to expect of it, historically speaking? When we read the exodus story, what historical information are we to get out of it?" The modern study of Exodus has driven home for Protestants vital and unavoidable questions about the historical character of the Old Testament that require a synthetic approach between Protestant faith and biblical criticism.

One Protestant's Perspective

How Protestants relate to biblical criticism is not an academic curiosity for me. Much of my writing and speaking has grown out of my process of working through the matters of faith and scholarship, and my experiences are hardly unique.

Although I was raised in a rather eclectic immigrant German Lutheran home, in my teenage years I entered the world of evangelical Christianity, where the authority of Scripture was assumed. The more I began to explore Scripture, the more I began to question whether things were quite so straightforward. I later enrolled in an evangelical Christian college where my faith was both confirmed and challenged. I was exposed to different ways of thinking and began to see, among other things, that I was not alone in my questions and that there was a big world out there, where people thought about the very same things that I was thinking about. To make a long story short, this began a process of study and reflection where, even before I attended seminary, I was already—albeit naively—synthesizing my faith with points of view that pushed the boundaries of that faith. After a fairly restless period, I entered seminary at the age of twenty-four to devote several years to learning more about Scripture, theology, church history, and other matters that might give me a better intellectual grounding from which to engage my questions.

As others have quipped, seminarians begin their studies with ten vital questions they want answered, but before the first semester is over, those ten are replaced with fifty others, more pressing and unexpected. It was mainly my grounding in the biblical languages that led me to see that the Bible can actually be a very tricky book to understand. English translations, as necessary as they are, tend to mask those interpretive challenges. Which is to say, "The Bible loses something in the original." Efforts to nail down what a passage is saying typically became exercises in playing with the interpretive flexibility of the text, especially the Hebrew Bible, born out of legitimate ambiguities that, I would later come to learn, are the very fuel of the long history of Jewish and Christian interpretation of Scripture.

I remain thankful for those early stages of my journey, and my time at seminary was foundational for much of what was to come—even if the lessons learned during those years would eventually prove inadequate for me, because the challenges of Scripture were often tamed too quickly in favor of preserving deeply held theological convictions. It was not until I began my doctoral work in Hebrew Bible and the ancient Near East, for what proved to be a five-year process of deep intellectual exploration, that I was truly forced to face some of the shortcomings of my background. From virtually the first week of my course work, I was brought into conversation with ways of thinking about Scripture, which addressed the questions I had (and others I did not yet have), that were clearly coherent and well thought out but also diametrically opposed to some nonnegotiable positions I had been taught. Entering this more mature stage of my quest for synthesis was unsettling but also exciting.

Many questions crossed my mind during my doctoral work, perhaps the most pressing were the two topics I chose to address in this chapter: how the Christian Bible achieves coherence, and the historical problems of the Old Testament. The latter issue was not unknown to me. Evangelicals tend to know something about the historical problems of the Old Testament, because an unintended consequence of their apologetics is to draw attention to them. (Two evangelical classics are *Encyclopedia of Bible Difficulties* and *The Big Book of Bible Difficulties*.)[17] Nevertheless, I never really had unfiltered, face-to-face, access to biblical criticism. Once I did, as so many have experienced, it was clear that historical questions about the Bible are not baseless impositions by a conspiring band of hostile scholars committed to undermining the faith but, stem from careful historical study and legitimate issues raised by a close reading of the biblical texts.

I had not been exposed, however, to the former issue, and this raised a new set of questions for me. I remember distinctly when and where that process began. During my second year of course work, I was a teaching assistant for a wildly popular undergraduate course of over six hundred students taught by my doctoral advisor, James Kugel, called "The Bible and Its Interpreters." Kugel would lecture on the major episodes in the Hebrew Bible and then look at those episodes from the point of view of how ancient interpreters handled those stories vis-à-vis modern biblical critics. In one lecture, Kugel's topic was the miraculous supply of water from the rock during Israel's wilderness wanderings in Exodus 17 and Numbers 20. Kugel read from several early Jewish sources from the first two centuries CE that spoke of how the Israelites had some constant, mobile source of water while they wandered in the desert. One of these sources actually spoke of the rock moving around with the Israelites from place to place. Presumably, the fact that the water from a rock is mentioned twice in the Pentateuch, at the beginning and end of the wilderness period, led some ancient interpreters to conclude that the two rocks were one and the same: the rock rolled around in the desert for forty years like a portable drinking fountain.

I chuckled inwardly at hearing this and appreciated the entertainment value of these ancient Jewish interpreters. But then Kugel followed with words that I realize in retrospect altered not only my career path but also my life: "Turn to 1 Corinthians 10:4." Now things were getting personal. In that passage, Paul speaks of the rock in the desert that nourished the Israelites. Of course, such episodes are simply waiting to be drawn into the Christian story, and so Paul identifies that rock in the Old Testament with Christ himself, as if to say that the rock that gave

Israel water in the desert was in fact Christ who also sustained them spiritually—the same Christ who now nourishes the church.

Nothing unexpected there, although verse 4 has a curious detail that I had never noticed in my years of reading Scripture, but it now leapt off the page like it was spring-loaded. Paul says, ". . . the rock *that followed them* was Christ." The clear implications of those three words (in English; a single word in Greek) encapsulated for me the process of spiritual and intellectual reorientation I had been living through for years, and that would now take a more serious turn. Paul was clearly aware of this Jewish legend of a rock moving in the desert. In fact, he seems to accept it quite casually—as if almost an afterthought, certainly in no need of defense or explanation. This created a dilemma for me. How could Paul, inspired by God himself, say something so fanciful, so silly, as a rock moving about in the desert? Not only was such a "moveable well" completely foreign to the Old Testament (we read of no rock rolling about in the desert), yet Paul passes on such a fable seemingly without a second thought. In short, my Bible was not behaving in an accurate, inerrant, inspired, unique way. The Bible started to look quite ordinary.

I knew that I had left familiar, comfortable territory and quickly surmised that my theology would never be quite the same again. I also knew instantly that I had a decision to make. I could:

1. Ignore the implications of what I heard and go about my life.
2. Dedicate my career to showing why what I heard could not possibly be true; that Paul could not possibly mean what he clearly says.
3. Accept what I heard and commit myself to doing the hard work of bringing faith and criticism into dialogue.

Avoidance, defensiveness, synthesis: those were my three options. I chose the third, and while this path has not always been easy to follow, it has been well worth taking. Along the way, I have learned some valuable lessons.

The Bible is not the center of the Christian faith. The Bible has always played an unimpeachable role in Christianity, and I certainly do not mean to suggest otherwise. It is not, however, the central focus of Christian faith. That position belongs to God, and Christians are called to trust him. Of course, as Christians believe, Scripture bears witness to God and what he has done in Christ, but Scripture's witness-bearing role should not be confused with the one to whom Scripture bears witness—and when the American landscape is dotted with "Bible" churches and seminaries, we see such confusion in full swing. Scripture is to be read with all diligence and respect, but the diverse interpretive conclusions reached throughout the history of the church and throughout the Christian world should alert us that "getting the Bible right" may not be possible—or even the point. Coming to the realization the Gospel is not at stake with every interpretive challenge will encourage a fruitful dialogue between religious and critical readings of Scripture.

Fear can quickly derail the dialogue between faith and critical readings of Scripture. Not every critical reading of Scripture is convincing or of equal value. Biblical scholarship has its share of trends and sloppy thinking. But critical scholarship has also brought significant clarity to the study of Scripture. Discerning between the two takes patience and learning, but fear too often comes into play. At the risk of oversimplifying, I think that fear of being wrong about ultimate reality has been a frequent problem in the Protestant tradition and often accounts for what are sometimes mislabeled theological and biblical disputes. When dialogue is stifled and aggressive responses quickly follow—whether by popular opinion or prevailing power structures—lurking not too far beneath the surface is an unstated fear: familiar, protective, theological boundaries are being threatened. Biblical criticism is fear inducing, and one of the challenges some iterations of the Protestant faith will have to continue working through is how to create spiritual climates where fear in the face of biblical criticism no longer dominates.

An unsettled faith is a maturing faith. When familiar patterns of thinking begin to look less convincing, spiritual distress can result, and it is a natural tendency to want to ease the discomfort as quickly as possible. Yet the monastic and contemplative traditions of the Christian faith—typically not part of the Protestant consciousness—attest to the power of spiritual struggle as an expected and valuable part of the spiritual life (modeled on such biblical precedents as Qohelet [Ecclesiastes],

Job, lament psalms, and Jesus himself). In fact, spiritual alienation can be a period of necessary spiritual purging of one's views of God and the Bible that have become caricatures, mere reflections of one's ego that need to be left behind. Such periods may feel like a loss of faith when, in fact, they are merely exposing an immature faith.

Response by Marc Zvi Brettler

Much in Professor Enns's essay resonated deeply with me. We even begin with the same problem—that it is not so easy to define the very heterogeneous religious group (Protestants, Jews) that we are exploring. I admire Enns's solution of "focusing on Protestants who are most likely to have an interest in how faith and biblical criticism can be in dialogue," a "middle group," of those "taking the Bible seriously." I am not sure, however, who might make up such a group of Jews, and I sense that it is proportionately a much smaller group than it is within Protestantism. Also, "taking the Bible seriously" would need to be defined quite differently within Judaism and Protestantism (and Catholicism).

Yet even the casual reader of my essay and Enns's will come away with many clear, determinative differences between the Jewish critical and Protestant critical reading of the Bible. The first of these concerns the place of the Bible. Enns notes that "in Protestantism the Bible is pressed into the role of supreme religious authority." This is not the case in Judaism. First of all, to the extent that there is any such "supreme religious authority," it is not the entire Bible, but the Torah, which within Judaism has always been seen as first among equals. Moreover, it is not the Torah text that has been the "supreme religious authority." That would be the case for the Karaites, who reject rabbinic texts and law. For Jews, the *interpreted* Torah has been supremely important—but there is no single authoritative interpretation of it. Rabbinic literature in the Talmudim and elsewhere is characterized by disagreement—phrases such as "another opinion" occur frequently. The rabbinic Bible has many divergent commentaries on each page. Although there have been some codifications of Jewish laws, there has not been a codification of Jewish biblical interpretation. That would fly in the face of central rabbinic principles concerning the pluriformity of meaning of the Bible. It is very difficult to have a pluriform "supreme religious authority."

In fact, the Protestant expectation that Enns notes—that the Bible should "be generally clear and consistent"—is foreign to most Jewish biblical interpretation. The Bible is given, according to the rabbinic view, "to be expounded," and the rabbis inherited and developed various rules of interpretation. The plain sense, so important to Protestants through-out their history, has hardly been important throughout the long history of Jewish biblical interpretation. Searching for the plain sense and using historical-critical methods are not identical, but they share some similar-ities. This means that contemporary Protestants, as compared to Jews, have significant traditions and interpretations on which to build when engaging in historical-critical study.

The Bible's clarity to Protestants, as Enns suggests, exists because "the Bible is ultimately a coherent grand narrative that tells one and only one story with a climax: the crucified and risen Son of God brings Isra-el's story to completion." Protestant scholarship typically sees the Bible as a single story with a climax; neither classical nor modern Jewish bib-lical scholarship shares this view. This is an important example of how even though both communities believe they are reading the same book, they are not.

Enns's description of "Protestant Identity in the Nineteenth Cen-tury," especially the "battle for the Bible," was new to me and invites comparison to Judaism. For various historical reasons, most aspects of this battle hardly took place in Judaism in the nineteenth century—they are instead taking place now.

As I noted in my essay, Darwin had a very different effect in the Jew-ish community than he did among Protestants. This is fundamentally connected to how each community read the Bible—Protestants typically read it as literal history, while for most Jews, the historical veracity of its details was less important, since it should be read more broadly, using a variety of interpretive methods. Some traditional Jews have noted simi-larities between evolution and rabbinic or mystical traditions, making evolution even more acceptable within that Jewish group. Yet many tra-ditional Jews feel uncomfortable with the idea of natural selection and believe that after the divine creation of the world—however that happened (because most Jews do not read Genesis 1–3 literally)—there has been continuous divine control.

Similarly, Enns expends considerable effort dealing with "the difficult historical problems that beset the Old Testament." This is not a core problem for Judaism, because for Jews, the Bible is not primarily a book of history to be interpreted literally. I suspect that more Jews than Protestants will agree with Enns's "one Protestant's perspective" that "Exodus is a theological statement that uses idioms of the day to paint a portrait of Israel's glorious beginnings and of the God they serve." This is quite similar to my (Jewish) mentor's comment: "The biblical writers were not consciously engaged in what we would consider history writing . . . Their concern was with the didactic use of selected historical traditions for a theological purpose."[18] This perspective sidesteps the issue of the Bible's historicity.

The second aspect of the "battle for the Bible" noted by Enns, the influence of Wellhausen and his school, has only recently begun to have an impact on Judaism. The work of Wellhausen and other critics was written in the world of the Protestant faculties of theology, largely in German and British universities. Jews certainly did not study there to be ministers, and only in unusual situations took courses there. I do not mean to imply that Jews were not at all influenced by source criticism in the late nineteenth and early twentieth centuries—a small number were. But Jewish contact with these ideas was mostly in the form of polemic rather than careful engagement. This is understandable given that many of the Protestant practitioners of these new methods, including Wellhausen, wove supersessionism deeply into their critical observations.

Of the three issues that Enns mentions, only the final aspect of the battle for the Bible, namely, the discovery of ancient Near Eastern documents and their comparison to the Bible, had significant resonance within the Jewish community. The Babel-Bibel affair of Friedrich Delitzsch in the early twentieth century, in which Delitzsch offered a series of public, widely publicized lectures attempting to show the superiority of Mesopotamia to the Hebrew Bible and Judaism, could not be ignored, and the Jewish press in both the German- and English-speaking world responded to his claims in great detail.

Enns highlights the Protestant concern with maintaining the traditional authorship of biblical books, noting that the Torah, Isaiah, and Daniel were "the most famous examples" of biblical criticism. Jews, too, were concerned about such issues but not to the same extent. As my essay made clear, the question of Mosaic authorship of most of the Torah is on a different plane from, for example, Isaiah's authorship of the entire Book of Isaiah. After all, Abraham ibn Ezra already hinted that chapters 40ff. of Isaiah were not by the same authors as the previous chapters. Following his precedent, the existence of Deutero-Isaiah was debated among some Jewish scholars in the nineteenth century and seen as fundamentally different from issues concerning the sources of the Torah. Some Jewish scholars argued for the division of Isaiah as strongly as they argued for the unity of the Torah.

Enns notes that from the Protestant perspective "God is the author of all of Scripture." Although there is a popular conception among some Jews that this is a Jewish belief, this is not so. As my essay shows, many Jewish sages thought that prophets authored their own oracles and books after receiving a divine vision, but the book itself was not authored by God. Similarly, according to Judaism, biblical books were canonized because they were authoritative, not because they were perceived as being divinely inspired. This difference in perspective explains many other fundamental differences between how Jews and Protestants view the Bible, and why certain aspects of critical scholarship are more readily accepted by Jews than by Protestants, especially outside the Torah.

Of course, Jews depart from Protestant interpretation as they do from Catholic interpretation concerning the belief that the focus of the whole Bible, Old and New Testaments combined, is "the central mystery of the Christian faith: the incarnation of Christ." Enns observes that "the Christian Bible, in other words, is a unified, coherent two-part story beginning with Israel and ending with Jesus." For Jews, the "story" element of the Bible is less significant, and that story certainly does not end with Jesus. The fact that the Writings or Ketuvim, the final part of the Hebrew Bible or Tanakh, are not in chronological order, and end with either Chronicles or Ezra-Nehemiah, highlights the extent to which it is not history. In fact, if I had to paraphrase Enns's observation in relation to the Jewish Bible, I would say that it is a thematically diverse collection beginning with creation and no defined ending.

I found Enns's choice of biblical texts to expound very telling: Hosea 11:1, Habakkuk 2:4, and Genesis 15:6. The first two are prophetic texts, reflecting the importance of the prophets, rather than the Torah, especially its legal sections, within Protestantism. A Jewish selection of three texts to illustrate Hebrew Bible and rabbinic connections would look different. This second and third text both use the Hebrew root *'mn*, "to believe," "to have faith." This reflects a Protestant choice of a core biblical word.

I am not being critical here but want to reinforce the simple, but crucial, point that Harrington made as well—that different religious communities see different sections of the Bible as being most important. Not only is it the case that Jews, Catholics, and Protestants have different Bibles, but even when they share the same books, they value them differently. When, for the *Jewish Study Bible*, my co-editor and I needed to find contributors, we could choose among many possible contributors for Torah books but finding Jewish contributors for the prophetic books was much more difficult.

Much of my response has focused on the different Jewish and Protestant conceptions of the Bible: differences that would inform how Jews and Protestants understand historical-critical study and religious commitment. But there are some similarities that I believe Jewish and Protestant perspectives share.

Like Harrington, Enns offers some comparison between the New Testament and the Talmud. I discussed this analogy in relation to Harrington's essay but would like to highlight here Enns's point of comparison: "both the Talmud and the New Testament share a similar posture toward Scripture: it is to be read in light of sudden and unplanned-for paradigm-shifting events." I would generalize this point differently, and pose it as a problem, one which I believe all three of us are attempting to address: reading a text religiously means connecting it to your community in the present, as Harrington notes in his essay. In contrast, reading a text from a historical-critical perspective means connecting it to its original author and setting. The main question with which we are all engaged is how can we constructively connect the past and the present in a manner that does justice to both (what Enns calls "a true synthesis between Protestant religious readings of Scripture and critical readings")?

We must do this, because as Enns noted correctly, "historical questions about the Bible are not baseless impositions by a conspiring band of hostile scholars committed to undermining the faith but stem from careful historical study and legitimate issues raised by a close reading of the biblical texts." We must look for answers by taking into account both historical-critical methods and our religious traditions. Like him, I wish to engage and encourage others to engage in "doing the hard work of bringing faith and criticism into dialogue."

The final comments of Professor Enns resonate very strongly with me. I repeat them here, sometimes with small changes, each with a brief addition explaining my Jewish perspective:

> "*The Bible is not the center of Jewish faith* . . . That position belongs to God."

And the Bible and its interpretation offer us complex understandings of that God, and it is our religious obligation to explore and integrate these.

> "*Fear can quickly derail the dialogue between faith and critical readings of Scripture.*"

But recall that seventy-five times the Hebrew Bible insists: "Fear not." This is a major biblical theme dispersed throughout the Hebrew Bible.

> "*An unsettled faith is a maturing faith.*"

Although some medieval formulae speak of *'emunah shelemah*, complete faith, that phrase or its equivalent is absent from the Hebrew Bible. Unsettled faith is faith nevertheless.

Response by Daniel J. Harrington, S.J.

My goal here is not to critique the author's tradition or his views on it but rather to explore points that are similar to and (especially) are different from the Catholic tradition, taking the opportunity to try to enrich the discussion.

While acknowledging the indispensable character of the historical-critical method, here I give particular attention to showing why and how there can be other interpretive approaches both in antiquity and today.

Ancient Parallels to the Use of the Old Testament in the New Testament

Professor Enns uses three examples to illustrate how the New Testament writers used various Old Testament texts. Hosea 11:1 is used in Matthew 2:15 to show that Jesus was God's Son even from his infancy and that his flight into and return from Egypt were in accord with the divine plan for Israel in the Exodus. In Galatians 3:11, Paul cites Habakkuk 2:4 out of context and with a different meaning of "faith" to provide the biblical basis for justification by faith and for Gentiles not needing to undergo circumcision. In Romans 4, Paul uses the example of Abraham in Genesis 15:6 to prove that Gospel faith was embedded in the beginning of salvation history—an idea that would have been foreign to the earlier biblical writer.

As Enns notes, such interpretations would not pass muster in most current Old Testament introduction courses. The reason is that such courses are now generally taught in accord with the historical-critical method. In such courses, the goals are to read texts in their original historical contexts and to determine as closely as possible the author's original intention and how the original audience would have understood the text. I have taught such courses many times and believe wholeheartedly in the value and indispensable character of this approach.

However, I am also aware that the historical-critical approach to Scripture is not the only approach. In fact, it is a recent development. The New Testament was not written in a cultural vacuum but reflects many of the Jewish attitudes and assumptions about Scripture that were in vogue at the time. Those attitudes and assumptions are on display in Jewish writings that were contemporary with Jesus. The Dead Sea Scrolls provide some good examples. In particular, the group of writings known as the *Pesharim* is perhaps most instructive.[19]

The *Pesharim* look something like modern biblical commentaries. They give a verse or two of the biblical text and provide an interpretation. The Qumran texts are mainly concerned with passages from the Old Testament Prophets or Psalms. They are often obscure biblical texts, some of which have baffled interpreters for centuries. The word *pesher* has come to mean "interpretation." But *pesher* is also used in the context of the interpretation of dreams or visions in the book of Daniel, where the content to be interpreted is called a *raz*—that is, a mystery to be solved. In the Qumran *Pesharim* the biblical text is taken to be a mystery to be solved, and the solution is often found in the history and everyday life of the community (probably Essene) that produced the *Pesharim*.

The example of the Qumran *Pesharim* shows that in Jesus' time, Jews were not especially concerned with establishing the literal, historical sense of Scripture. They may have regarded such a concern as too obvious or unimportant. They were, instead, more interested in texts they found puzzling and in finding correlations between those texts and their own communal life. Their own history and daily life became the hermeneutical key whereby the mysteries of obscure biblical texts might be resolved.

A similar process seems to have been at work in early Christian circles, as the three examples cited above show. According to the New Testament writers, Christ was the key to the Scriptures. The Bible in the early church was what we now call the Old Testament. Whether it was read in Greek or Hebrew, that Bible was viewed as a source for understanding Jesus' life and teachings. Indeed, some have speculated that the Qumran people made *Testimonia*, or lists of biblical quotations focused on particular themes. It is very likely that early Christians did the same and applied them to Jesus and the Christian community. Such activity seems to have been at the root of the promise and fulfillment or from shadows-to-realities approaches to the Old Testament that became so prominent in the patristic writings and have remained so in Catholic and Orthodox Christian circles.

Both the Qumran community and the early Christians aimed at a similar goal: to find significance for the present in what had become authoritative (in some sense) texts from the past. What they were doing could be classed as an example of the search for the "religious" meaning of the Scriptures. There is certainly nothing wrong with this. Indeed, it is what preachers do regularly. What is important for those who study the Scriptures today is to recognize that there are and always have been different ways of reading these texts and that much depends on the attitudes and assumptions that the various interpreters brought to the texts.

Hermeneutical Theory

The tension between the original meaning of the ancient text and its contemporary significance is not simply a phenomenon of the distant past or of biblical study. Indeed, it is part of the modern hermeneutical debate that has its proper home in philosophy. "Hermeneutics" is a term for the process or art of interpretation. While theoretically a topic for philosophers, it has obvious relevance for biblical scholars and theologians.

The hermeneutical debate concerns the nature of a text and what the reader can and should do with it. One position, represented by E. D. Hirsch, describes what happens in most critical-biblical scholarship today.[20] The first task, according to Hirsch, is to explain the text in its original historical context, using all the literary and historical methods to arrive at the *meaning* of the text. The second and separate task is to try to articulate the *significance* of the text. That is, what relevance (if any) it may have for today. Having established objectively what the text says and means, the interpreter is free to decide whether what it says is true or significant. For example, one may provide an objective literary and historical reading of the biblical accounts of the exodus and arrive at their meaning in their original context. Then one has to ask and answer: Are they true? Did it happen that way? Did the original author think that it did happen that way? Does it make any sense today?

At the other end of the hermeneutical spectrum is the view represented by Paul Ricoeur, who stresses the autonomy of the text once it is "published."[21] This view regards the historical study of a text to be of comparatively small importance. As a philosopher rather than a historian, Ricoeur was mainly interested in ideas and regarded as most important what Hirsch might call the significance of the ideas in the text. This approach is concerned primarily with the text as a vehicle for thought. It affirms that once the text has been made public in whatever form, it has become separated from its author and the author's original context, and it can mean whatever the reader or readers want to make out of it. With respect to the biblical exodus accounts, Ricoeur might say that the author's intention is beyond what we can know and is therefore irrelevant, that what is the proper object of interpretation is the text as we have in the Bible (Exod 14–15 and elsewhere), and that what matters is the story's message of God's saving care for his people and their liberation from the power of evil.

A mediating hermeneutical position is taken by Hans-Georg Gadamer, who developed the concept of the fusion of horizons.[22] He wants to take seriously the world behind the text (the original historical context), the text as we have it today, and the world in front of the text (what the reader might make of it today). He regards the art of interpretation as bringing together or fusing the horizons of both the author and the reader through the medium of the text. The most obvious example would be the preacher taking a biblical passage and applying it to the current needs of a specific religious community. But it also applies to musicians, lawyers, actors, and many other kinds of interpreters. Musicians work with musical scores, and their interpretation and execution of them constitute a performance. Lawyers try to interpret their clients' cases in the light of legal precedents and written laws. Actors read scripts and develop their characters as they see fit. In all these cases, the goal is to bring together a text of some sort and the experiences of real people here and now, in other words, in the fusion of horizons.

How does all this hermeneutical theory illuminate what the Qumran people and the early Christians were doing with biblical texts? They were not doing the kind of historical criticism we do today. Whatever concept of biblical authority they might have had, it led them to take very seriously texts that are part of what we now call the Hebrew Bible or Old Testament. However, they were also convinced that they now possessed a hermeneutical key—the life and times of the Qumran community, or the person of Jesus of Nazareth—that could open up and reveal the true meaning of those texts. And so they were led to make a fusion of horizons between the ancient texts of the Bible and their own community's faith and life.

The Analogy of the Incarnation

In talking about the "down to earth" character of the Bible, Peter Enns appeals to the analogy of the "incarnation" of Christ as the central mystery of Christian faith. The word "incarnation" refers to the Christian belief that Jesus as the Son of God took on human flesh and so became truly human as well as truly divine. The clearest New Testament foundation appears in John 1:14: "And the Word became flesh and lived among us." While the language of John 1:1–18 (and Col 1:15–20, Heb 1:3, and Phil 2:6–11) echoes the Old Testament passages that describe wisdom personified (Prov 8:22–31, Sir 24:1–34, Wis 7), in Catholic theology, John 1:14 has been taken very seriously and concretely as affirming that Jesus, the second person of the Blessed Trinity, the Son of God, became one of us, died for us and for our sins, and now reigns in glory.

In his essay here and in his fine book, *Inspiration and Incarnation*, Enns uses the analogy of the incarnation to deal with the Old Testament's relationship to ancient Near Eastern literature.[23] His point was that the Bible's story of ancient Israel took place in the linguistic and conceptual frameworks of the ancient Near East and so was strongly influenced by them. Likewise, in modern Catholic documentation it has become customary to describe the Bible as "the word of God in human language." At a critical point in discussing the divine inspiration of Scripture and its interpretation, Vatican II's *Dei Verbum* 13 invokes the analogy of incarnation: "For the words of God, expressed in human language, have become like unto human speech, just as the Word of the eternal Father, when he took on himself the flesh of human weakness, became like unto human beings."

The analogy of the incarnation can help Christians to imagine how they can hold that their Bible is divine and human at the same time, and that therefore they should welcome the ancient Near Eastern parallels and influences that historians and archaeologists may bring to their attention as part of the world in which the Bible as the word of God took shape. The thrust of John's Gospel is that Jesus is the revealer and the revelation of God, that God has revealed who God is and what God wills through Jesus the Word made flesh, and that the incarnation took place in a particular land and people and at a particular time. For believing Christians the task of historical criticism is to learn as much as possible about the conditions under which the Word became flesh.

Further Reading

Armerding, Carl E. *The Old Testament and Criticism*. Grand Rapids, MI: Eerdmans, 1983. Overview of the main methods of critical-biblical scholarship, while advocating a "moderately critical approach" for evangelical-biblical scholarship.

Bartholomew, Craig, C., Stephen Evans, Mary Healy, and Murray Rae, eds. *"Behind" the Text: History and Biblical Interpretation*. Grand Rapids, MI: Zondervan, 2003. Collection of thoughtful essays, with responses, reassessing the value of historical criticism for biblical interpretation in view of recent emphases on literary methods, postmodernism, and a renewed interest in how theology influences our view of history.

Enns, Peter. *Inspiration and Incarnation: Evangelicals and the Problem of the Old Testament*. Grand Rapids, MI: Baker, 2005. Employs an incarnation model of Scripture to help evangelicals come to terms with the various aspects of biblical criticism, namely, the Old Testament's ancient Near Eastern setting, theological diversity in the Old Testament, and the use of the Old Testament by the New Testament writers.

Harvey, Van A. *The Historian and the Believer: The Morality of Historical Knowledge and Christian Belief*. New York: Macmillan, 1966. Classic and influential discussion of the tensions between modern historical inquiry and Christian faith.

Levenson, Jon D. *The Hebrew Bible, The Old Testament, and Historical Criticism*. Louisville, KY: Westminster/John Knox, 1993. Collection of Levenson's essays on the relationship between the "traditional" study of Scripture and historical criticism, advocating that the latter is largely a product of liberal Protestant scholarship and therefore should not replace the former for Judaism.

Noll, Mark A. *Between Faith and Criticism: Evangelicals, Scholarship, and the Bible in America*. 2nd ed. Grand Rapids, MI: Baker, 1991. A study of evangelical biblical scholarship and the challenges of religious faith amid critical skepticism.

Smith, Christian. *The Bible Made Impossible: Why Biblicism Is Not a Truly Evangelical Reading of Scripture*. Grand Rapids, MI: Brazos, 2011. Evangelical biblicism does not address adequately the diverse biblical data but continues to survive because of its historical role in establishing evangelicalism's sociological boundary markers.

Sparks, Kenton L. *God's Word in Human Words: An Evangelical Appropriation of Critical Biblical Scholarship*. Grand Rapids, MI: Baker, 2008. Scholarly treatment by an evangelical scholar arguing that his fellow evangelical scholars need to be more deliberate and open in appropriating critical methods and results in their own writing.

Postscript

IN THIS VOLUME, we have tried to demonstrate through our personal experiences how religious and critical readings of the Bible can coexist. We feel that such a synthesis is both compelling and necessary, given the widely recognized developments in biblical criticism and the sincere commitments we each have toward our respective religious traditions. As professional biblical scholars, these two worlds are in constant dialogue for us—as it is for the countless women and men of faith who live in the modern world and revere an ancient text.

As the essays and responses indicate, we each have different understandings of what the Bible is, how it should be interpreted, what the historical-critical method means, and the extent to which our religious tradition has incorporated such methods and is at home with them. Despite these differences, however, there are many commonalities and potential commonalities. After all, the Bible, though defined and functioning differently, is the core text of Jews, Catholics, and Protestants. We learned a great deal from one another as we engaged in this project and have come to believe that, in many cases, such comparative study yields increased mutual understanding of the similarities and differences between these three great traditions.

While better mutual understanding is the primary goal of much ecumenical and interreligious dialogue, it also encourages better understanding of, and appreciation for, our own traditions. Expanding our gaze beyond our own community of discourse often yields unexpected theological insights or solutions. Thus, we expect that this dialogue will result not only in better mutual understanding but also in better understanding of ourselves and the religious traditions we belong to.

We hope that we have demonstrated and illustrated how biblical criticism, properly understood, need not be regarded as a threat to religious believers. Indeed, at different times in our lives, such "criticism" has taught each of us how to view and comprehend biblical texts from fresh angles and has increased our appreciation of what a rich resource the Bible really is. We hope that it will serve a similar function for our readers.

Notes

INTRODUCTION

1. John Barton, *The Nature of Biblical Criticism* (Louisville, KY: Westminster John Knox, 2007).

2. Edmund Leach and D. Alan Aycock, *Structuralist Interpretations of Biblical Myth* (Cambridge: Cambridge University Press, 1983), 3.

3. Jeffrey H. Tigay, ed., *Empirical Models for Biblical Criticism* (Philadelphia: University of Pennsylvania Press, 1985).

4. Benjamin Sommers, *A Prophet Reads Scripture: Allusion in Isaiah* (Palo Alto, CA: Stanford University Press, 1998), 40–66. On inner-biblical interpretation more generally, see Michael Fishbane, *Biblical Interpretation in Ancient Israel* (Oxford: Oxford University Press, 1985); and Bernard M. Levinson, *Deuteronomy and the Hermeneutics of Legal Innovation* (New York: Oxford University Press, 1997).

5. Geza Vermes, *The Complete Dead Sea Scrolls* (New York: Penguin, 2004).

6. Günter Stemberger, *Introduction to the Talmud and Midrash* (Edinburgh: T&T Clark, 1966), 17–34.

7. Kenneth Hagen, *The Bible in the Churches: How Different Christians Interpret the Scriptures* (New York: Paulist, 1985), 3–34.

8. Michael Legaspi, *The Death of Scripture and the Rise of Biblical Studies* (New York: Oxford University Press, 2010).

9. Baruch Spinoza, *Tractatus Theologico-Politicus* (Gebhardt Edition, 1925), trans. Samuel Shirley (Leiden: Brill, 1989).

10. Richard Simon, *Histoire Critique du Vieux Testament* (Paris, 1678). See the English translation published as Richard Simon, *A Critical History of the Old Testament* (London, 1682), http://www.archive.org/details/SimonRichard1638-1712 ACriticalHistoryOfTheOldTestament1682.

11. The classic treatment by Albert Schweitzer, *The Quest of the Historical Jesus* (repr., Minneapolis, MN: Fortress, 2001).

12. Ernst Troeltsch, "Historical and Dogmatic Method in Theology," in *Religion in History/Ernst Troeltsch*, ed. James Luther Adams and Walter E. Bense (Minneapolis, MN: Fortress, 1991), 11–32.

13. Douglass A. Knight, ed., *Methods of Biblical Interpretation* (Nashville, TN: Abingdon, 2004); and Martin Buss, *Biblical Form Criticism in Its Context* (Sheffield, UK: Sheffield Academic Press, 1999).

14. For example, Hector Avalos, *The End of Biblical Studies* (Amherst, NY: Prometheus Books, 2007); and Philip R. Davies, *Whose Bible Is It Anyway?* (London: T&T Clark, 2004).

15. In English-speaking academic circles in recent years, the main target has been the Albright School and in particular John Bright, *History of Israel*, 3rd ed. (Philadelphia: Westminster, 1981).

16. Legaspi, *The Death of Scripture and the Rise of Biblical Studies*, 169.

CHAPTER 1

All abbreviations used in the following notes follow *The SBL Handbook of Style*.

1. Throughout this essay, I use the term "Bible" for what others would call the Hebrew Bible. I have no other Bible, so, for me, these books are simply the Bible. On the Bible as "a fundamentally cryptic book," see James L. Kugel, *The Bible as It Was* (Cambridge, MA: Harvard University Press, 1997), 18. *Peshat* and the historical-critical method have some similarities but are certainly not identical. On *peshat* and *derash*, see David Weiss Halivni, *Peshat and Derash: Plain and Applied Meaning in Rabbinic Exegesis* (New York: Oxford University Press, 1991); along with the review of Baruch J. Schwartz, "Of *Peshat* and *Derash*, Bible Criticism and Theology," *Prooftexts*, 14 (1994): 71–88. The assumptions of *derash* are clearly explained in Kugel's *The Bible as It Was*, 1–49 and in his *In Potiphar's House: The Interpretive Life of Biblical Texts* (San Francisco: HarperSanFrancisco, 1990). For an overview of Jewish biblical interpretation, see the essays in Adele Berlin and Marc Zvi Brettler, ed., *The Jewish Study Bible* (New York: Oxford University Press, 2004), 1829–1919. More extensive information is found in Magne Sæbø, *Hebrew Bible/Old Testament: The History of Its Interpretation* (Göttingen: Vandenhoeck & Ruprecht, 1996–); and the forthcoming *New Cambridge History of the Bible*.

2. The Frymer Kensky quotation is from her "The Emergence of Jewish Biblical Theologies" in *Jews, Christians, and the Theology of the Hebrew Scriptures*, ed. Alice Ogden Bellis and Joel S. Kaminsky (Atlanta: Society of Biblical Literature, 2000), 111. The Smith quotation is from *What Is Scripture: A Comparative Approach* (Minneapolis, MN: Fortress, 2005), 113.

3. Mordecai M. Kaplan, *The Religion of Ethical Nationhood* (New York: Macmillan, 1970), 1; and in much greater detail, his *Judaism as a Civilization* (New York:

Macmillan, 1934). I adopt his definition without adopting the surrounding theological framework.

4. For the quotation from Kugel, see James L. Kugel, *How to Read the Bible: A Guide to Scripture, Then and Now* (New York: Free Press, 2007), 681; and the trenchant review by Benjamin D. Sommer, "Two Introductions to Scripture: James Kugel and the Possibility of Biblical Theology," *JQR*, 100 (2010): 153–182. On the "messy self," see Jennifer Rosner, *The Messy Self* (Boulder, CO: Paradigm, 2007).

5. The quotations are from Robert A. Orsi, *Between Heaven and Earth: The Religious Worlds That People Make and the Scholars Who Study Them* (Princeton, NJ: Princeton University Press, 2005), 192, 14. The entire book is instructive on how critical study may be combined with religious engagement.

6. On written versus oral law, see *b. Shabbat 31a*; Kugel, *The Bible as It Was*, 402–407; Martin S. Jaffee, *Torah in the Mouth: Writing and Oral Tradition in Palestinian Judaism, 200 BCE–400 CE* (New York: Oxford University Press, 2001); and the extensive discussion of Benjamin D. Sommer, "Unity and Plurality in Jewish Canons: The Case of the Oral and Written Torahs," in *One Scripture or Many: Canon from Biblical, Theological and Philosophical Perspectives*, ed. Christine Helmer and Christof Landmesser (Oxford: Oxford University Press, 2004), 108–150. On the analogy between rabbinic tradition and the New Testament, see Smith, *What is Scripture?* 296, n. 65. On canonization and the differing natures of the Hebrew Bible and the Old Testament, see Marc Zvi Brettler, "The Canonization of the Bible," in *The Jewish Study Bible*, Berlin and Brettler, 2072–2077; Adele Berlin and Marc Zvi Brettler, *How to Read the Jewish Bible* (New York: Oxford University Press, 2007), 273–278; Roger Brooks and John J. Collins, eds., *Hebrew Bible or Old Testament? Studying the Bible in Judaism and Christianity* (Notre Dame: University of Notre Dame Press, 1990); and Marvin A. Sweeney, "Jewish Biblical Theology," in *The Hebrew Bible: New Insights and Scholarship*, ed. Frederick E. Greenspahn (New York: New York University Press, 2008), 195–198.

7. On the Karaites, see Meira Polliack, "Medieval Karaism," in *The Oxford Handbook of Jewish Studies*, ed. Martin Goodman (Oxford: Oxford University Press, 2002), 295–326. On R. Jacob's position, see Ephraim Kanarfogel, "On the Role of Bible Study in Medieval Ashkenaz," in *The Frank Talmage Memorial*, vol. 1, ed. Barry Walfish (Haifa: Haifa University Press, 1993), 151.

8. For the quotation from Heine, see Jaacov Shavit and Mordechai Eran, *The Hebrew Bible Reborn: From Holy Scripture to the Book of Books*, Studia Judaica 38, trans. Chaya Naor (Berlin: de Gruyter, 2007), 38. On the development of modern Jewish biblical scholarship, see my essay with Edward Breuer in vol. 4 of the forthcoming *New Cambridge History of the Bible*. On Jewish biblical theology, see the works of Marc Zvi Brettler, Moshe Goshen-Gottstein, Tamar Kamionkowsy, Jon Levenson, Benjamin Sommer, and Marvin Sweeney, esp. Marvin A. Sweeney,

TANAK: A Theological and Critical Introduction to the Jewish Bible (Minneapolis, MN: Fortress, 2012).

9. Maimonides' principles are here translated according to the rendition of Joel Hoffman in *My People's Prayer Book*, in vol. 6, *Tachanun and Concluding Prayer*, ed. Lawrence A. Hoffman (Woodstock, VT: Jewish Lights, 2002), 162. For the poetic version in *Yigdal*, see vol. 5, *Birkhot Hashachar (Morning Blessings)* (Woodstock, VT: Jewish Lights, 2001), 99. On *Yigdal*, see Menachem Kellner, *Must A Jew Believe Anything?* (London: Littman Library of Jewish Civilization, 1999), 153; and Marc B. Shapiro, *The Limits of Orthodox Theology: Maimonides' Thirteen Principles Reappraised* (Oxford: Littman Library of Jewish Civilization, 2004), 17–19.

10. Schwartz, "On *Peshat* and *Derash*," 79.

11. Biblical translations in this essay follow the Jewish Publication Society *Tanakh* translation or are my modifications of that translation. For the conflict between Maimonides and the historical-critical method, see the opinions adduced in Louis Jacobs, *Principles of the Jewish Faith: An Analytical Study* (New York: Basic Books, 1964); Menachem Kellner, *Dogma in Medieval Jewish Thought: From Maimonides to Abravanel* (Oxford: Oxford University Press, 1986); Kellner, *Must A Jew Believe Anything?*; and Shapiro, *Limits of Orthodox Theology*. On the meaning of *torah* in Leviticus and in Deuteronomy 4:44, see Jacob Milgrom, *Leviticus 1–16*, The Anchor Bible (New York: Doubleday, 1991), 382–383; and Moshe Weinfeld, *Deuteronomy 1–11*, The Anchor Bible (New York: Doubleday, 1991), 234–235. More broadly, see William M. Schniedewind, *How the Bible Became a Book: The Textualization of Ancient Israel* (Cambridge: Cambridge University Press, 2004), esp. 118–138.

12. See Reuven Hammer, *Entering Jewish Prayer: A Guide to Personal Devotion and the Worship Service* (New York: Schocken Books, 1994), 232.

13. On the meanings of these terms, see Abraham Joshua Heschel, "Torah from Heaven," in *Heavenly Torah as Refracted through the Generations*, ed. and trans. by Gordon Tucker (New York: Continuum, 2005), 368–386. The phrase *Torah min haShamayim* is first attested in Mishnah Sanhedrin 10:1. Heschel expands on the notion that "the original denotation of the term *the heavenly Torah* was the Ten Utterances heard at Mount Sinai, but . . . Rabbi Akiva expanded the term to include all of the words of the Pentateuch" (59). On conceptions of revelation in the Bible, see Benjamin D. Sommer, "Revelation at Sinai in the Hebrew Bible and in Jewish Theology," *JR* 79 (1999): 422–451; Marc Zvi Brettler, "The Many Faces of God in Exodus 19," in *Jewish and Christian Biblical Theology*, ed. Joel Kaminsky and Alice O. Bellis (Atlanta: Scholars Press, 2000), 353–367; and Marc Zvi Brettler, "Revelation at Sinai: Biblical Perspectives" in *The Significance of Sinai: Traditions About Sinai and Divine Revelation in Judaism and Christianity*, ed. George J. Brooke et al. (Leiden: Brill, 2008), 15–28. How and when the Torah became authoritative is debated, see James W. Watts, *Persia and Torah: The Theory of Imperial Authorization of the Pentateuch* (Atlanta: SBL, 2001).

14. On these marginal readings (*Qere-Kethib*), see Emanuel Tov, *Textual Criticism of the Hebrew Bible* (Minneapolis, MN: Fortress, 1992), 58–64.

15. See David A. Glatt-Gilad, "The Status of the Law (Book) of Moses within the Deuteronomistic History," in *Mishneh Todah: Studies in Deuteronomy and Its Cultural Environment in Honor of Jeffrey H. Tigay*, ed. Nili Sacher Fox et al. (Winona Lake, IN: Eisenbrauns, 2009), 185–199.

16. See for example, Sara Japhet, *I & II Chronicles* (London: SCM Press, 1993), 561, 585, 646, 976; for an opposing view, see Judson R. Shaver, *Torah and the Chronicler's History Work: An Inquiry into the Chronicler's References to Laws, Festivals, and Cultic Institutions in Relationship to Pentateuchal Legislation* (Atlanta: Scholars Press, 1989).

17. On the text of 1 Kings 8:65, see Mordechai Cogan, *1 Kings*, The Anchor Bible (New York: Doubleday, 2000), 290. On the Sukkot text of Lev 23, see Israel Knohl, *The Sanctuary of Silence: The Priestly Torah and the Holiness School* (Minneapolis, MN: Fortress, 1995), 13, 20–21, 27.

18. See e.g., Andrew E. Hill, *Malachi*, The Anchor Bible (New York: Doubleday, 1998), 360–371.

19. On Philo, see Yehoshua Amir, "Authority and Interpretation of Scripture in the Writings of Philo," in *Mikra*, ed. Martin Jan Mulder (Assen: Van Gorcum, 1988), 429–433; on Josephus, see, e.g., *Judean Antiquities 1–4*, translation and commentary by Louis H. Feldman (Leiden: Brill, 2000), 4.318 on p. 471.

20. For the definition of dogma, see *Oxford Dictionaries Online*, s.v. dogma, http://oxforddictionaries.com/definition/dogma. On Maimonides, see Kellner, *Dogma*, 17. On Christian creeds, see Philip Schaff, *The Creeds of Christendom, with a History and Critical Notes*, vol. 1 (Grand Rapids, MI: Baker Book House, 1966), 14–29; Jaroslav Pelikan and Valerie Hotchkiss, eds., *Creeds & Confessions of Faith in the Christian Tradition*, vol. 1 (New Haven, CT: Yale University Press, 2003).

21. On a religion of law versus a religion of belief, see, e.g., "Law and Religion in Judaism" in *Christianity and Law: An Introduction*, ed. John Witte, Jr., and Frank S. Alexander (Cambridge: Cambridge University Press, 2008), 33–53. On the grammatical problems of the beginning of the Shema, see my "A 'Literary Sermon' in Deuteronomy 4," in *"A Wise and Discerning Mind": Essays in Honor of Burke O. Long*, ed. Saul Olyan (Atlanta: Scholars Press, 2000), 42 n. 39.

22. The literature on the Decalogue is vast; see esp. *The Ten Commandments in History and Tradition*, ed. Ben-Zion Segal (Jerusalem: Magnes, 1990); David H. Aaron, *Etched in Stone: The Emergence of the Decalogue* (New York: T&T Clark, 2006); the comments scattered in Moshe Weinfeld, *Deuteronomy 1–11*, The Anchor Bible (New York: Doubleday, 1991); and William H. C. Propp, *Exodus 19–40*, The Anchor Bible (New York: Doubleday, 2006). On the Decalogue in Second Temple Judaism, see Lee I. Levine, *The Ancient Synagogue: The First Thousand Years* (New Haven, CT: Yale University Press, 2000), 156, 521–522.

23. On Maimonides as "the first dogmatist," see Shapiro, *Limits of Orthodox Theology*, 6. On Kellner concerning Karaite and Christian influence, see *Dogma in Medieval Jewish Thought*, 3, 215. On Graetz and Renan, see Jacobs, *Principles*, 2; and concerning Mendelssohn, see Moses Mendelssohn, *Jerusalem, or, On Religious Power and Judaism*, trans. Allan Arkush (Hanover: Brandeis University Press, 1983), 100–101. Schechter's position is articulated in Solomon Schechter, "The Dogmas of Judaism," in his *Studies in Judaism, First Series* (Philadelphia: Jewish Publication Society, 1896), 147–181. The quotations from Kellner are in *Must a Jew Believe Anything?* 9, 43. On the Maimonidean controversies, see the *Encyclopedia Judaica* article, "Maimonidean Controversy," Jewish Virtual Library, http://www.jewishvirtuallibrary.org/jsource/judaica/ejud_0002_0013_0_13046. html.

24. Isadore Twersky, *A Maimonides Reader* (New York: Behrman House, 1972), 420–421.

25. For the Levenson quotation, see Jon D. Levenson, *The Hebrew Bible, the Old Testament, and Historical Criticism: Jews and Christians in Biblical Studies* (Louisville, KY: Westminster/John Knox, 1993), 64. For scholars who disagree with Maimonides, see Shapiro, *Limits of Orthodox Theology*, 91–121.

26. B.B.B. 15a and parallels; see Shapiro, *Limits of Orthodox Theology*, 104–105; and Moshe Greenberg, "Jewish Conceptions of the Human Factor in Biblical Prophecy," in his *Studies in the Bible and Jewish Thought* (Philadelphia: Jewish Publication Society, 1995), 407–408, 113; see also Yaakov Elman, "The Book of Deuteronomy as Revelation: Nahmanides and Abarbanel," in *Ḥazon Naḥum: Studies in Jewish Law, Thought, and History Presented to Dr. Norman Lamm on the Occasion of His Seventieth Birthday*, ed. Yaakov Elman and Jeffrey S. Gurock (New York: Yeshiva University Press, 1997), 229–250.

27. Levy, *Fixing God's Torah*, 156. For a recent discussion on changes in the biblical text, see Hanne von Weissenberg et al., eds., *Changes in Scripture: Rewriting and Interpreting Authoritative Traditions in the Second Temple Period* (Berlin: de Gruyter, 2011); for a more accessible discussion, see Emanuel Tov, *Textual Criticism of the Hebrew Bible* (Minneapolis, MN: Fortress, 1992), 8–13.

28. See *Ibn Ezra's Commentary on the Pentateuch: Genesis (Bereshit)*, trans. H. Norman Strickman and Arthur M. Silver (New York: Menorah Pub., 1988), 151; Shapiro, *Limits of Orthodox Theology*, 92–103; and Levy, *Fixing God's Torah*.

29. See esp. Nahum M. Sarna, "Hebrew and Bible Studies in Medieval Spain" in his *Studies in Biblical Interpretation* (Philadelphia: Jewish Publication Society, 2000), 81–125; see also Moshe Greenberg, "Hermeneutical Freedom and Constraint in Jewish Bible Exegesis," in *Mishneh Todah*, 509–524. The quotations from Sarna are from 81, 107.

30. The translation of Sanhedrin 10:1 follows Jacob Neusner, *The Mishnah: A New Translation* (New Haven, CT: Yale University Press, 1988), 604. On "locus classicus," see Jacobs, *Principles*, 11. Schechter discusses the passage in "The

Dogmas of Judaism," 157. Kellner's observations are from *Must A Jew Believe Anything?* 33–38. For a collection of texts presuming post-Sinaitic revelation, see Bernard J. Bamberger, "Revelations of Torah after Sinai: An Aggadic Study," *HUCA*, 16 (1941): 97–113.

31. The Jacobs quotation is from *Principles*, 259, 289–290. For rabbinic texts that suggest textual changes in the torah, see Levy, *Fixing God's Torah*, esp. 159–160, on Deuteronomy 6:20, where the Septuagint preserves the text found in early versions of the Passover Haggadah; and Nahum M. Sarna, "Variant Scriptural Readings in Liturgical Texts," in *Solving Riddles and Untying Knots: Biblical, Epigraphic, and Semitic Studies in Honor of Jonas C. Greenfield*, ed. Z. Zevit et al. (Winona Lake, IN: Eisenbrauns), 203–206.

32. Under the influence of Moshe Greenberg, I prefer to speak of more original, rather than *the* original, which we cannot attain, see Greenberg, "The Use of the Ancient Versions for Interpreting the Hebrew Text" in his *Studies in the Bible and Jewish Thought*, 209–225. For the Fackenheim quotation, see Emil L. Fackenheim, *Quest for Past and Future* (Boston: Beacon, 1968), 71. Samuelson's book is *Revelation and the God of Israel* (Cambridge: Cambridge University Press), 2002; the quotations are from 221 and 238. Levenson's quotation is from "What Do American Jews Believe? A Symposium," *Commentary* 102:2 (August 1996): 8. For a broad discussion of revelation and religion, see C. Stephen Evans, "Faith and Revelation," in *The Oxford History of Philosophy of Religion*, ed. William J. Wainwright (Oxford: Oxford University Press, 2005), 323–343.

33. Fleischacker, *Divine Teaching and the Way of the World* (New York: Oxford University Press, 2011), 281, 303.

34. Sommer, "Two Introductions to Scripture," 182. (The end of the quotation is an allusion to the story in b. Shabbat 31a of Hillel teaching a potential convert the entire Torah on one foot.)

35. On Frankel, see Joseph E. Heller and Yehoyada Amir, "Frankel, Zacharias," in *Encyclopedia Judaica*, 2nd ed., ed. Michael Berenbaum and Fred Skolnik (Detroit: Macmillan Reference USA, 2007), 7.200–201; Ismar Schorsch, "Zacharias Frankel and the European Origins of Conservative Judaism," in his *From Text to Context: The Turn to History in Modern Judaism* (Hanover, NH: Brandeis University Press, 1994), 255–265; the quotation of Frankel is from Louis Jacobs, *Principles of the Jewish Faith*, 297. On Schechter and Catholic Israel, see "Solomon Schechter," My Jewish Learning, http://www.myjewishlearning.com/history/Modern_History/1700-1914/Denominationalism/Conservative/Solomon_Schechter.shtml, quoting Louis Jacobs; the quotation is from Schechter, introduction to *Studies in Judaism* (London: Black, 1896), xviii.

36. The quotations from Rosenzweig are from his letter, later published as "The Unity of the Bible: An Argument between Orthodoxy and Liberalism"; see Franz Rosenzweig, Alan Udoff, and Barbara Ellen Galli, *Franz Rosenzweig's*

"The New Thinking" (Syracuse, NY: Syracuse University Press, 1999), 183; Franz
Rosenzweig, "The Unity of the Bible: A Position Paper vis-à-vis Orthodoxy and
Liberalism," *Scripture and Translation*, ed. Lawrence Rosenwald and Everett Fox
(Bloomington: Indiana University Press, 1994), 25.

37. For the early Reform platforms, see Walter Jacob, "The Influence of the Pittsburgh Platform on Reform *Halakhah* and Biblical Study," in *The Changing
World of Reform Judaism: The Pittsburgh Platform in Retrospect: Papers Presented
on the Occasion of the 100th Anniversary of the Pittsburgh Platform, February, 1985
and the Proceedings of 1885* (Pittsburgh: Rodef Shalom Congregation, 1985), 35,
26. For later and recent Reform positions, see the symposia on Jewish belief in
Commentary, reprinted as *The Condition of Jewish Belief: A Symposium Compiled
by the Editors of* Commentary *Magazine*; and "What Do American Jews Believe?
A Symposium," *Commentary* 102:2 (August 1996).

38. For the history of this belief within Conservative Judaism, see Ismar Schorsch,
"Coming to Terms with Biblical Criticism," *Conservative Judaism*, 2005,
3–22. For the quotation from Schechter's address, see *Seminary Address and
Other Papers* (Cincinnati: Ark Publishing, 1915), 36, also at biblicalia, http://
www.bombaxo.com/blog/?p=1453; for a broader perspective on Schechter,
see the forthcoming article by David Starr, "Loving is Believing: Solomon
Schechter and the Bible." The quotations at the end of the paragraph are from
Robert Gordis, *Understanding Conservative Judaism* (New York: The Rabbinical
Assembly, 1978), 67, 63, 64, 69.

39. The initial summary is from Milton Steinberg, *Basic Judaism* (Northvale, NJ:
Jason Aronson, 1987 [1947]), 32. The following citations from Yeshiva University professors are from Moshe J. Bernstein, "The Orthodox Jewish Scholar and
Jewish Scholarship: Duties and Dilemma," *Torah u-Madda Journal*, 3 (1991–
1992): 20, 24; Mordechai Z. Cohen, "'The Best of Poetry . . .': Literary Approaches to the Bible in the Spanish Peshat Tradition," *Torah U-Madda Journal*,
6 (1995–1996): 15–57; Barry L. Eichler, "Study of Bible in Light of Our Knowledge of the Ancient Near East," in *Modern Scholarship in the Study of Torah*, ed.
Shalom Carmy (Northvale, NJ: Jason Aronson, 1996), 98. On textual criticism,
see Yeshayahu Maori, "Rabbinic Midrash as Evidence for Textual Variants in the
Hebrew Bible: History and Practice," in *Modern Scholarship*, ed. Carmy, 101–129;
Levy, *Fixing God's Torah*. Rackman's comments may be found in *The Condition
of Jewish Belief*, 180; and Levy's "The State and Directions of Orthodox Bible
Study," in *Modern Scholarship*, ed. Carmy, 78. On ArtScroll, see esp. B. Barry
Levy, "Our Torah, Your Torah, and Their Torah: An Evaluation of the ArtScroll
Phenomenon," in *Truth and Compassion: Essays on Judaism and Religion in
Memory of Rabbi Dr. Solomon Frank*, ed. H. Joseph, J. Lightstone, and M. Oppen-
heim (Ontario: Wilfred Laurier University Press, 1983), 137–189; and Jeremy
Stolow, *Orthodox by Design: Judaism, Print Politics, and the ArtScroll Revolution*
(Berkeley: University of California Press, 2010).

40. In English, see Meir Ekstein, "Rabbi Mordechai Breuer and Modern Orthodox Biblical Commentary," *Tradition* 33:3 (Spring 1999): 6–23; Shalom Carmy, "Introducing Rabbi Breuer," in *Modern Scholarship*, ed. Carmy, 147–158; and Mordechai Breuer, "The Study of Bible and the Primacy of the Fear of Heaven: Compatibility or Contradiction?" in *Modern Scholarship*, ed. Carmy, 159–180. The quotations at the end are my translations from Joseph Ofer, ed., *The "Aspects Theory" of Rav Mordechai Breuer: Articles and Responses* (Alon Shevut: Higyonot, 2005), 7, 35.

41. Snayer Z. Leiman, "Response to Rabbi Breuer," in *Modern Scholarship*, ed. Carmy, 185.

42. The quotations are from Tamar Ross, *Expanding the Palace of Torah: Orthodoxy and Feminism* (Hanover, NH: University Press of New England, 2004), 197; Moshe Greenberg, "Biblical Criticism and Judaism," *Commentary*, March 1953, 304; and Nahum M. Sarna, *Understanding Genesis* (New York: Schocken Books, 1966), xxiv.

43. The initial quotation is from David Weiss Halivni, *Revelation Restored: Divine Writ and Critical Responses* (Boulder, CO: Westview, 1997), 2. This book builds upon his earlier insights in *Peshat and Derash*; see the trenchant review of Baruch J. Schwartz, "Of *Peshat* and *Derash*, Bible Criticism and Theology," *Prooftexts*, 14 (1994): 71–88. The final quotation is from *Revelation Restored*, 10.

44. See Frank Moore Cross and Shemaryahu Talmon, eds., *Qumran and the History of the Biblical Text* (Cambridge, MA: Harvard University Press, 1975), 187–188; Tov, *Textual Criticism*, esp. 110–117; and James C. VanderKam, *The Dead Sea Scrolls and the Bible* (Grand Rapids, MI: Eeerdmans, 2012), esp. 1–24.

45. I critique the view that Judaism must be separated from biblical religion in "Judaism in the Hebrew Bible? An Exploration of the Transition from Ancient Israelite Religion to Judaism," *Catholic Biblical Quarterly*, 61 (1999): 429–447. My ideas concerning how Judaism evolves are similar to the model of "punctuated equilibrium" in evolution, see http://en.wikipedia.org/wiki/Punctuated_equilibrium. On the origins of Rabbinic Judaism, see, e.g., Shaye J.D. Cohen, "The Significance of Yavneh: Pharisees, Rabbis, and the End of Jewish Sectarianism," *Hebrew Union College Annual* 55 (1984): 27–53; David Goodblatt, "The Place of the Pharisees in First Century Judaism: The State of the Debate," *JSJ*, 20 (1989): 12–30.

46. On Rosenzweig and *rebeinu*, see note 36; and Louis Jacobs, *A Jewish Theology* (Springfield, NJ: Behrman House, 1973), 209.

47. The quotations are from Menachem Elon, *Jewish Law: History, Sources, Principles*, vols. 1–4 (Philadelphia: Jewish Publication Society, 1994), 1.285, 286, 300.

48. On Hirsch, see Tova Ganzel, "Explicit and Implicit Polemic in Rabbi Samson Raphael's Bible 'Commentary,'" *HUCA* forthcoming; the quotations are from Samson Raphael Hirsch, *The Pentateuch: Exodus* (New York: Judaica, 1971), 289, 288. Little is available on Hoffman in English—see esp. his introductions to

Leviticus and Exodus. On Halevy, see O. Asher Reichel, *Isaac Halevy (1847–1914): Spokesman and Historian of Jewish Tradition* (New York: Yeshiva University Press, 1969), esp. "The Architect of Agudath Israel," 103–122.

49. Jay Harris, *How Do We Know This? Midrash and the Fragmentation of Modern Judaism* (Albany: SUNY Press, 1995), 3. See his entire book as well as the summary of it in his "Midrash Halakhah," *The Cambridge History of Judaism*, vol. 4, *The Late Roman-Rabbinic Period* (Cambridge: Cambridge University Press, 2006), 336–368. See also Paul Heger, *The Pluralistic Halakhah: Legal Innovation in the Late Second Commonwealth and Rabbinic Periods* (Berlin: de Gruyter, 2003); and Eliezer Shimshon Rosenthal, "Tradition and Innovation in the *Halakha* of the Sages," *Tarbiz*, 63 (1994): 321–374; Hebrew with English summary, xix–xx, esp. 343, 349–350, 366:

> Exegesis of the Torah was the means through which the Rabbis established the authority of the extrabiblical laws and practices they apparently inherited; they employed this medium in order to create new laws in their own times . . . Certainly, some and probably most midrashic passages strike one as inconceivable unless one assumes that the legal conclusion was already known . . . In this [Talmudic] passage and in hundreds like it, one is left with the impression that exegesis represents nothing more than the personal preference of different sages and, therefore, one might conclude that its results cannot be considered part of the essential message of the divine lawgiver.

See more recently Azzan Yadin, "Resistance to Midrash? Midrash and *Halakhah* in the Halakhic Midrashim," in *Current Trends in the Study of Midrash*, ed. Carol Bakhos (Leiden: Brill, 2006), 52: "Though interpretive in form, it should now be clear that the midrash of the Sifra serves to support existing *halakhot* rather than interpretively generate new legal conclusions."

50. The first comprehensive study on this is Lawrence H. Schiffman, *The Halakhah at Qumran* (Leiden: Brill, 1975); on *tosefet Shabbat*, see 84–87; more recently, see Aharon Shemesh, *Halakhah in the Making: The Development of Jewish Law from Qumran to the Rabbis* (Berkeley: University of California Press, 2009); on *tosefet Shabbat*, see 74–75. On p. 75 he notes: "This shared tradition . . . may be the result of parallel developments within different Jewish groups at the time of the Temple and thereafter."

51. The term "creative philology" is borrowed from Isaak Heinemann, *The Methods of Aggadah* (Jerusalem: Magnes, 1954), 4–7 (Hebrew). For the traditional rabbinic interpretation of "for ever" in Exodus, see Jacob Z. Lauterbach, *Mekhilta de-Rabbi Ishmael* (Philadelphia: Jewish Publication Society, 2004), 2.366. For Rashbam's commentary, see Martin I. Lockshin, *Rashbam's Commentary on Exodus* (Atlanta, GA: Scholars Press, 1997), 230, and n. 22; see also p. 17. The quote from Weiss Halivni is from Halivni, *Peshat and Derash*, 172. For more on Rashbam, see Halivni, *Peshat and Derash*, 168–171; and "Introductory Essay: *Peshat*

and *Derash* in Northern France," in *Rashbam's Commentary on Deuteronomy: An Annotated Translation*, ed. Martin I. Lockshin (Providence: Brown Judaic Studies, 2004), 1–25.

52. Scholem's essay is found in his *The Messianic Idea in Judaism and Other Essays on Jewish Spirituality* (New York: Schocken, 1971), 282–303. The texts cited are from b. Menachot 29b (see Scholem, 283); Tanhuma Buber 2.60a (see Scholem, 289); and b. Baba Metziah 59b (see Scholem, 291–292). The final midrash cited is translated in Jacob Neusner, *Lamentations Rabbah: An Analytical Translation*, Brown Judaic Studies 193 (Atlanta, GA: Scholars Press, 1989), 14 (at 5B). See also Samuel Fleischacker, *Divine Teaching and the Way of the World: A Defense of Revealed Religion* (New York: Oxford University Press, 2011), 370–373, on the importance of practice rather than doctrine in Judaism.

53. Louis Jacobs, *Beyond Reasonable Doubt* (London: Littman Library of Jewish Civilization, 1999), 104–105.

54. On biblical history, see Marc Zvi Brettler, *The Creation of History in Ancient Israel* (London: Routledge, 1995), esp. 135–144. On revisions of history within the Bible, see ibid., 62–78; and David A. Glatt-Gilad, "The Re-Interpretation of the Edomite-Israelite Encounter in Deuteronomy II," *Vetus Testamentum* 47 (1997): 441–455. On Psalm 78, see Jeffrey M. Leonard, "Identifying Inner-Biblical Allusions: Psalm 78 as a Test Case," *Journal of Biblical Literature* 127 (2008): 241–265; on Psalm 105, see my "The Poet as Historian: The Plague Tradition in Ps 105," *Bringing the Hidden to Light: Studies in Honor of Stephen A. Geller*, ed. K. F. Kravitz and D. M. Sharon (Winona Lake, IN: Eisenbrauns, 2007), 19–28.

55. Concerning Job as a parable, see b. Baba Batra, 15a. On Rashi, see Avraham Grossman, "The School of Literal Jewish Exegesis in Northern France," in *Hebrew Bible/Old Testament: The History of Its Interpretation*, vol. 1, *From the Beginnings to the Middle Ages (Until 1300)*, ed. Magne Sæbø (Göttingen: Vandenhoeck & Ruprecht, 2000), 332–346. The interpretations of Rashi are cited from A. M. Silbermann, ed., *Chumash with Targum Onkelos, Haphtaroth and Rashi's Commentary* (Jerusalem: Feldheim, 1999), 45, 2. For recent discussions on nonliteral interpretation, citing older literature, including Sa'adya and Maimonides, see, e.g., Joshua L. Golding, "On the Limits of Non-Literal Interpretation of Scripture from an Orthodox Perspective," *Torah U-Madda Journal* 10 (2001): 3–59; Shubert Spero, "The Biblical Stories of Creation, Garden of Eden and the Flood: History or Metaphor?" *Tradition* 33:2 (Winter 1999): 5–18; Nathan Aviezer, *Fossils and Faith: Understanding Torah and Science* (Hoboken, NJ: Ktav, 2001); and Natan Slifkin, *The Challenge of Creation: Judaism's Encounter with Science, Cosmology, and Evolution* (Brooklyn: Zoo Torah, 2006), 103–122. On the controversy created by this book in some circles, see Natan Slifkin, "The Problem with Intelligent Design," *Jerusalem Post*, November, 15, 2006, http://www.jpost.com/HealthAndSci-Tech/ScienceAndEnvironment/Article.aspx?id=41414.

56. The initial quotation is from Michael Shai Cherry, "Creation, Evolution and Jewish Thought" (PhD diss., Brandeis University, 2001), 342. For a similar, but less extensive, treatment, see Raphael Shuchat, "Attitudes towards Cosmogony and Evolution among Rabbinic Thinkers in the Nineteenth and Early Twentieth Centuries: The Resurgence of the Doctrine of the Sabbatical Years," *Torah U-Madda Journal*, 13 (2005): 15–49. On "the rabbis eschewed," see Shai Cherry, "Jewish Origins: Cosmos, Humanity and Judaism," in *Routledge Companion on Science and Religion*, ed. James W. Haag et al. (London: Routledge: 2012), 428. The Slifkin quotation is from Natan Slifkin, *The Challenge of Creation*, 344. Kugel's quote is from *How to Read*, 673.

57. The classic passage opening the paragraph may be found in *Soncino Babylonian Talmud: Seder Nezikin: Tractate Baba Bathra*, vol. 1 (London: Soncino, 1976), 14b–15a. On its aggadic nature, see Levy, "The State and Directions of Orthodox Bible Study," 65, who notes that "the history of its interpretation leaves the impression that it was taken to have not greater authority than many other midrashim that could be accepted or rejected more or less at will." The ibn Ezra passage is translated in *The Commentary of Ibn Ezra on Isaiah*, vol. 1, ed. M. Friedländer (London: Pub. for the Society of Hebrew Literature, 1873), 169–171; his position was followed by some later Orthodox scholars, such as Nachman Krochmal and Jakob Barth. On the rabbinic attribution of Psalms to David, see b. Baba Batra 14b–15a. On medieval exegetes suggesting otherwise, see Israel M. Ta-Shma, "Bible Criticism in Early Medieval Franco-Germany," in *The Bible in the Light of Its Interpreters: Sarah Kamin Memorial Volume*, ed. Sara Japhet (Jerusalem: Magnes, 1994), 453–459 (Hebrew); and Ta-Shma, "Open Bible Criticism in an Anonymous Commentary on the Book of Psalms," *Tarbiz*, 66 (1997): 417–423 (Hebrew with English summary, vii–ix).

58. Concerning the order of biblical books, see Sid Z. Leiman, *The Canonization of the Hebrew Scripture: The Talmudic and Midrashic Evidence* (New Haven, CT: Archon, 1976), 51–52, with relevant footnotes there; the contrasting order in manuscripts is detailed in Christian D. Ginsburg, *Introduction to the Massoretico-Critical Edition of the Hebrew Bible* (repr. New York: Ktav, 1966), 1–8. On the connection between the divine revelation and the written prophetic word, see Greenberg, "Jewish Conceptions of the Human Factor in Biblical Prophecy," 405–419; the quotation is from 416.

59. On inspiration in a Jewish context, see the comments in Jacobs, *Principles*, 457–458; and Fleischacker, *Divine Teaching and the Way of the World*, 357–359. The quotation from Leiman is from 127; on 57, he discusses the name *kitvei qodesh*. According to its index, "holy spirit" is mentioned only three times in E. E. Urbach, *The Sages: Their Concepts and Beliefs* (Jerusalem: Magnes, 1975). For a detailed discussion of this term's meaning and use, see Peter Schäfer, *Die Vorstellung vom heiligen Geist in der rabbinischen Literatur* (München: Kösel-Verlag, 1972); and Menahem Haran, *The Biblical Collection: Its Consolidation to the End*

of the Second Temple Times and Changes of Form to the End of the Middle Ages, vol.
1 (Jerusalem: Bialik Institute and Magnes, 2003; Hebrew), 340–358.

60. See Tov, *Textual Criticism*, 12–13, 172, 174–176.

61. This paragraph builds on Brettler, *How to Read*, 280; and "Biblical Authority: A
Jewish Pluralistic View," in *Engaging Biblical Authority: Perspectives on the Bible as
Scripture*, ed. William P. Brown (Louisville, KY: Westminster John Knox, 2007),
1–9. This approach is called "canonical" and critiqued in Eryl W. Davies, *The
Immoral Bible: Approaches to Biblical Ethics* (London: T & T Clark, 2002), 63–110.

62. On the rabbinic abolition of the ḥerem, see Moshe Greenberg, "Ḥerem," *Encyclo-
pedia Judaica* (Jerusalem: Keter, 1971), 8.349. For Jefferson's New Testament, see
The Life and Morals of Jesus of Nazareth: The Jefferson Bible (Washington, DC:
GPO, 1904).

63. See esp. Barton, *The Nature of Biblical Criticism*, 120.

64. This section is based on my forthcoming commentary on Psalms 91–119, to be
published by the Jewish Publication Society. That commentary will contain
extensive technical material and notes, justifying interpretive decisions. As I
offer detailed notes on any biblical text, I often use words such as "possible" and
"most likely." This follows some rabbinic and medieval Jewish traditions, which
do not insist on certainty.

65. The exception that proves the rule about Jewish engagement with the Hebrew
text is ancient Alexandria, where the Greek Septuagint was seen as authoritative. This gave rise to various legends of how the Septuagint was composed,
indeed inspired; see Abraham Wasserstein and David J. Wasserstein, *The Legend of the Septuagint: From Classical Antiquity to Today* (Cambridge: Cambridge
University Press, 2006). On the confusion between the letters *yod* and *waw* in
ancient Hebrew, see Tov, *Textual Criticism*, 10, 13.

66. This principle was emphasized to me again and again by my late teacher,
Nahum M. Sarna; for its origin, see Pirke Avot 6: 6, which follows with a proof-
text from Esther 2:22.

67. On typologies in the Hebrew Bible, see Brettler, *Creation of History*, 48–61. On
Jewish-Christian continuities, see Amy-Jill Levine and Marc Brettler, eds., *Jew-
ish Annotated New Testament* (New York: Oxford University Press, 2011). For the
Midrash on Psalms, see *The Midrash on Psalms*, vol. 2, trans. William Braude
(New Haven, CT: Yale University Press, 1959), 215–222. On *torah* as instruction,
see Brettler, "Torah," in *The Jewish Study Bible*, 1–2.

68. Nahum N. Glatzer, *Franz Rosenzweig: His Life and Thought* (New York: Schocken,
1961), 246. See also the distinctions drawn in Uriel Simon, "The Religious Significance of *Peshat*," trans. Edward L. Greenstein, *Tradition* 23:2 (Winter 1988): 41–63.

69. On updating, see Stephen Garfinkel, "Applied Peshat: Historical-Critical Method
and Religious Meaning," *Journal of the Ancient Near Eastern Society of Columbia
University* 22 (1993): 19–28, and in a very different religious context, Krister Stendahl, "Biblical Theology, Contemporary," *The Interpreter's Dictionary of the Bible*

(New York: Abingdon Press, 1962), 1, 418–432. Reprinted: Stendahl, *Meanings: The Bible as Document and as a Guide* (Philadelphia: Fortress, 1984), 11–44. For excellent examples of changes over time in Jewish law, see Daniel Sperber, *On Changes in Jewish Liturgy: Options and Limitations* (Jerusalem: Urim Publications, 2010). James Kugel coined the term omnisignificant, and its use has been expanded and developed significantly in Yaakov Elman, "The Rebirth of Omnisignificant Biblical Exegesis in the Nineteenth and Twentieth Centuries," *Jewish Studies Internet Journal* 2 (2003): 199–249. The expression "seventy faces . . . " is first found in Numbers Rabbah 13:15, and the tradition concerning a hammer on a rock is in b. Sanhedrin 34a. For an important discussion comparing midrashic methods to literary theory, see Susan Handelman, *The Slayers of Moses: The Emergence of Rabbinic Interpretation in Modern Literary Theory* (Albany: SUNY Press, 1982). For more recent works on midrash and how it functions, see Harris, *How Do We Know This?* and Bakhos, ed., *Current Trends in the Study of Midrash.*

70. This identification of wisdom and Torah is first attested in the second century BCE work (The Wisdom of) Ben-Sira(c)h 24:23.

71. Philadelphia: Jewish Publication Society.

72. Norman Solomon's recent monograph *Torah from Heaven: The Reconstruction of Faith* (Oxford: Littman Library of Jewish Faith, 2012) overlaps somewhat with my perspectives but was published after this essay was in proofs. Solomon concludes that Torah from Heaven is true as a "foundational myth."

73. Richard J. Clifford, *Psalms 73–150*, Abingdon Old Testament Commentaries (Nashville: Abingdon, 2003), 191–194.

74. Clifford, *Psalms 73–150*, 194.

75. Dean Béchard, ed., *The Scripture Documents* (Collegeville, MN: Liturgical Press, 2002), 183–211.

76. Ibid., 19–33.

77. See volume 6 of Scott W. Hahn, ed., *Letter & Spirit* (Steubenville, OH: Emmaus Road, 2010).

78. Raymond E. Brown and Sandra M. Schneiders, "Hermeneutics," in *The New Jerome Biblical Commentary*, ed. Raymond E. Brown, Joseph A. Fitzmyer, and Roland E. Murphy (Englewood Cliffs, NJ: Prentice Hall, 1990), 1163–1164.

CHAPTER 2

1. For full documentation, see Dean P. Béchard, ed., *The Scripture Documents* (Collegeville, MN: Liturgical Press, 2002). For a general discussion, see Daniel J. Harrington, *How Do Catholics Read the Bible?* (Lanham, MD: Rowman & Littlefield, 2005).

2. For example, see Donald Senior and John J. Collins, eds., *The Catholic Study Bible*, 2nd ed. (New York: Oxford University Press, 2006).

3. For an introduction to these books, see Harrington, *Invitation to the Apocrypha* (Grand Rapids, MI: Eerdmans, 1999).

4. See the final text in Béchard, *The Scripture Documents*, 19–33. For the background and context, see John W. O'Malley, *What Happened at Vatican II* (Cambridge, MA: Harvard University Press, 2008).

5. Pope Benedict XVI, *Verbum Domini: The Word of God in the Life and Mission of the Church* (Ijamsville, MD: Word Among Us Press, 2010).

6. For another view, see the articles in volume 6 of Scott W. Hahn, ed., *Letter & Spirit* (Steubenville, OH: Emmaus Road, 2010).

7. Harrington, *Interpreting the Old Testament: A Practical Guide* (Wilmington, DE: Michael Glazier, 1981). See also my *Interpreting the New Testament: A Practical Guide* (Wilmington, DE: Michael Glazier, 1979).

8. Ernst Troeltsch, "Historical and Dogmatic Method in Theology," in *Religion in History/Ernst Troeltsch*, ed. James Luther Adams and Walter E. Bense (Minneapolis, MN: Fortress, 1991), 11–32.

9. Samuel Rolles Driver, *An Introduction to the Literature of the Old Testament* (New York: Meridian Books, 1956).

10. Joseph Blenkinsopp, "The Midianite-Kenite Hypothesis Revisited and the Origins of Judah," *Journal for the Study of the Old Testament* 33 (2008): 131–153.

11. J.-P. Sonnet, "Risquer sa vie sur des êtres de papier?" *Christus* 225 (2010): 16–27.

12. Joseph T. Lienhard with Ronnie J. Rombs, *Exodus, Leviticus, Numbers, Deuteronomy*, vol. 3, Ancient Christian Commentary on Scripture: Old Testament Series (Downers Grove, IL: InterVarsity Press, 2001), 9–29.

13. As a side issue, let me say here that "midrash" is defined differently by different scholars. Some use it exclusively to refer to specific Jewish midrashic *texts*, i.e., commentaries on Scripture. Others, such as myself, use the term more generally to indicate *approaches* to the text, well documented in ancient Judaism, that are marked by various creative and innovative ways of reading Scripture.

14. The critique of Arthur Allen Cohen, *The Myth of the Judeo-Christian Tradition and Other Dissenting Essays* (New York: Harper & Row, 1969), remains trenchant.

15 *Seder 'Olam Rabbah* §30; see also, e.g., b. Megillah 7a–b; b. Sotah 48b; b. Sanhedrin 11a; b. Yoma 9b.

CHAPTER 3

1. A distinction should be made between Protestant traditions and specific denominations. The main traditions coming out of the Protestant Reformation are Lutherans, Calvinists, Baptists, and Anabaptists, and somewhat indirectly Anglicans. Within these traditions grew subdivisions and denominations that number in the hundreds—or thousands—over the centuries.

2. A Google search of "future of evangelicalism" will reveal the attention this question is receiving in recent years among various types of evangelicals— traditionalists who wish to maintain older boundaries, and progressives who seek to push those boundaries further.

3. For example, Christians during the Civil War were divided over whether slavery could be defended on biblical grounds. I will not treat that issue here, but it illustrates the crisis of biblical authority at the time. The fact that both sides of the debate used the same Bible to make opposite ironclad cases raised an obvious issue for Protestants at the time: What good is biblical authority if it can be pressed into service to support opposite views? What good is an inerrant Bible if it can't help us solve such a pressing moral issue of our time? See M. A. Noll, *The Civil War as a Theological Crisis* (Chapel Hill: University of North Carolina Press, 2006).

4. This connection between the Protestant Reformation and higher criticism is commonly discussed. For example, Gerhard Ebeling, *Word and Faith* (Philadelphia: Fortress, 1963); John Barton, *The Nature of Biblical Criticism* (Louisville, KY: Westminster/John Knox, 2007).

5. The Protestant Bible is made of an Old Testament and New Testament. The Old is comprised of the same books that make up the Jewish Bible, but the order is different. The typical Protestant division is Pentateuch, Historical Books (Joshua through 2 Chronicles), Poetic/Wisdom books (Job, Psalms, Proverbs, Ecclesiastes, Song of Songs), and Prophets (the four Major Prophets with Lamentations, Twelve Minor Prophets). The Protestant Old Testament differs from the Catholic one in that the latter also includes the Apocrypha. Like the Catholics, the Protestant New Testament includes the four Gospels and the book of Acts, the letters of Paul (either written by him or attributed to him), the remaining letters (often called General or Catholic Epistles), and the apocalyptic book of Revelation.

6. Jon D. Levenson, *The Hebrew Bible, The Old Testament, and Historical Criticism* (Louisville, KY: Westminster/John Knox, 1993), 56. The quote is taken from chapter 2, "Why Jews Are Not Interested in Biblical Theology."

7. For a recent and succinct summary of the connection between the New Testament and Qumran *pesher* interpretation, see Maxine Grossman, "The Dead Sea Scrolls," in *The Jewish Annotated New Testament*, ed. Amy-Jill Levine and Marc Zvi Brettler (Oxford: Oxford University Press, 2011), 569–572.

8. Wellhausen's magnum opus *Prolegomena to the History of Israel* was first published (under a different title) in German in 1878 and in a revised version in 1883. It first appeared in English in 1885.

9. The fluctuations within evangelicalism's view of the Bible are not simply to be understood as theological debates but involve deep sociological factors. For a recent treatment see Christian Smith, *The Bible Made Impossible: Why Biblicism Is Not a Truly Evangelical Reading of Scripture* (Grand Rapids, MI: Brazos, 2011).

10. I develop this idea more fully in *Inspiration and Incarnation: Evangelicals and the Problem of the Old Testament* (Grand Rapids, MI: Baker, 2005). Roman Catholicism has a rich history of thinking of Scripture as analogous to the incarnation of Christ. A robust and engaging incarnational understanding of Scripture pervades part 1 of Pope Benedict XVI's apostolic exhortation, *Verbum Domini*

(2010), on the nature and function of Scripture. See also *Dei Verbum*, Vatican II's *Dogmatic Constitution on Divine Revelation* (1965).

11. For example, the fourth-century theologians Gregory of Nyssa and John Chrysostom. See *Dei Verbum* cited in the previous note. A succinct and readable article is Mary Healy, "Inspiration and Incarnation: The Christological Analogy and the Hermeneutics of Faith," *Letter and Spirit* 2 (2006): 27–41.

12. These statistics are compiled from the indices in Barbara Aland et al., eds., *The Greek New Testament*, 4th rev. ed. (Stuttgart: Deutsche Bibelgesellschaft, 1993), 887–900.

13. An excellent introduction to the issue is James L. Kugel and Rowan A. Greer, *Early Biblical Interpretation* (Philadelphia: Westminster, 1986).

14. "The Story of Si-nuhe," trans. John A. Wilson (James B. Pritchard, ed., *Ancient Near Eastern Texts Relating to the Old Testament* (Princeton, NJ: Princeton University Press, 1969), 18–22). "Sinuhe," translated by Miriam Lichtheim (William W. Hallo and K. Lawson Younger, eds., *The Context of Scripture* (Leiden: Brills, 1997), 1.77–82). A handy collection of ancient Near Eastern texts is by Bill T. Arnold and Bryan E. Beyer, eds., *Readings from the Ancient Near East* (Grand Rapids, MI: Baker, 2002). "Tale of Sinuhe" is on pages 76–82.

15. James K. Hoffmeier, *Israel in Egypt: The Evidence for the Authenticity of the Exodus Tradition* (New York: Oxford University Press, 1996); Kenneth Kitchen, *On the Reliability of the Old Testament* (Grand Rapids, MI: Eerdmans, 2003); Iain Provan, V. Phillips Long, and Tremper Longman III, *A Biblical History of Israel* (Louisville, KY: Westminster/John Knox, 2003).

16. "The Creation Epic," trans. E. A. Speiser (*ANET*, 60–72); "Epic of Creation," trans. Benjamin R. Foster (*COS*, 390–403). See also Arnold and Beyer, eds., *Readings from the Ancient Near East*, 31–50.

17. Gleason Archer, Jr., *Encyclopedia of Bible Difficulties* (Grand Rapids, MI: Zondervan, 1982); Thomas Howe and Gleason Archer, Jr., *Big Book of Bible Difficulties* (Grand Rapids, MI: Baker, 1992). New editions of these works appeared in 2001 and 2008, respectively.

18. Nahum Sarna in *Ancient Israel, Revised and Expanded Edition*, ed. Hershel Shanks (Washington, DC: Biblical Archaeology Society, 1999), 35.

19. For the texts, see Geza Vermes, *The Complete Dead Sea Scrolls* (New York: Penguin, 1997), 460–492.

20. Eric D. Hirsch, "Objective Interpretation," in his *Validity in Interpretation* (New Haven, CT: Yale University Press, 1967), 209–244.

21. Paul Ricoeur, "The Hermeneutical Function of Distanciation" and "Appropriation," in *Hermeneutics and the Human Sciences*, ed. J. B. Thompson (Cambridge: Cambridge University Press, 1981), 131–144, and 182–193.

22. Hans-Georg Gadamer, *Truth and Method* (New York: Seabury, 1975), 235–240, 245–278, 289–294, and 325–341.

23. Peter Enns, *Inspiration and Incarnation: Evangelicals and the Problem of the Old Testament* (Grand Rapids, MI: Baker, 2005).

Glossary

actualization The process of bringing the meaning of the Bible into the present.

aggadah Literally "telling" (Hebrew). 1. A homiletical tale. 2. The collective unit of Aggadah—rabbinic lore that includes proverbs and tales.

Akkadian An extinct Semitic language used in ancient Mesopotamia, known through texts discovered in archaeological excavations.

aliyah Literally "ascent" (Hebrew). Being called up to recite the blessings over the Torah; both the physical ascent to where the Torah is read and the participation in this ritual.

allegory A method of interpreting parables and other texts as symbolic representations of general truths.

Apocrypha Literally "hidden things" (Greek). The term is used to describe those Old Testament books in the Catholic and Orthodox canons but not in the Jewish and Protestant canons of Scripture. Also known as Deuterocanonicals.

apophatic Relating to the belief that God can only be known to humanity in terms of what God is not; also called negative theology.

Atrahasis Eighteenth-century BCE Akkadian epic featuring accounts about creation and a great flood, with parallels to early parts of Genesis. It influenced the eleventh tablet of Gilgamesh.

Babylonian captivity The exile of ancient Judah's political and religious elite in Babylon in the early sixth century BCE.

Babylonian Talmud Edited in the fifth to seventh centuries in Babylonia, the Talmud is the core source of Jewish law. The first complete English translation was *The Soncino Talmud* (1935–1948).

biblical criticism The scholarly process of establishing the original, contextual meaning of biblical texts and of assessing their historical accuracy.

Calvin, John (1509–1564) French Protestant Reformer and theologian, he sought to establish a theocracy in Geneva and wrote commentaries on many books of the Bible.

canon Literally "reed" or "measuring stick" (Greek). A list of sacred writings whose content provides rules or norms for faith and practice.

Chronicles The biblical book(s) that contain genealogies from Adam to postexilic Judah and retell the stories of David, Solomon, and the kings of Judah from a postexilic point of view.

Church Fathers Christian thinkers and leaders active from the second to the seventh century CE.

Daniel The biblical book containing narratives and visions in which Daniel is the central figure.

Dead Sea Scrolls Ancient Hebrew, Aramaic, and Greek manuscripts found at various sites (especially Qumran) near the Dead Sea, especially in the late 1940s and 1950s.

demythologization To move past the mythological elements of a biblical passage to reveal the underlying and abiding message.

Deuteronomistic history Abbreviated DtrH. Refers to the book of Deuteronomy and the following books, Joshua, Judges, 1 and 2 Samuel, and 1 and 2 Kings, which reflect key terminology and theological concerns of the book of Deuteronomy. These books were likely first edited together in the late seventh century BCE and reedited in the Babylonian exile (sixth century).

documentary hypothesis The theory that the Pentateuch was gradually composed over several hundred years on the basis of at least four major written sources: Yahwist (J), Elohist (E), Deuteronomist (D), and Priestly (P).

Enlightenment A philosophical movement prominent in Europe between the seventeenth and nineteenth centuries that emphasized rationalism and rejected traditional religious, social, and political ideas.

Enuma Elish A Babylonian account about creation and a great battle between the forces of order and chaos, with some parallels to the creation story in Genesis 1. The date is disputed, with some scholars favoring a date in the eighteenth century BCE and others around 1100 BCE.

form criticism The method that analyzes and identifies the literary genres used in the Bible and tries to locate their "setting in life" (*Sitz im Leben*).

gaon Literally "pride" (Hebrew). An honorific title given to the head of the Jewish academies in Babylon.

Gilgamesh A Sumerian king and legendary hero of Sumerian stories and a later Akkadian epic. He sought immortality but failed to find it, with parallels to Noah and his ark in Genesis 6–9. The Akkadian version is dated to the early second millennium BCE with earlier Sumerian Gilgamesh stories dating to the end of the third millennium.

Haggadah Literally "telling" (Hebrew). The Haggadah, which is recited out loud, is the text of the Passover Seder. The Haggadah includes biblical passages about the exodus from Egypt, as well as postbiblical prayers, questions and answers, rituals over food, and commentaries by sages.

halakhah 1. An authoritative ruling of rabbis on a certain case. 2. The collective unit of Halakhah—the entire body of rabbinic law.

Haskalah Literally "enlightenment" (Hebrew). The Jewish Enlightenment of the eighteenth century, which began in Germany and spread throughout Europe. The Haskalah exhibited a renewed interest in the Hebrew Bible, as well as in Western literature and philosophy.

hermeneutics The study of the principles and theories of the interpretation of biblical texts and their significance for people today.

Hexateuch Literally "six books" (Greek). The first six books of the Jewish and Christian Bible (Genesis, Exodus, Leviticus, Numbers, Deuteronomy, Joshua).

historical-critical method A way of investigating biblical texts that focuses on their original historical setting and what they meant in those contexts.

historical Jesus Scholarly reconstructions of Jesus as a historical figure, based on methods of historical criticism that engage the theologically driven Gospel accounts but are not limited to them.

Holy Spirit The presence of God within individuals and communities, inspiring and empowering them. In Christian theology, the term refers to the third person of the Blessed Trinity.

Ignatian contemplation The method of reading and praying on Gospel texts that gives special attention to the use of the senses and the imagination.

incarnation The core Christian theological conviction that Jesus of Nazareth is God in the form of human flesh (see John 1:14).

inculturation Communicating Scripture to reach people in their own cultural contexts.

inerrancy The understanding of Scripture as conveying the truth without error of any sort.

inspiration The understanding of Scripture in Christianity as having been written under the guidance of the Holy Spirit.

Isaiah The eighth-century BCE prophet active in Judah, and the book that bears his name, even though chapters 40–66 probably originated in the sixth century or later.

Justify To declare someone to be righteous or in right relationship with God. Paul argued that all people can enjoy such a relationship with God through Jesus' death and resurrection and faith in him (see Rom 3:21–26 and 4:25).

Karaites Literally "scripturalists" (Hebrew). A Jewish group that developed in the second half of the first millennium and rejected rabbinic authority and texts (for example, the Talmud).

Kenites An ethnic group based in northern Sinai that included Moses' father-in-law, Jethro/ Hobab. Some scholars have argued that Moses learned about YHWH from the Kenites (the Kenite hypothesis).

lectio divina The monastic method of reading Scripture involving reading, meditating, praying, and contemplating and/or acting.

legend of Sargon The story of the birth of Sargon (King of Akkad, ca. 2300 BCE), which is quite similar to the later account of Moses' birth in Exodus 2:1–10.

literal sense The plain meaning of Scripture expressed directly by the human authors.

Luther, Martin (1483–1546) The founder of the Protestant Reformation and translator of the Bible into German; he insisted that faith in Christ alone justifies one before God, not works.

Magisterium The official teaching office of the Roman Catholic church consisting of the bishops and headed by the pope as bishop of Rome.

Maimonides (1135–1204 CE) Rabbi Moshe Ben Maimon (Rabbi Moses son of Maimon), noted medieval Jewish philosopher, theologian, physician, and codifier of Jewish law. Leader of the Jewish community in Cairo and a prolific writer. Among his influential works, three central texts are his commentary on the Mishnah, his code of law entitled the *Mishneh Torah*, and his philosophical *Guide for the Perplexed*.

Marcion (died ca. 160 CE) Early Christian teacher who rejected the Old Testament and the Creator God depicted in it as having nothing to do with the Christian God of love. In the New Testament, he accepted only the Gospels and the letters of Paul, excluding the Pastoral Epistles (1 and 2 Timothy and Titus).

Masoretic Text (MT) The biblical text assembled by the Masoretes, a group of scholars from the sixth to tenth centuries CE. The standard Jewish version of the Hebrew Bible is attributed to the Masoretes; it includes the consonantal text, vowel-points, cantillation marks, and marginal notes highlighting unusual word forms.

midrash (plural midrashim) Literally "exposition" (Hebrew). 1. A rabbinic manner of instruction or elaboration upon a biblical story where an idea develops from an interpretation of a biblical verse. 2. A homiletic teaching that utilizes interpretations of individual words/phrases to ground the argument. 3. A collection of traditional Jewish interpretations of the Bible into books that look like biblical commentaries.

Mishnah Literally "that which was recited" (Hebrew). An early compilation of rabbinic laws edited in the land of Israel in the late second century.

modern Orthodoxy The centrist position within Jewish Orthodoxy; it subscribes to the notion of *Torah uMadda*, "Torah and science." This phrase underlines the dual values of adherence to halakhah, or Jewish law, and engagement with secular society.

Oral Torah (*Torah shebe'al peh*) Jewish religious teachings that, according to traditional teachings, were received at Sinai alongside the Written Torah and later formed part of the Mishnah and Talmud.

parallelism The characteristic feature of biblical poetry. Parallelism refers to the linguistic association of part of a line or a full line with one or more other lines. The grammatical structure may be the same or there may be a semantic relationship.

paschal mystery In Christian theology, the saving significance of Jesus' death and resurrection (around Passover time), a theme developed especially by Paul.

Pentateuch Literally "five books" (Greek). The first five books of the Jewish and Christian Bible (Genesis, Exodus, Leviticus, Numbers, Deuteronomy).

peshat A Hebrew term used in medieval Jewish biblical interpretation for the contextual or simple meaning of the text.

Pesher (plural Pesharim) Literally "interpretation" (Hebrew). In texts from Qumran, pesher is the interpretation that typically follows a biblical quote, showing how it is actualized or fulfilled in the author's own period. In this way, Pesharim at Qumran designates a specific type of literary interpretation and biblical exegesis that treats verse after verse.

Pirke Avot Literally "Sayings of the Fathers" (Hebrew). A commonly cited collection of rabbinic teachings from the Mishnah. Familiar quotes include "If I am only for myself, *what* am I?" (1:14); and "The world stands on three things: Torah, [religious] service, and acts of loving kindness" (1:2).

Pontifical Biblical Commission The group of Catholic biblical scholars charged with advising the pope and other church officials on biblical matters.

Rashi (1040–1105 CE) Rabbi Shlomo Yitzhaki (Solomon ben Isaac), medieval exegete from northern France and author of a central Bible commentary and the main commentary on the Babylonian Talmud. Rashi's Bible commentary is largely unoriginal, compiled from a wide range of earlier rabbinic sources, though it shows some interest in grammar and in *peshat,* in contrast to much of earlier interpretation, which was very atomistic.

redaction criticism The method that tries to identify the contributions of the editors of biblical books and their distinctive theological positions.

Seder Literally "order" (Hebrew). The Seder is the family or communal meal that forms the main activity of the festival Passover. The Seder both refers to the order of rituals that make up the Passover tradition, as well as to the gathering of family and friends around the festive table. The Seder represents the symbolic way to commemorate the biblical exodus.

Septuagint (LXX) Literally "seventy" (Greek). Greek translation of the Hebrew Bible which began gradually in the third century BCE for the benefit of diaspora Jews. Diverse traditions were streamlined somewhat in the centuries that followed, but no one final Greek Old Testament likely ever existed. The name stems from a legend that claimed the translation was completed by seventy-two translators (six from each of the tribes of Israel) in seventy-two days.

Shabbat The Jewish Sabbath, from approximately sunset on Friday until after sunset on Saturday night.

Sitz im Leben Literally "setting in life." This German term from biblical form criticism refers to the sociological setting from which a biblical text originally arose.

source criticism The method that tries to identify traditional written material edited together by the biblical writers, especially concerning the Pentateuch (see *documentary hypothesis*).

Spinoza, Baruch or Benedict(us) (1632–1677) Influential and controversial Jewish philosopher, eventually excommunicated from the Amsterdam Jewish community.

Centuries after his death, Spinoza's *Tractatus Theologico-Politicus* became fundamental to nineteenth-century biblical criticism and remains pivotal in the history of modern biblical interpretation.

supersessionism The Christian theological view that the church has replaced (super-
seded) Israel as the people of God and that the people of Israel no longer has
significance in God's plan for salvation.

synoptic problem Significant differences between parallel historical accounts, especially among the four Gospels in the New Testament, and sometimes the two
histories of Israel (Chronicles and the Deuteronomistic history) in the Hebrew
Bible/Old Testament.

Talmud (plural "Talmudim"): Literally "learning." See **Babylonian Talmud** and **Talmud of the Land of Israel**.

Talmud of the Land of Israel Also called the Jerusalem or Palestinian Talmud, this
corpus, written in Palestinian Aramaic, was compiled in northern Israel in the
fourth century CE. While the Mishnah of the Jerusalem Talmud largely parallels
that of the Babylonian Talmud, the Gemara (the rabbinic expositions) differs in
extent, content, and narrative style.

Talmudic Pertaining to the Jewish traditions, especially those contained in the Mishnah and in the Babylonian Talmud and the Talmud of the Land of Israel.

Targum Literally "translation" or "interpretation" (Hebrew). An Aramaic translation
of the Bible or a book of the Bible. The three Targumim (Targums) to the Pentateuch are Targum Onkelos, Targum Pseudo-Jonathan, and Targum Yerushalmi.

textual criticism The process of gathering and analyzing the ancient witnesses to the
biblical text and determining which reading best represents the wording of the
earliest text.

theological exegesis A recent movement to recapture the theological relevance of
Scripture for the church rather than focusing exclusively on historical-critical
and other academic issues.

Torah Literally "instruction" (Hebrew). 1. The Five Books of Moses (Genesis through
Deuteronomy), also known as the "Written Torah." 2. The collective body of
authoritative Jewish teachings, consisting of the Written and Oral Torah.

Tosafists Literally "those who added." Medieval rabbis of Germany and France who
wrote explanatory glosses on portions of the Talmud.

tradition history Study of the use and reuse of biblical materials from their earliest
forms and life settings down to their final form in the Bible.

Wellhausen, Julius (1844–1918) German Protestant biblical scholar and orientalist
who popularized the documentary hypothesis of the Hexateuch.

Zohar Literally "splendor" (Hebrew). The central work of Jewish mysticism and a
commentary on the Torah (Five Books of Moses). Although attributed to Shi-
mon son of Yohai (second century CE), most scholars agree that the Zohar,
written in medieval Aramaic and Hebrew, represents a compilation by a group
of mystics including Moses de Leon (ca. 1250–1305).

Index